PRAISE FOR
FIRST AMONG EQUALS

"Extraordinary…thoughtful…provocative…adept…persuasive…
informative, insightful, and a valuable addition to
Supreme Court literature."
—*Baltimore Sun*

"Captivating, perceptive, fair minded…accessible to lay readers and
brimming with insights for experienced Court-watchers."
—**Stuart Taylor, columnist,** *National Journal* **magazine,
and contributing editor,** *Newsweek*

"Colorful…part memoir, part layman's law book and part scholarly
analysis…surveys the Court's positions on affirmative action,
suspects' rights, and other hot topics."
—*Philadelphia Inquirer*

"Eminently readable and informative…I can say that this is not just
the best treatment of the Court after Warren, but that it is likely to
have that distinction for a long, long time."
—**Judge David B. Sentelle,
United States Circuit Judge**

"Written in a clear, nontechnical style accessible to a
wide readership."
—*Publishers Weekly*

"Excellent…informative…perceptive, focused…thoughtful."
—*Library Journal*

FIRST AMONG EQUALS

THE SUPREME COURT IN AMERICAN LIFE

KENNETH W. STARR

WARNER BOOKS

An AOL Time Warner Company

Copyright © 2002 by Kenneth W. Starr
All rights reserved.

Warner Books, Inc., 1271 Avenue of the Americas,
New York, NY 10020
Visit our Web site at www.twbookmark.com.

W An AOL Time Warner Company

Originally published in hardcover by Warner Books, Inc.
Printed in the United States of America
First Trade Printing: October 2003
10   9   8   7   6   5   4   3   2   1

The Library of Congress has cataloged the hardcover edition as follows:

Starr, Kenneth
    First among equals : the Supreme Court in American life / Kenneth W. Starr.
        p. cm.
    Includes index.
    ISBN 0-446-52756-4
        1. United States. Supreme Court—History. 2. Judicial power—United States. 3. Judicial process—United States. 4. Courts of last resort—United States. I. Title.

KF8748.S815 2002
347.73'26—dc21   200201896

ISBN: 0-446-69130-5 (pbk.)

Book design by Giorgetta Bell McRee
Cover design by Brigid Pearson
Cover photo by Terry Ashe/TimePix

To Alice, my loving wife, who was as always beautifully supportive throughout this and countless other efforts, and to our dear, now-grown children, Randy, Carolyn, her husband, Cameron, and to our high-school senior, Cynthia, who will soon be studying the nation's highest court

CONTENTS

PREFACE

THURGOOD MARSHALL THUNDERED at me from the bench. In Justice Marshall's waning years on the Court, he spoke up only rarely in oral argument. But he was always focused. The eye contact was the dead giveaway. The great civil rights lawyer who led the legal fight against Jim Crow in *Brown v. Board of Education* was in the sunset of his career, but he was still sharp. The advocate could not escape his glare. He watched you, closely.

The nine justices who sit on our Supreme Court are remote from American society. They don't go on *Larry King Live*. They give occasional speeches, but mostly to legal audiences. In an age of celebrity, the only justice who might be recognized in the checkout line of a grocery store is the first woman ever appointed to the High Court, Justice Sandra Day O'Connor.

We know the justices from their appearances on the bench, when they hear and decide cases. That is what they do. With the exception of the chief justice, that is all they do. The Constitution inserts the chief into impeachment proceedings when the president is in the dock: He is to preside over the Senate trial. We saw a chief justice in this job in early 1999, when Chief Justice William H. Rehnquist presided over the Senate impeachment trial of President Clinton. Yet even during that historic event, the chief said little. He held no press conferences to explain the process, much less to set forth his own views about it. At the end of each trial day, the chief slipped back to the Court and thus away from the media glare.

The justices speak to the public in their written opinions. But before they decide cases and compose their opinions, they hear arguments from lawyers representing the contending sides. Seated behind a long bench in order of seniority, though always with the chief justice occupying the center chair, the justices permit each advocate at least to begin a sentence. But soon enough one justice, and then another, and another ask questions that are carried throughout the courtroom over the stereo Surround Sound public-address system.

The justices physically lean forward in their huge, large-backed chairs. They make clear that they are engaging the lawyer who hopes to win his case. At once they are both testing the advocate and exploring the issues at hand. You have to respond—quickly. Time at the podium is rapidly fleeting. Beating around the bush, stalling for a better moment, is never an option.

On this day, Justice Marshall was outraged. The question was whether the Oklahoma City public schools were still segregated. Almost forty years earlier, Marshall himself had stood where I was now, presenting the historic argument in *Brown v. Board of Education,* that public-school segregation was unconstitutional. Years ago, Oklahoma City schools had been ordered by the federal courts to dismantle the old, unconstitutional dual system of public education. The elected school board had carried out the order conscientiously and transformed the schools. Or at least that was what the federal judge in Oklahoma City had concluded. The U.S. Court of Appeals for the Tenth Circuit, which sits in Denver, had disagreed, holding that the school system had to remain under the supervision of the federal courts.

"General Starr, you don't think segregation is constitutional?" Fighting words, especially coming from this justice. The United States, which I represented as the solicitor general, had taken the side of the school board in asking to end the long regime of court-ordered supervision. Justice Marshall himself had once served as solicitor general, the government's top advocate in the Supreme Court. As the Justice Department's third-ranking (now fourth-ranking) officer, Thurgood Marshall had been in the hot spot many times, fending off attacks from justices who were hostile to the government's position.

Now it was my turn. During the allotted one hour, the argument centered on one question: What is the meaning of "segregation"? Is a minority-dominated school that reflects the racial makeup of its neighborhood still considered "segregated" under law? Or does it take more than demographics to reach that conclusion? Might government (state or local) have done something to cause the racial imbalance? Justice Marshall was interested in results, in numbers about race. He was resolute: The school board should not be permitted to come out from under federal court supervision.

The argument concluded, and the SG's team repaired to what I called the "recovery room," a small office adjacent to the lawyers' lounge (an amusing contradiction in terms) used by the government lawyers who argue, day in and day out, before the Supreme Court. The argument had been intense. As the postmortem was getting under way, the door to the public hallway opened. In walked Ronald Day, the lawyer for the Oklahoma City school board, escorting his client, the board's chair. An African American elected by the people of Oklahoma City, she thanked me effusively: "General Starr, thank you for helping us get our schools back."

Here were two starkly competing visions. The locally elected school board wanted control, full control, over the school system. The federal judiciary had been resistant. Justice Thurgood Marshall made clear where he stood on the issue: not a chance, as far as he was concerned. If the racial numbers for individual schools didn't match those for the district as a whole, then the federal courts had to remain the cop on the beat, even almost forty years after *Brown*.

Justice Marshall failed to carry the day. Eventually the Court, by a divided 5–3 vote, held in 1991 that the school board—located a thousand miles from the nation's capital—had satisfied the necessary conditions to eliminate the need for federal court supervision. Racial imbalance, without some causal action by the government, was not enough. Oklahoma City would once again have control of its schools.

Merits aside, the contrast between Marshall's view of the law and the school board's could not have been more dramatic. This clash of perspectives is the stuff of constitutional litigation, issues that reach the Supreme Court for what is almost always final resolution. That has been a large part of my professional world for many years and continues to this day.

I first thought about becoming a lawyer when I was in high school in the 1960s. What drew me toward the law was the Supreme Court and the sharply joined issues then before it—issues of the kind I found myself arguing years later in the Oklahoma City case. The Court has long held a strong fascination for me, and this book is a product of my reflections on the highest court in the land.

I have been very fortunate to have worked in capacities

that enabled me to see the Court from a variety of perspectives. From 1975 to 1977, I was one of several freshly minted lawyers who clerked for Chief Justice Warren E. Burger. To say we saw the Court in its daily labor is an understatement. A "term" of Court runs from the first Monday in October through the end of the following June (when all remaining opinions are issued) and through the summer until the Court returns from its summer recess. It was our job during the two terms I served to read the papers filed in the cases the Court considered reviewing as well as, of course, those the Court actually accepted for review. We did legal research and helped with the opinion-writing.

From 1981 to 1983 (after a stint in private law practice), I served as counselor to William French Smith, President Reagan's first attorney general. As a matter of law, an attorney general oversees the solicitor general. I worked with Attorney General Smith and Rex Lee, the solicitor general during the first Reagan term, focusing on a number of high-profile cases before the Court. The urgency was to think about the task of persuading the Court—a quite different one from that in which I was engaged as a law clerk. As Smith's counselor, I also assisted him in carrying out a job attorneys general have been asked to do since the 1850s: Help the president select federal judges. In April 1981 (still recovering from John Hinckley's assassination attempt), President Reagan was informed by Bill Smith, in a private conversation in the residential quarters of the White House, of Justice Potter Stewart's intention to step down in the summer of that year. Sandra Day O'Connor was Reagan's eventual choice to fill the seat, and in our internal process I found myself reviewing every bit of information our team collected about her. At the attorney general's behest, I flew to Arizona, joined my Justice Department colleague Jonathan

Rose, and interviewed then Judge O'Connor for the better part of a day.

In the fall of 1983, President Reagan appointed me to the U.S. Court of Appeals for the District of Columbia, one of thirteen courts of appeals around the country. These are the courts situated between the district or trial courts and the Supreme Court. During my five-plus years on the D.C. Circuit, there was seldom an issue on which the court above ours—the Supreme Court—had not pronounced, either directly or indirectly. It was daily fare for me and my colleagues, who included future Justices Antonin Scalia (whom Reagan appointed to the High Court in 1986) and Ruth Bader Ginsburg (whom President Clinton appointed in 1993), to adhere to the Court's precedents and to reason from them in cases raising new issues. Here I saw the Court from below, as a federal judge bound by the judgments of the justices.

In 1989, President George Bush asked me to return to the Justice Department as solicitor general. This is a small but special law office. There were only eighteen lawyers on our staff, yet in a given term we participated in as many as half of the cases the Court decided in those years (about one hundred, a number now down to about seventy-five). Often one of us argued before the Court—as I did in the Oklahoma City school-desegregation case. After fours years as SG, I joined a private law firm and mainly handled federal cases, including some reviewed by the Supreme Court. In 1994, I was appointed independent counsel in the Whitewater matter, which itself generated two cases ultimately reviewed by the justices. Since then, I have continued to practice before the Court as a "private" lawyer, as well as to teach constitutional law at New York University and George Mason University.

So what is this special court? The Supreme Court was created by the Constitution, and has thus been with us since 1789, when the first justices were appointed. My focus in this book is on the Court I know best, which is the Court of the past three decades, the Court as it has been variously composed since 1969, when the most influential justice in the twentieth century, Chief Justice Earl Warren, stepped down. The years since 1969 have given us the Burger Court (1969–1986) and now the Rehnquist Court. These are the Courts I write about in this book, the Rehnquist Court especially, with appropriate and necessary references to the Warren Court and its groundbreaking work.

I should emphasize that this book (some readers will be happy to know) is not a manual on Supreme Court practice. My goal is more modest and, I hope, more interesting: to introduce many of the key decisions of the modern Supreme Court; to describe the legal tools the justices have used in interpreting the law and deciding cases; to explain the big ideas that have moved the justices; to identify the sharpest divisions among them; and to show the difference that the vote of a single justice has so frequently made.

Throughout the book I pursue a much larger theme— that of the role the post-Warren Supreme Court has played in American life. That role was much smaller a century ago, and during the Warren Court it grew so large that commentators—friendly and hostile alike—spoke of it as a "revolutionary" court. Among other things, the Warren Court ended Jim Crow laws (state-sponsored segregation); ordered the reapportionment of the U.S. House of Representatives (and also of state legislatures and local governmental bodies) according to a "one-person, one-vote" standard; changed key aspects of federal and state criminal procedure (enhancing the rights of the accused in the process); expanded First Amendment protections for free speech; and insisted on a stricter separation of church and state, by ordering an end to prayers and Bible readings in the public schools. No one disputes that in boldly reshaping whole areas of the law, the Warren Court distinguished itself—for better or for worse—from its predecessors, insinuating itself deeply into American life. By doing so, it provoked a profound—and continuing—argument about the proper role of the Court in American life and the kind of justices a president should appoint.

In 1973, the Burger Court handed down a decision with the look and feel of a Warren Court ruling in *Roe v. Wade*. *Roe* voided the abortion laws of all fifty states by announcing that the Constitution protects a woman's right to abortion. But the Burger Court was, as it had to be, given its membership, different from the Warren Court. It was, in short, a less "revolutionary" body. And the Rehnquist Court, with its membership changing too, has been different again. My aim is to identify the kind of Court we have had, and to specify the role it has played in American life, since Earl Warren's retirement.

Many things can be said about the post-Warren Supreme Court, not least that it has evolved into a more lawyerly tribunal and that it has become increasingly dedicated to stability and moderation. But one thing that may not be said about the Court today is that it has abandoned its central role in American life, which was established so firmly by the Court under Earl Warren. *Bush v. Gore,* a case that most Americans recognize, makes the point. That case was decided in December 2000, and it effectively resolved the presidential election. The Court didn't have to decide *Bush v. Gore;* that the Court stepped in at all demonstrated its willingness to exercise judicial power in a way that foreclosed action by Congress and the state of Florida.

Bush v. Gore illustrated the modern Court's most abiding characteristic. It is one identified time and again in the pages of this book. Ultimately in our system of government, the Supreme Court is first among equals.

INTRODUCTION

ON NOVEMBER 7, 2000, AMERICANS went to the polls and elected a new president. Or at least we thought we did. Late that night—actually, early the next morning—we realized that the presidential race had no clear winner. Al Gore narrowly led George W. Bush in the popular vote. But he hadn't won enough states to give him the 270 electoral votes necessary to prevail in the electoral college and become president. Nor, though he trailed in the popular vote, had Bush. Florida, with its 25 electoral votes, was in doubt. In the first official tally of the state's popular vote, Bush led Gore by 1,784 votes out of almost 6 million cast. The machine recount required under Florida law narrowed Bush's lead to a mere 327 votes. Exercising his rights under Florida law, Gore then sought hand recounts in four counties. Gore believed that there were uncounted votes that had been cast for him, and that if they were counted, they would give him Florida and its electoral votes, and thus the presidency. We now know the rest of the story: After a tumultuous five-week dispute over vote-counting in Florida, the Supreme Court of the United States resolved the controversy, and George W. Bush became the nation's forty-third president.

The irony was plain. The Supreme Court itself had been an issue during the campaign. Both Bush and Gore had discussed the kind of justices they would appoint should vacancies occur. Governor Bush wanted justices who would interpret the law, not make it up. Vice President Gore wanted justices who would keep the Constitution in tune with changing times. Governor Bush held up Justices Antonin Scalia and Clarence Thomas as models. Vice President Gore cited the late Thurgood Marshall, who was appointed by President Lyndon Johnson and served until 1991. This was an issue on which Bush and Gore sharply disagreed. But who would have thought that the Supreme Court would in effect pick the individual who would in turn pick the next justices?

The irony invites us to think more closely about the Supreme Court. The Constitution we adopted more than two centuries ago created the Court, just as it created the Congress and the presidency. Elections settle (or are supposed to settle) who sits in Congress and the White House. The justices of the Supreme Court, by contrast, are appointed by the president, subject to Senate approval. In civics courses we're told that we govern ourselves through our elected officials, not the appointed ones. But a case like *Bush v. Gore* suggests that things are more complicated. Those appointed justices seem to be more powerful than the textbooks allow, especially if they can, in effect, install someone in the White House.

As it happens, the justices exercise power in countless arenas—and have done so for some while. Under Chief Justice Earl Warren, who served from 1953 to 1969, the Court abandoned the more limited role it had maintained through most of its history and assumed a more assertive one—even a revolutionary one. Even its friends acknowledged that it was a Court on a mission, interested in doing what was good and fair. To its foes, the Warren Court was the most activist Court in the nation's history. By activist, the Court's critics meant that the Court had acted in ways that exceeded, and sometimes wildly so, its appropriate and legal authority as an unelected branch of government. In other words, judges were acting more in a legislative or policy-making role, not simply resolving legal issues in the course of litigation.

Many books have been written about the Warren Court, but there are fewer about the Courts that came after it. This is a book about those Courts, which is to say the modern Court, the Court first under Chief Justice Warren E. Burger (1969–1986) and then under Chief Justice William H. Rehnquist, who succeeded Burger in 1986. For most of us, the post-Warren Court has a less distinct profile than its predecessor. This book aims to draw a clearer picture of this Court, especially as it is composed today.

Like the Warren Court, the post-Warren Court has been accused of activism. This is so even though the Republican presidents since Earl Warren retired—Richard Nixon, Gerald Ford, Ronald Reagan, and George Bush (the elder)—sought through the ten justices they appointed (the other two were appointed by President Clinton) to produce a Court that would not be activist but restrained. The fact is, however, that the Court of the past thirty years has at times engaged in activism. The 1973 case of *Roe v. Wade,* in which a majority announced that the Constitution protects the right to abortion, is a prime example. The Court's 2000 decision in the presidential-election litigation was likewise regarded as activist not only by liberals but by many conservatives as well.

Nonetheless, it is a mistake to regard the post-Warren Court simply as an extension of the Warren Court, as a continuing exercise in activism. Whatever else may be said about it, the post-Warren Court has lacked its predecessor's almost missionary zeal to reshape society. The justices appointed to the Court since Earl Warren stepped down have proved more lawyerly than those who sat on the Warren Court and much less inclined to act as reform-minded legislators. They have generally been cautious and moderate in their decision-making; so much so, in fact, that they have declined to overrule the most controversial cases of the 1960s and early 1970s. They have sought principles or standards that will bring greater unity and coherence to their work, in particular the principle of equality. Perhaps most remarkably, the Court has not withdrawn from the most controversial and divisive issues of social policy. To the contrary, through its power to say what the law is, the Court has insisted that its pronouncements are superior to those of the other branches and the states. Moreover, as *Bush v. Gore* makes clear, the Court is willing to step in—actually, over the states and Congress—and resolve a presidential election.

Chapter One begins not with recent cases, but with one from 1803. Until that time, the Court had little occasion to exercise the judicial power assigned to it by the Constitution. John Jay was our first chief justice, yet the job was so undemanding that he left his judicial duties and traveled to England to negotiate the treaty named after him. Not until 1803, under our fourth chief justice, John Marshall, did the Court decide the case that ensured its political relevance and indeed its enduring role in American life. The case was *Marbury v. Madison*. It stands as one of the Court's greatest decisions. The Court was faced with a conflict between a law of Congress and a provision in the Constitution. What was the Court to do? The unanimous Court, with Marshall writing the opinion, ruled that the congressional statute was inferior to the Constitution and thus must be set aside. In explaining the decision, Marshall expounded the doctrine of judicial review, under which it is the province of the judiciary to declare what the law is.

Without judicial review, the Court and our politics would have been very different. Consider that the Court would not have been in a position to decide *Brown v. Board of Education* (the 1954 Warren Court decision that outlawed public-school segregation), or *Roe v. Wade,* or *Bush v. Gore.* So while this is a book about the post-Warren Court, I begin in Chapter One by telling the story of *Marbury v. Madison.* This chapter also sketches briefly the Court's exercise of judicial review, showing how judicial supremacy has sometimes been the result. Chapter One thus provides a constitutional and historical prologue.

Throughout the book I discuss most of the justices of the past thirty years. Seventeen have served since 1969, including six who were holdovers from the Warren Court. As the Court opens the twenty-first century, five loom as the most influential figures. Chapter Two introduces this group: Chief Justice Rehnquist, and Justices O'Connor, Scalia, Kennedy, and Breyer. It then introduces the remaining four justices, including the Rehnquist Court's most original thinker, Clarence Thomas.

Chapters Three through Fifteen treat major Supreme Court cases of the past three decades, with the first nine chapters examining individual-rights cases in particular. The cases focused on in these chapters are ones in which individuals sought protection for rights they claimed were protected by the Bill of Rights or the Fourteenth Amendment, which guarantees equality and due process of law. The rights are familiar ones: free speech and religious liberty, for example, or privacy and equal protection.

Although they are the most visible and recurring, individual-rights cases are by no means the only kind the Court decides. Indeed, an important part of the Court's business, especially in recent years, has concerned the structure of government itself, specifically the nature and scope of powers assigned to Congress, the presidency and the executive departments and agencies, and finally the states. Chapters Twelve through Fifteen discuss what can be called the Court's structural work—its interpretation of laws of Congress; its changing views of the role of Congress vis-à-vis the states; its judgments about the scope of executive power, including its landmark rulings in the 1974 Nixon tapes case and in the Reagan-era litigation over the constitutionality of the independent-counsel law; and, last but not least, its recent work in the unprecedented litigation that settled the 2000 election.

One theme of this book concerns the continuity between the Warren Court and its two successors. In a number of areas, the Warren Court advanced new understandings of the law that broadened and deepened the federal judiciary's influence. These understandings have largely survived the Burger and Rehnquist Courts. Consider, for example, the First Amendment, where the Warren Court adopted a decidedly more libertarian view of the free-speech and free-press guarantees. This view, as I show in Chapter Three, has by no means been overturned by the post-Warren Court but, to the contrary, has been strengthened. Likewise, the Warren Court developed the body of law prohibiting state-sponsored religious exercises from the public schools. That law hasn't been reversed, as many conservatives argued it should have been. To the contrary, as I discuss in Chapter Five, it has been reaffirmed and indeed extended in its applications.

Consider, too, the Warren Court's two most famous cases on criminal procedure. In *Mapp v. Ohio* (1961), the Court imposed on the states the exclusionary rule, under which evidence obtained in violation of an individual's Fourth Amendment rights (against an unreasonable search or seizure) must be excluded from trial. Warren Burger, who replaced Chief Justice Warren, was eager to overrule *Mapp,* as I relate in Chapter Ten, but the five necessary votes were never there. To be sure, the more cautious Burger and Rehnquist Courts have limited the reach of the exclusionary rule, but *Mapp* itself remains the law of the land. So does the other case, *Miranda v. Arizona* (1966), in which the five-member majority, over vehement dissenting opinions, held that the Fifth Amendment privilege against compelled self-incrimination extends to custodial interrogations by police, which the Court said are inherently coercive. To ensure against coercion in this context, the majority announced its famous *Miranda* warnings. In his 1968 campaign for the presidency, Richard Nixon made the Court an issue, and *Miranda* in particular drew his wrath. But *Miranda,* while not extended in its reach, has not been jettisoned. Indeed, in 2000, Chief Justice Rehnquist, who was first appointed to the Court by Nixon, wrote the opinion upholding *Miranda* and strengthening the foundation of what had long been seen as a principal example of Warren Court excess.

Continuity can also be seen with what came to be called the "right" of privacy. In the 1965 case of *Griswold v. Connecticut,* the Warren Court held that the Constitution contained a right of privacy (though precisely where it dwelled was unclear). The occasion for the *Griswold* holding was a challenge to a state law forbidding the prescription of contraceptives to married couples. Eight years later in *Roe v. Wade,* the Burger Court, with Nixon appointee Harry Blackmun writing the opinion, used *Griswold*'s right of privacy to declare a much more controversial right to abortion.

Of the decisions the Court has rendered since 1970, *Roe v. Wade* above all has the look and feel of a Warren Court ruling. The Court was subsequently asked on several occasions by Republican administrations to overrule *Roe*. I personally presented that argument—unsuccessfully—in 1992, in a case called *Planned Parenthood v. Casey*. But as with *Miranda,* a cautious Court declined to cast *Roe* aside. Ironically, three appointees of Presidents Reagan and Bush wrote the crucial opinion. So it was that the Rehnquist Court chose not to break from the Burger Court.

There would not have been as much continuity had the composition of the post-Warren Court been different. As recent confirmations have reminded the nation, it matters, fundamentally and decisively, who serves on the Court. Conversely, it matters a great deal who is not permitted to serve, whose nomination is blocked by the Senate or withdrawn prior to confirmation hearings by the president, or even who is not chosen by the president in the first place. It thus matters, deeply, how important the president and his advisers view the nomination of a justice. What purpose is the president trying to achieve with the appointment? Is he trying to shift the jurisprudential direction of the Court—a long-term goal—or is he aiming to achieve a more immediate political or public-relations goal, say by appointing the first woman? That was the choice before President Reagan in 1981, when he directed the attorney general to focus exclusively on women as prospective nominees. Left behind: the overwhelming choice of the Reagan Justice Department, Robert Bork. That presidential decision, driven entirely by political considerations, changed the course of the Court's modern history, since there is little doubt that the Republican-controlled Senate in 1981 would have confirmed Bork handily.

Likewise, the Senate's view of a president's nominee also matters. In 1987, the Democratic Senate successfully opposed Bork, the nominee for Justice Lewis F. Powell, Jr.'s seat, on grounds of ideology (or judicial philosophy). Anthony Kennedy, less conservative than Bork, was eventually appointed instead. Had Bork made it to the Court, either in 1981 or in 1987, a number of rulings would likely have gone the other way. In particular, it is very likely that *Roe v. Wade*—the Burger Court's most important decision—would have been overruled.

Today, not only does *Roe* still stand, so do the most controversial decisions of the Warren Court. Indeed, the

Court today still aggressively chooses to assert power over virtually the same range of subjects as the Warren Court. It remains very much in business in the most divisive areas of our national life.

This theme is found elsewhere in the Court's work. Consider race. The Court in recent decades has not shied from the burden the Warren Court first accepted in *Brown* to declare what the law of equal protection is for all citizens at all levels of government. The Court, especially in recent years, has backed away from the kind of law that it countenanced during the 1980s—law, shaped by the last liberals from the Warren Court era, that allowed governments, for the sake of getting beyond racism or promoting diversity, to allocate opportunities with race in mind. Here again, the Court has proved more restrained than the Warren Court would have been. Still, what is striking in this area of the law is that the Court is willing to say no to those who deviate from the almost-colorblind law it has been expounding.

The Court has also made the same assertion in cases involving the presidency and the states. In 1974, at the height of Watergate, President Nixon asked the Court, in effect, to tell the special prosecutor to withdraw his request for the fateful White House tapes. Fourteen years later, in 1988, the Reagan administration joined in a challenge to the independent-counsel law, passed in the wake of Watergate, as an unconstitutional usurpation of presidential authority. Finally, in 1996 President Clinton asked the Supreme Court, in the Paula Jones case, to immunize a sitting president against a civil action brought against him concerning alleged conduct preceding his term of office. On all three of these occasions, the Court rebuffed a sitting president.

But the Court today is also one that regularly tells Congress no. In a series of cases in which the Court reviewed challenges to laws of Congress said to infringe upon state prerogatives, the Court invariably found those laws unconstitutional. These cases are typically seen as ones in which state authority is vindicated. But what should not be missed is that the Court time and again has proved willing to stand up to the branch of government closest to the people and treated first in the Constitution: the Congress.

Finally, the Court is also willing to tell the states no, even when state courts are interpreting state law. This, indeed, is what it did in the litigation between the two presidential candidates five weeks after the votes were counted on Election Day 2000. The Supreme Court was confronted with a state court—the Florida Supreme Court— that had made a mess of Florida election law in order to remedy perceived wrongs—or to vindicate the intent of the voters. The Rehnquist Court would not allow what it appeared to deem a runaway court to hijack a presidential election by riding roughshod over state law. That is what the Florida litigation ultimately was about.

Today's Court, then, while more restrained in doctrine than the Warren Court, reigns supreme. Still, there are pivotal differences between the Warren Court and the Court of today. The post-Warren Court, no doubt in response to the freewheeling decision-making of its predecessor, has been self-consciously struggling for greater rigor and persuasiveness in its doctrine. This is a task for lawyers, and it is striking that the only people whom the appointing presidents, starting with Nixon, have named to the Court have been lawyers working at lawyers' jobs. Here we see a sharp break with the past. It was not uncommon before the Nixon presidency for a president to appoint to the Court a senator (consider Senator Hugo Black of Alabama, whom FDR appointed) or a governor (Earl Warren himself, appointed by Dwight Eisenhower). But every appointee since Warren E. Burger has been a person of the law, not of politics, most frequently a judge on a federal court of appeals. This is true of the only two justices appointed by a Democratic president. In 1993, President

Clinton considered senators (including George Mitchell) and a sitting governor (Mario Cuomo) before settling on a judge from my old court, Ruth Bader Ginsburg. In 1994, he chose a judge from the U.S. Court of Appeals for the First Circuit in Boston, Stephen Breyer. Both Ginsburg and Breyer were highly respected as careful appellate judges.

The choice by presidents since Nixon to appoint workaday judges to our nation's highest tribunal has dramatically shaped the Court's work. It has become more and more lawyerly, another theme of this book, as the justices' disputes over how to interpret law illustrate. Text, structure, constitutional history, and precedent (past decisions of the Court): These are the basic tools in the judicial workshop. Working with these tools of interpretation, the justices have traveled far from the wide-open approach of the Warren Court. The lawyerly rigor has only increased with time, with the occasional looseness of the Burger Court (especially on race and religion) replaced by more stringent, careful analysis. The Rehnquist Court tends to shy away from overt "balancing" of competing interests (with some key exceptions, in particular the independent-counsel case, *Morrison v. Olson*). That process, common during the Burger Court years, has the feel of policy-making, of legislating rather than judging. So, too, none of the current justices would be inclined to say, as Thurgood Marshall reportedly did when asked about his judicial philosophy, "I do what I think is right and let the law catch up to me."

That being said, the current Court is moved by large ideas, such as equality. Some of these ideas cut across ideological and philosophical lines to a considerable degree, if only imperfectly. In watershed cases, such as *Bush v. Gore,* the justices seek common philosophical ground, identified at a high level of generality—say, all voters should be treated equally, just as all speakers should likewise be so treated. Or, as a corollary to equality, aid to faith-based institutions should be upheld if the governmental program is widely available on a neutral, nondiscriminatory basis. Large principles, in short, can bring surprising results in their application. So, too, the principle of individual conscience looms large, drawing together a solid majority (although not all) of the justices in the sensitive arena of school prayer or other religious observances in public schools, just as it protects flag burning as a form of free expression. At other times, the Court has invoked the grand traditions of "restraint," the principle that unelected courts should be highly deferential to the judgments of the political branches.

These big ideas both animate the Court and serve as ammunition for justices who find themselves outvoted and thus relegated to preparing a dissenting opinion. For example, in two important areas, federalism and the 2000 presidential election case, "restraint" has been the rallying cry for dissenting justices upset by the Court's invalidating congressional regulation of state interests (federalism) or its overturning the Florida Supreme Court's second decision in the epic *Bush v. Gore* struggle.

So this is the Court today: It is a judge's Court, a Court of lawyers. A Court where history, which Henry Ford once dismissed as "bunk," is treated with genuine respect. A Court dedicated to stability, not change; moderation and incrementalism, not liberalism or progressivism. The Rehnquist Court's stability has been especially evident in its dedication to the principle of *stare decisis*—the doctrine that courts should follow earlier judicial decisions, even if the prior holdings are viewed as wrongly decided. At the same time, it is a Court moved by large, unifying ideas. And a Court that, while remote from the hustle and bustle of American life, remains engaged in virtually all areas of our national life. It is, as *Bush v. Gore* demonstrated, first among equals, the branch of government with the authoritative role in vital issues that deeply affect American life and politics.

FIRST AMONG
EQUALS

PART ONE

The Supreme Court

Then and Now

Chapter One

★

ORIGINS

THE CONSTITUTION CREATES THE SUPREME COURT. Other federal courts may come and go, in Congress's discretion, but only the Supreme Court is ordained in the founding document itself. Even so, the early years of the Supreme Court were not busy ones. John Jay, the first chief justice, took time away from his duties to negotiate the much-despised Jay Treaty with England. When he returned home, Jay resigned from the Court to accept the post of governor of his native New York. The second chief justice, Oliver Ellsworth, was soon bored. He stepped aside in 1800 only weeks after Thomas Jefferson was elected president.

Jefferson's triumph over John Adams brought about a seismic shift in national politics—a political revolution, as the new president saw it. During the nation's first twelve years, battles had been fought over the enduring question of the power of the federal government as opposed to that of the states. Throughout his eight years as president, George Washington remained above the fray, but below—in the trenches of cabinet-level disputes—the struggle between competing visions of national versus state power had been fierce. Alexander Hamilton, the first secretary of the treasury, led the pro-nationalist forces. In Hamilton's view, the central government should be strong, active, energetic, moving ahead with programs to build the young nation. Hamilton pressed successfully for the establishment of a Bank of the United States, an institution he thought necessary for the nation's economic development but that was destined to be challenged in court early in the nineteenth century. For his part, the president—in Hamilton's vision—needed to be energetic, showing strong leadership in promoting a sense of genuine nationhood throughout the country. The people should look to the national capital, first New York, then Philadelphia, and finally the new city of Washington, D.C., for the establishment of policies and institutions that would enable the country to thrive.

Like Hamilton, Jefferson also served in Washington's cabinet. He was the loser in these early battles. His vision of a federal government strictly confined to the powers enumerated in the Constitution had failed to carry the day during Washington's two terms. Jefferson then lost a hard-fought, bitter contest to John Adams in 1796. But Jefferson was tenacious, determined to best the centralizing forces of the Federalist Party epitomized by his adversary, now President Adams. In 1800, his defeat of Adams, a virtuous, principled man lacking in political skills, finally brought the states' rights advocates—the so-called Anti-Federalists—to power. The "Revolution of 1800," as Jefferson dubbed the election, occurred after twelve successive years of Federalist domination.

The business of the Supreme Court now began to pick up. Not only was there more work to do at the Court itself, but the justices often found themselves "riding circuit." They would literally ride on horseback or take coaches to various cities and preside at trials.

Not surprisingly, the Court, stocked as it was with

Washington's and then Adams's appointees, was strongly pro-Federalist. Chief Justice Oliver Ellsworth's resignation in late 1800 gave the Federalists the opportunity to deepen their influence upon the judiciary. Notwithstanding his lame-duck status, President Adams took advantage of the Ellsworth resignation and nominated a brilliant, loyal Federalist from Virginia, John Marshall, to become chief justice. Adams also rushed through nominations of other judges to the lower courts. The "midnight appointees," as they came to be known, were destined to dominate the federal courts for years to come. But no other appointment in history had the enduring impact of John Marshall's.

More than any other figure save for Washington himself, John Marshall gave shape to the national government. In particular, Marshall affirmed the power of the nation's highest court to interpret the Constitution and federal law. Known as the power of judicial review, it was first given full expression in the 1803 case of *Marbury v. Madison*. The underlying dispute was simple: Was William Marbury entitled to a commission that, upon delivery, would permit him to take the oath of office as a justice of the peace in the new District of Columbia? From that tiny legal dispute a mighty doctrine grew.

The issue is this: In a constitutional democracy, the Constitution is the ultimate authority, binding on all branches and levels of government. But the Constitution, since it is a written document, must be interpreted. Who is to do that? May each branch of government interpret the Constitution for itself? What if the president or Congress reads the Constitution differently from the Supreme Court? Which branch prevails?

In the case that resolved this issue, William Marbury invoked a measure passed by Congress and signed into law by George Washington. The statute was the Judiciary Act of 1789. That law, among other things, created the attorney general's office. It created the United States Marshals. It created lower federal courts.

But another provision of that law—and one invoked by would-be Justice of the Peace Marbury—said that the Supreme Court could hear as an "original" matter (that is, without any lower court passing on the case) certain legal actions, namely lawsuits seeking a writ of mandamus. Mandamus is an ancient writ at common law and is still in active use today. To "mandamus" someone is to secure an extraordinary directive requiring an official (including judges) to take certain action, or to cease and desist from a court taking certain action (called in bygone years a writ of prohibition).

Invoking the mandamus provision, William Marbury filed a petition in the Supreme Court to mandamus the incoming secretary of state, James Madison, to deliver the justice-of-the-peace commission that had been authorized by outgoing President John Adams and signed by then Secretary of State John Marshall. Marshall, who hadn't delivered Marbury his commission, was now chief justice.

Marbury doubtless entered the High Court brimming with optimism. This was, after all, a Federalist bench from top to bottom. These were the appointees of Washington and Adams. The commission was surely his.

There was a huge problem, however, one unanticipated by Marbury's argument. The issue had to do with the Supreme Court's authority to hear the case, what lawyers and judges call "jurisdiction." Jurisdiction is a fundamental issue for courts. Judges routinely ask: Do we have power—i.e., jurisdiction—to hear this lawsuit? Are the litigants in the right court? Does this plaintiff have "standing" (some legally recognizable injury) to mount the legal challenge in question? Is there a statute, passed in accordance with the Constitution, conferring power on the courts to resolve the particular case?

In particular, federal courts (including the Supreme Court) worry about their authority in a federal system: "Counsel, what right does your client have to be here?" The basic point is this: In our system of government, courts are limited in their authority. Although within their sphere of authority they are powerful indeed, courts can do only what the law creating them authorizes. To go beyond that power is to behave lawlessly.

Occasionally, judges will be insufficiently attentive to what they consider jurisdictional niceties. An episode during my service in the 1980s as a judge on the U.S. Court of Appeals in Washington, D.C., illustrates the point. One of the giants of the district court in Washington at the time was Gerhard Gesell, son of the renowned Yale child psychologist and a distinguished lawyer in his own right at Washington's prestigious Covington & Burling. Before his appointment to the bench, Gesell had been one of the nation's premier antitrust advocates. He was smart and shrewd. Each year, he would sit by designation for several days as a guest judge on the court of appeals in Washington. On one such occasion, as we were chatting in the judges' robing room just behind the courtroom, Gesell was complaining about recent opinions from our court tightening up the rules of standing, saying, "Let's get on with these cases, get to the merits, instead of wrestling with all this technical stuff." Gesell was a bit testy on the point. He seldom hesitated to speak his mind, but he seemed especially agitated over this trend toward "technical" decisions. I was amused, but listened politely. I liked Gerry a lot, and respected his opinions. The presiding judge that morning was Robert Bork. Always quick, Judge Bork reminded the venerable district judge that these recent opinions didn't simply reflect some hypertechnical approach: "Well, Gerry, it is constitutionally required, you know." What Judge Bork was saying is this: Courts are limited, by Article III of the Constitution, to deciding actual cases and controversies. Gesell snorted. Here was the practical, common-sense district judge who wanted to move the cases along and get them decided, on the one hand, pitted against the principle, rooted in the idea of a limited judiciary, that judges can't decide anything and everything parties might choose to bring them.

This was the problem that confronted Marbury. He had brought his case to the Supreme Court instead of some lower court because the Judiciary Act of 1789 told him he could. But this, Chief Justice Marshall concluded, was impermissible. The text of the Constitution itself—in Article III setting forth the judicial power and creating the Supreme Court—designated the specific categories of cases in which the Supreme Court enjoyed "original" (that is, firsthand) jurisdiction. What Marbury was seeking— mandamus—was not within those categories.

Thus, the 1789 statute tried to expand what the Constitution itself established. The categories of original jurisdiction created by the Constitution were closed (barring, of course, a constitutional amendment). Congress could not depart from the text of Article III and devise additional categories of original jurisdiction. Obviously, the statute was inconsistent with what the Constitution provided. Both could not be law.

The final step in John Marshall's analysis represented the inexorable conclusion: If a statute passed by Congress is inconsistent with the Constitution, then the statute must be set aside. Otherwise, ordinary legislation would render ineffectual the very law that sets up Congress and the rest of the government—the Constitution. And, Marshall added, it was the job of judges to say, finally, what was the law of the land.

The Federalist midnight appointee John Marshall had ruled against his philosophical comrade. But in the process of disappointing Marbury, the great chief justice (as he came to be called) had established the fundamental role of the judiciary in a constitutional democracy—to interpret the Constitution finally and authoritatively, even when one of the other branches of government (or both) had come to a contrary view.

To Jefferson, the *Marbury v. Madison* approach was profoundly wrong. Each branch, he thought, was co-ordinate and co-equal. It would not do to have a regime of judicial supremacy in which the unelected, third branch of government stood over the two elected branches. A new aristocracy would rule the two branches most responsive to the people.

But President Jefferson's sense of foreboding was to no avail. Congress made no effort to overturn *Marbury* through constitutional amendment. Nor was a more modest measure seriously pursued, such as one requiring that the Court be unanimous before striking down as unconstitutional an act of Congress or an action of the executive branch.

Marbury v. Madison was the seminal decision of John Marshall's tenure. But it began a long series of Marshall's contributions. In case after case, spanning over three decades of service, Marshall guided the Court in a way that upheld national power over the country. That is, when the issue involved the power of the Congress as against the claims of the states, Marshall was a reliable supporter of the federal government. In particular, his interpretation of one pivotal provision in the Constitution—the Commerce Clause—paved the way for Congress to be free to regulate the economy in the myriad ways that have now become commonplace.

Much of what Congress does falls under the category of

regulating "commerce." The Constitution's language in this respect is simple: Article I, section 8 provides that the national legislature is empowered "[t]o regulate Commerce with foreign Nations, and among the several states, and with the Indian Tribes." In an early landmark testing the extent of this power, Marshall, in a characteristically broad interpretation of congressional authority, dealt a serious blow to state authority (*Gibbons v. Ogden* [1824]). In that case, the Marshall Court struck down a New York law giving a monopoly to a steamboat company carrying passengers on the Hudson River. In overturning the law, Marshall gave the pivotal term *commerce* a sweepingly broad definition, thus maximizing federal power at the expense of the states.

Marshall's pro-Federalist vision likewise triumphed in an early case involving Maryland's challenge to the controversial remnant of Hamilton's program from the prior century, the Bank of the United States. To the Anti-Federalist defenders of states' rights, most prominently Jefferson, the Bank embodied the evils of national concentration of power. Nowhere in the Constitution was the Bank either generally or specifically mentioned. The legality of the Bank thus went to the heart of the Constitution's structural arrangements. The Constitution, after all, laid out in elaborate detail the various powers of Congress. To the Anti-Federalists, its silence about national financial institutions resolved the question of Congress's power: If the Constitution was silent, then the power did not exist.

This narrow approach to interpreting the Constitution is frequently referred to as "strict construction." A strict constructionist, as the term is generally used, is a judge or justice who discerns the meaning of the Constitution in its text, structure, and history. Many nominees for judicial office will march under the banner of strict construction, since it suggests a modest, limited role for judges in a democratic society. Judges, advocates of strict construction say, should not import their own views of good and sound policy into the clauses and phrases of the supreme law of the land.

Despite its popular appeal, strict construction has only episodically characterized the Supreme Court's work. The enduring approach toward constitutional interpretation was outlined by John Marshall in the landmark decision involving the Bank of the United States. The case was *McCulloch v. Maryland*, decided in 1819. Showing its hostility toward the national bank, Maryland imposed a tax on all banks or branches operating in the state that had not been chartered by the state legislature in Annapolis. The cashier of the Baltimore branch of the national bank, James McCulloch, issued notes on which no state tax had been paid, and the Maryland authorities filed an action in state court to collect the taxes due. The state courts ruled in favor of Maryland, and the case found its way to the Marshall Court.

The Court, speaking through Marshall, invoked a provision in the Constitution that Maryland had largely ignored. The "Necessary and Proper" Clause—the final clause of Article I, section 8—provided that Congress was empowered "to make all Laws which shall be necessary and proper for carrying into Execution the foregoing Powers," which were specifically listed. In broad language that has stood the test of time, Marshall wrote that the "Necessary and Proper" Clause gives great latitude to Congress in working its will. "Let the end be legitimate," wrote Marshall, "let it be within the scope of the Constitution, and all means which are appropriate, which are plainly adapted to that end, which are not prohibited, but consistent with the letter and spirit of the Constitution, are constitutional." This was an open-ended approach that would allow Congress and the president to work their will on the nation. Hamilton's dream would live on.

More important for the future, John Marshall's approach

to interpreting the Constitution would stand as one of the great legacies of his tenure. The Constitution was to be interpreted broadly, not narrowly. In Marshall's approach, the Constitution was quite different from ordinary law. In criminal law, for example, one of the rules of interpretation is that criminal statutes should be construed narrowly. The "rule of lenity" puts a thumb on the scales in favor of individual liberty. An individual should not, under our system of law, be charged with a crime unless the nature of the criminal offense is clear to an ordinary person. Ambiguity or uncertainty in the criminal law is to be interpreted against the government and in favor of the individual. The opposite approach applies, however, when the Constitution, rather than a criminal statute, is being interpreted. As Chief Justice Marshall put it, "We must never forget that it is a Constitution that we are expounding." The Constitution, in short, must be interpreted in a generous, reasonable manner, with the judge aware that the Constitution was intended to set forth a workable, practical structure of government. The frame of mind of the interpreting justice, in this view, is one of flexibility and practicality, with the operations of government clearly in mind.

And it is the judiciary's interpretation that ultimately counts. As Marshall wrote in *Marbury v. Madison,* "It is emphatically the province of the judicial department to say what the law is."

These were Marshall's enduring legacies. National power—especially the power of Congress—would be interpreted generously, to allow Congress and the president to fashion policies and programs that met the felt necessities of the time. At the same time, it was the role of the courts, ultimately the Supreme Court, to be the final arbiter of the meaning of the Constitution.

Chapter Two

★

THE JUSTICES

THE SUPREME COURT SINCE EARL WARREN stepped down has been a different Court—more lawyerly, and less activist. There's no mystery why. Republican presidents opposed to the Warren Court's activism were able to make the large majority of the appointments of the past three decades.

President Nixon made the first four appointments. In 1969, he replaced Earl Warren with Warren Burger, and then, in 1970, he replaced Abe Fortas with Burger's fellow Minnesotan, Harry Blackmun. Two years later Nixon made his other two appointments, as Lewis Powell, Jr., succeeded Hugo Black and William Rehnquist took the seat vacated by John Marshall Harlan II. In 1975, President Ford replaced William O. Douglas with John Paul Stevens. Then an appointments drought set in: Jimmy Carter became the first president ever to serve a full term without making an appointment to the Supreme Court. A vacancy did occur soon after Ronald Reagan took office, as Potter Stewart (appointed by Eisenhower) stepped down. Reagan took the historic step of naming the first woman: Sandra Day O'Connor. The next vacancy occurred in 1986, when Chief Justice Burger retired. President Reagan elevated Associate Justice Rehnquist to Burger's center seat and then appointed Judge Antonin Scalia, of my former court, to take Rehnquist's now empty chair. A year later, a second member of the Burger Court, Lewis Powell, retired; Reagan appointed Anthony Kennedy. In 1990, President Bush, moving to fill the seat vacated by William J. Brennan, Jr., who had served since 1957, tapped David Souter. A year later, Bush replaced Thurgood Marshall, an appointee of President Johnson, with Clarence Thomas. So it was that from 1969 through 1991, only Republican presidents had picked Supreme Court justices. In his first term, President Clinton got the chance to appoint the next two, and most recent, justices, replacing Byron White (the last holdover from the Warren Court) with Ruth Bader Ginsburg in 1993 and Harry Blackmun with Stephen Breyer in 1994.

Today's Court, the Rehnquist Court, thus includes, in addition to Chief Justice Rehnquist, Justices Stevens, O'Connor, Scalia, Kennedy, Souter, Thomas, Ginsburg, and Breyer. Each justice has made distinctive contributions. Yet some have proved, and promise to continue to prove, more influential than the rest. They are, in their order of appointment: the chief justice, O'Connor, Scalia, Kennedy, and Breyer. They are the justices to watch most closely. Over the past decade, their influence and power have been pivotal in determining the Court's direction. But the other four, especially Clarence Thomas, are not to be overlooked. As we will see, each has made his or her own mark.

William Hobbs Rehnquist, sixteenth chief justice of the United States, moved to the pivotal center seat at the Court in September 1986 after fifteen years as a very productive associate justice. At the time widely regarded as the smartest justice in the courthouse, he became Chief Justice Burger's go-to colleague.

In a courthouse filled with suits, lawyerly formality being de rigueur at the time, Rehnquist wore Hush Puppies and sport coats. Efficient at getting the work done, he was at the same time easygoing and well liked around the Court. It was a formidable combination. Brilliant, first in his class at Stanford Law School, yet unstuffy and down-to-earth, then Justice Rehnquist was hugely popular, even among the clerks from liberal chambers. He was especially popular at the "take-a-justice-to-lunch" sessions, a pleasant, informal tradition in which each chambers' set of law clerks would invite, over the course of the term, each of the other justices to an informal, off-the-record lunch. This was viewed as a priceless benefit of being a clerk at the Court. The easygoing, unassuming justice from Arizona—a close friend of the Court's most liberal member, William O. Douglas, a holdover from the Warren Court years—filled his dance card quickly. No fancy restaurants. Cheeseburger and a beer was a favorite combo, befitting his roots in Milwaukee. He was interesting, direct, and friendly, but never overly chummy or ingratiating. He was not a slap-you-on-the-back type, nor was he gregarious, like the elfish, much-beloved Justice Brennan, an Eisenhower appointee and faithful lieutenant to Chief Justice Warren, who became the longtime leader of the post-Warren Court's liberal wing. The cerebral Rehnquist would saunter around—taking walks with his clerks, unnoticed by tourists—perhaps with an Anthony Trollope novel under his arm.

The casual, no-airs friendliness of this native Wisconsinite transplanted to Arizona did not in the slightest dilute his uncompromisingly conservative judicial philosophy. Rehnquist was greatly admired by then Chief Justice Burger, who for his part was more deeply conservative

than his voting behavior indicated. The two were so philo-
sophically in agreement that it was natural for writing assignments to flow easily from Burger in Justice
Rehnquist's direction. And Rehnquist was gutsy. He didn't
seem to mind if he was in solitary dissent. He became
known as the "Lone Ranger." He was willing to stand
up—all by himself—against the crowd of justices moving
in a different direction.

As President Nixon's youngest appointee (at age forty-
seven), Rehnquist was seen as situated at the vanguard of
change, of movement away from the recently concluded
Warren Court years. As a junior justice, he attacked Warren Court precedents with relish, sought to narrow them
at every turn, and dissented deeply—as he did in *Roe v.
Wade*—when the Burger Court itself engaged in activism.
He was decidedly not a centrist, even though the Court
under Chief Justice Burger was moving in that direction.
The trend lines were especially strong due to the powerful
centrist influence of Justice Lewis Powell, Jr. The order of
the day was a quiet departure or backing off from Warren
Court precedents, but only in the sense of not pursuing
their logic further. This was, as one student of the Burger
Court put it, the "counterrevolution that wasn't."

This genteel moderation did not appear to sit well with
the Court's youngest, and newest, member. He wanted to
move more aggressively, to clean out the precedents litter-
ing the pathways of constitutional law.

Justice Rehnquist made his views known outside the
courthouse, where he openly criticized liberal theories of
constitutional law. For example, in a 1976 *Texas Law Review* article, he lampooned the idea of the "living Constitution," calling it an invitation to judicial lawmaking.
Judges, in Rehnquist's view, should not interfere with the
representative process. They should allow democratic self-
rule. Rehnquist's understanding of the judicial power

echoed, ironically, President Franklin Roosevelt's criticism of the "Nine Old Men" who had struck down important measures passed, at FDR's urging, by the New Deal Congress.

In 1986, when Reagan decided to appoint Rehnquist chief justice, he also settled on Antonin Scalia as Rehnquist's successor. Scalia had distinguished himself as a powerful intellectual voice on the U.S. Court of Appeals in Washington and through his decisions had endeared himself to legal conservatives. The expectation was, at least inside the Reagan administration, that Rehnquist, with the considerable help of Scalia, would move the Court significantly to the right.

It was not to be. Soon, the Rehnquist judicial tone changed. While he continued to articulate certain core beliefs, most importantly his consistent view that *Roe v. Wade* was wrongly decided and should be overruled, he was no longer speaking out, and seldom if ever in solitary dissent. His lectures at law schools railing against judicial excesses likewise were now a thing of yesteryear. Instead of continuing the conservative fight, his long-standing interest in history came to the fore. Chief Justice Burger had read widely, especially in history and biography. But Rehnquist not only read, he wrote. He turned out a charming book on the Court published in 1987. After that successful initial outing, and in a remarkable twist of irony, he began to steep himself in the history of impeachment. Little could he have sensed that he was preparing himself for his own role in presiding over the 1999 Senate impeachment trial of President Clinton.

Not only had he turned to more genteel pursuits, Rehnquist soon showed that his philosophy of judicial restraint had an unexpected effect. Other than *Roe v. Wade,* few issues so inflamed Reagan administration lawyers as those involving federalism and separation of powers. The principles emphasize, respectively, (1) the rights of states to carry on their policies free from federal interference and (2) the separation of powers at the national level among the executive, legislative, and judicial branches. These were seen as seminal conservative principles. Terry Eastland, a Reagan administration alumnus, later wrote a book about the importance of a strong executive branch, drawing from ideas first put forth by Alexander Hamilton, titled *Energy in the Executive*. Part of the received wisdom was that Congress was ever seeking to aggrandize its power, particularly at the expense of the executive branch.

This presumption carried over into the Bush administration. When coming on board as solicitor general, I was summoned over to the White House on one occasion to meet with Boyden Gray, counsel to the president. The sole subject of discussion was separation of powers. This was discussed generally, not in the context of a specific case. Gray made this clear: Restoring the balance between Congress and the president was an overarching concern requiring the careful attention of senior lawyers in the executive branch.

The Burger Court had struck down as unconstitutional important congressional initiatives—which the executive branch regarded as power plays—such as the long-used legislative veto (whereby a single House, or even a single committee, invalidates a set of agency regulations). But soon after Rehnquist became chief justice, the Court handed the Reagan administration a bitter separation-of-powers defeat. The Court held that the independent-counsel law, already enshrouded in controversy by virtue of Judge Lawrence Walsh's unfolding investigation into Iran-Contra, was *not* unconstitutional.

The omens had seemed favorable finally to rid the system of this unwanted post-Watergate "reform." The Reagan administration had early on disagreed with the independent-counsel law, and urged that it be allowed to lapse—in testimony before Congress presented by future mayor and then Associate Attorney General Rudy Giuliani. And then the D.C. Circuit had struck it down, albeit by a 2–1 vote. Impressive voices, such as those of former Attorneys General Griffin Bell, Edward Levi, and my former boss at the Justice Department, William French Smith, condemned the law as misguided and unconstitutional. The United States—through the solicitor general—argued that the independent-counsel law improperly invaded the sphere of the executive branch in a core constitutional function: carrying on criminal investigations and making prosecutorial decisions based on those investigations.

Nonetheless, Chief Justice Rehnquist voted to uphold the law. Even more, he wrote the majority opinion and did so in a worrisome way. He invoked a vague sort of balancing test, an approach ordinarily anathema to conservatives, who prefer articulation of clear principles and faithfully sticking with them. A man who had once headed the office where executive branch power is most zealously guarded, the Office of Legal Counsel of the Justice Department, now, as chief justice of the United States, authored an anti–executive power opinion, and for an overwhelming seven-vote majority. (Justice Anthony Kennedy, then new to the Court after the unsuccessful nominations first of Judge Bork and then Judge Douglas Ginsburg, to succeed the retiring Lewis Powell, Jr., did not participate.) Only newcomer Antonin Scalia, who had likewise headed OLC, was in dissent. A passionate and fervent dissent it was, eminently quotable as so many Scalia opinions have proved, but Scalia was all alone. No longer was Chief Justice Rehnquist the Lone Ranger. To the contrary, the Court's liberals and centrists were rallying under his leadership.

This enormous setback for conservatives in 1988 was then hugely compounded years later in 2000 as the chief authored the opinion reembracing one of the icons of the Warren Court era, the *Miranda* decision (discussed in detail in Chapter Eleven). Reagan administration alumni watched in disbelief as Rehnquist wrote, in a pithy opinion, that *Miranda* would stand. The contrast between the early Rehnquist (the associate justice) and the later Rehnquist (the chief justice) was vivid. As associate justice—on assignment from Chief Justice Burger—Rehnquist had authored a pivotal opinion (which won majority support on the Court in 1974) that the *Miranda* principle was not a core constitutional holding. But as chief, he embraced the idea that *Miranda* was a constitutional holding that could not be amended by Congress (much less overruled).

This contrast between the early and the later Rehnquist duly noted, however, it is emphatically not the case that the chief justice experienced the sort of complete philosophical transformation seen in the cases of Justice Harry Blackmun and, more recently, Justice David Souter. Nixon appointee Blackmun wound up voting consistently with the most liberal members of the Court. So has Bush appointee Souter. But not Rehnquist. The chief has been, above all, at the vanguard of restoring, as he sees it, the appropriate balance in the constitutional structure between the federal government and the states. This—the concept of federalism, aimed at keeping Congress within its enumerated powers under the Constitution—has been Rehnquist's signature issue. Rehnquist has been to federalism what his predecessor, Chief Justice Burger, was to separation of powers. As chief justice, Rehnquist has been a tireless and effective defender of what he sees as the rightful domain of the states.

On the social-issues front as well, the Court's widely discussed opinion in June 2000 in the Boy Scouts case—

whether the Boy Scouts could exclude a gay-rights activist as an assistant scoutmaster—instructively reminded observers of the chief justice's instinctive conservatism. On social issues, the chief is reliably traditional. He will not use judicial power to alter long-standing social institutions.

This, then, appeared to be the chief's guiding philosophy: No upsetting the apple cart. That, it seems, has been at the core of the chief's mission over the course of his fifteen years in the center seat. No wild gyrations if he can help it, which in its own way is a "conservative" approach even if it does not necessarily lead to "conservative results." To be sure, there remains a flicker of the flame that burned brightly during his days as a franchise junior member of the Court, the justice on whom Chief Justice Burger so heavily relied. In particular, Chief Justice Rehnquist remains quite eager to cure certain pivotal excesses (as he sees it) in the law, most particularly the unspeakably unacceptable *Roe v. Wade* and church-state decisions infected with an anti–religious freedom strain.

Nonetheless, when taken in the entirety of his work over the past fifteen years, Rehnquist as chief justice appears willing to accept much of modern-day constitutional law. He has, in surprising ways, been willing to follow principles of *stare decisis*—even if, as with *Miranda,* he wouldn't have agreed with the case to begin with. This, then, is the chief as judicial pragmatist, a respecter of legal precedent, wary of sudden change. He has set the tone of the current Court.

"He has been called the Arnold Schwarzenegger of the American judiciary." Graham Zellick, the vice chancellor of the University of London, got the audience's attention with his unexpected, clever introduction of the Supreme Court's most colorful, quotable member. Justice Antonin

Scalia had swept into London in the summer of 2000 to make several summertime speeches, this one a dinner address to a human-rights seminar. The next day, he would be moving about London with Lord Wolff, England's highest judge and one of the justice's many friends across the Atlantic.

As usual, the justice spoke without notes, revealing himself to be the natural teacher he is, witty, clever, and easy to understand. "I hate to be the skunk at the garden party," he said, obviously relishing the role. He had come from Vienna with a warning. Beware of sweeping statements of human rights, however noble and uplifting, when the enforcement mechanism will be an unaccountable judiciary. The ancient law of England and Wales, which the United States had inherited, was soon to have formally incorporated into it a super-layer of European human-rights law, effective October 2, 2000. The "New Labor" government of Tony Blair had warmly embraced the concept with little debate or discussion. Now the clock was ticking on British control of its own centuries-old body of law.

The Scalia theme was a familiar one. It transcended national boundaries. Be fearful, he suggested, of putting power in a judiciary—by design unaccountable to the people—to interpret "rights." Although protecting human rights is a noble goal, judges in interpreting a codified set of "rights" can—and do—fashion social policies that are then removed from the arena of democratic debate. The danger, Justice Scalia emphasized, is fundamental in a democratic society; judicial power tends to rob the people of the ability to decide for themselves how they would live and what kind of society they would have.

Justice Scalia thus raised the enduring issue before a constitutional court charged with interpreting the meaning of the Constitution. It is on this issue that the justices of the Supreme Court tend, without much open discussion, to divide sharply. Antonin Scalia takes a side in this debate, and he tirelessly trumpets it as he did on a summer evening in London. Of the sitting members of the Court, Justice Scalia has articulated the most systematic view of the way judges should go about interpreting the Constitution. His vision has by no means predominated; this is not the Scalia Court. The Court today is more of a centrist Court, and Justice Scalia is not a centrist. But the Supreme Court—and American constitutional law more generally—has been strongly influenced by his views. Scalia's express aim is to curb judicial power and maximize democratic self-government.

Although summarized in his remarks in London, the most comprehensive statement of Scalia's philosophy is found in his 1997 essay *A Matter of Interpretation*. His point is simple: The justices of the U.S. Supreme Court inherited a legal culture that we can call, simply, the common-law tradition. That tradition developed in England and migrated to the United States as an integral part of our early legal institutions. Simply put, the idea of the common law is that judges, in the course of deciding cases, develop principles of law that bind not only the parties in the particular case but other judges handling future cases. The judges' work is, in theory, subject to review and modification by legislatures. As it happened, the decisions of English (and then American) judges were usually left uncorrected. The judges, collectively, thus were able to develop bodies of law binding on everyone. Judges, in short, became lawmakers in the course of deciding cases. These principles of judge-made law (outside the context of the Constitution and its meaning) have governed important relationships in society. The world of business and commerce operates under the law of contract. Injuries caused by intentional acts or through negligence are redressed through the law of tort.

Common law is the mother's milk of beginning law students. Every year, 100,000 fresh new faces embark on an intense nine-month study of judge-made law in the 200 or so law schools around the United States. Here they learn to "think like a lawyer." They engage in a reasoned analysis of cases, whether in contract, property, or tort (along with a few other subjects), and learn to discern in those cases both the various principles of law (the rules themselves) and the reasons justifying those principles.

Justice Scalia summarizes the common-law tradition, as absorbed by first-year law students, this way: "[T]his system of making law by judicial opinion, and making law by distinguishing earlier cases, is what every American law student, every newborn American lawyer, first sees when he opens his eyes. And the impression remains for life. . . . That image of the great judge remains with the former law student when he himself becomes a judge, and thus the common-law tradition is passed on." With this tradition Justice Scalia is at peace. "I am content to leave the common law, and the process of developing the common law, where it is."

But along the way of common-law development, something very important happened. With greater frequency as the years went by, Congress and state legislatures passed laws covering a wide (and ever-growing) range of subjects. But law students, guided by their professors, largely went on as before, living in the world of the common law. Little attention was paid to the development of statute law. This was odd, Justice Scalia notes, because statutes abound. Yet, even in law-school courses where the analysis of statutes was unavoidable, say, in the law of employment discrimination, the focus remained on case law. The upshot of this decided educational tilt toward cases, rather than statutes, is that statutory interpretation remained a distant cousin, receiving little notice in the law schools. In

short, as common-law development became ever more re-
fined, statutory interpretation remained primitive, so
much so that settled rules of statutory interpretation were
never agreed upon. Indeed, the Scalia school emphasizes,
the legal system has never agreed on what the *basic mission* of statutory interpretation should be. Is the purpose
in analyzing statutes to determine the legislature's intent in
passing the law? Or something else?

Justice Scalia has a clear and carefully worked out answer. His "mission statement" for statutory interpretation
pours directly over into his theory of constitutional interpretation. It is, in a word, "textualism." For Scalia, textualism is not to be confused with what is frequently called
strict construction, discussed in Chapter One. Political
camps, reflecting the ongoing debate within the law, tend
to divide into warring sides. For those favoring generous
interpretation of "rights" provisions in the Constitution
and the Bill of Rights, the watchwords are *the living Constitution*. The theory goes like this: As society evolves over
time, our "understanding" of the Constitution likewise
evolves. The Constitution embodies "values," which then
guide the judge in articulating what they are in the current
age.

The living-Constitution school of judging is a very ex-
citing one, Scalia observes, for under that school's philosophy, judges enjoy substantial latitude in interpreting the
Constitution. Consider, for example, the key constitutional word *liberty*, whose meaning the justices have con-
tentiously debated. Abortion, physician-assisted suicide,
grandparents' visitation rights, gay and lesbian rights—all
these, and more, are analyzed and decided under the
rubric of "liberty." But the issue is, Who decides what the
governing social policy will be? Judges or legislatures? For
the Scalia school, the answer is fundamental. Liberty, in
the ultimate constitutional sense, means at its core the

freedom of a democratic society to govern itself. In the main, judges should stay on the sidelines while the other branches are out on the playing field of government. In contrast, the living-Constitution school—illustrated by the Warren Court and its admirers—encourages judges to engage in the game.

For opponents of bold, muscular judging, a living Constitution represents a judicial license to read into the Constitution what he or she thinks is right, or just, or good. Uncomfortable with this more freewheeling approach to constitutional interpretation, conservative critics frequently insist on strict construction, as we saw in the previous chapter.

Justice Scalia shies away from this description of his judicial philosophy. In *A Matter of Interpretation* he writes: "I am not a strict constructionist, and no one ought to be—though better that, I suppose, than a nontextualist." He elaborates: "A text should not be construed strictly, and it should not be construed leniently; it should be construed reasonably, to contain all that it fairly means."

How did this great divide in the law come to be? It is, as Justice Scalia sees it, the temptation to carry on the common-law tradition. Keep making the law. Judges weave contract law, tort law, property law, so why not the "higher law" of the Constitution? Scalia explains: "The Constitution, however, even though a democratically adopted text, we formally treat like the common law." Scalia instead urges: Remain true to the text. Text and structure will yield up answers if we will be lawyerly and rigorous in our approach. The Constitution is law, and it should be treated as law. Avoid, in short, the common-law tradition of judging.

How does textualism work? First, writes Scalia in his essay, context is critical. "In textual interpretation, context is everything, and the context of the Constitution tells us not to expect nit-picking detail, and to give words and phrases an expansive rather than narrow interpretation— though, not an interpretation that the language will not bear." Take freedom of speech and the companion First Amendment liberty, freedom of the press. Justice Scalia engages in a textualist interpretation this way: "Hand-written letters, for example, are neither speech nor press. Yet surely there is no doubt they cannot be censored. In this constitutional context, speech and press, the two most common forms of communication, stand as a sort of synecdoche for the whole. That is not strict construction, but it is reasonable construction." In the textualist approach, then, the constitutional freedoms of speech and press are about *communication*. The reasonable judge thus does not limit the terms *speech* and *press* to their most narrow meanings. That might be strict construction, but it is not textualism. Rather, the textualist judge, using reason and logic, discerns that these two constitutional watchwords were designed to protect communications more broadly.

Symbolic acts of protest that convey a message—like wearing an armband in protest or burning the flag—are forms of communication. So too art and music. All these, and more, thus enjoy the protection of the First Amendment.

This is, in shorthand, the textualist effort to discern meaning—the original meaning as embodied in the text. It is not, however, "intent." We do not ask, in a proper textualist analysis, what the framers of the Constitution "intended." We inquire, rather, into what the words they chose to employ mean. And that meaning is controlling. Nor is the textualist overly wedded to the Court's prior cases and their holdings. This is very much a matter of judgment, or degree, as to how much respect the applicable set of judicial precedents should enjoy. But as a matter of judgment, and as a matter of degree, the common-law value of precedent—*stare decisis*—ranks lower on the textualist value scale. Scalia's passionate and continuing opposition, year after year, to *Roe v. Wade* illustrates the relative weakness of *stare decisis* for a textualist. That, then, is textualism, or the Scalia school.

Like Justice Scalia, Justice Anthony Kennedy is charming and witty, continually displaying a boyish enthusiasm that belies his proud status as grandfather. He has an uncanny ability to connect with an audience. In his inaugural days as a justice, Kennedy appeared before the Supreme Court Historical Society and made a picture-perfect fifty-minute presentation in the courtroom itself of the period when President Franklin D. Roosevelt tried to "pack" the Court with a majority of justices. This unique episode, prompted by the Court's invalidation of critical portions of FDR's New Deal, is one of fascination and intrigue to Court watchers. Stymied by the Court's adverse decisions, FDR sent a message to Congress in February 1937 calling for appointment of an additional justice for each justice aged seventy or over. The idea, of course, was to bring about a Supreme Court less hostile to New Deal programs. The plan failed, and it buttressed the independence of the Supreme Court from Congress and the president. Kennedy laid out the saga with ease. It was an altogether impressive performance. The audience was effusive, uttering comments like "A tour de force" and "Can you believe that he didn't use a note?"

Justice Kennedy's assiduous focus on the justices and the constitutional case law of the 1930s signaled much more than a commonly shared judicial interest in constitutional history. Time and again in the course of his opinions, he focuses extensively on the Court's case law. He reasons and analogizes from what is already found in the

Court's jurisprudence. He distinguishes, carefully, cases handed down by prior Courts. Kennedy is, in short, a common-law constitutionalist. He appears most offended when the Court departs from what he sees as the logic and thrust of its prior opinions. On the last day of the 2000 term, the justice, in a rare display of wounded feelings, railed against the majority opinion in an abortion-related free-speech case (*Hill v. Colorado*). From the bench, he lamented as "profoundly disappointing" the Court's rejection of pro-life activists' challenge to a Colorado statute limiting their ability to engage in leafleting and sidewalk counseling outside abortion clinics. Kennedy spoke with considerable authority, for he has fashioned himself—in the manner of the common law—as a champion of First Amendment freedoms. A vigorous free-speech advocate, he has built upon the Court's growing body of free-speech precedent. Moved mainly by Kennedy's free-speech opinions, Burt Neuborne, former litigation director of the ACLU and law professor at New York University, has pronounced the current Supreme Court "the most profoundly pro–First Amendment Court in the nation's history."

In the 2000 free-speech case, Justice Kennedy's pristine common-law methodology was abundantly evident as he moved through the lengthy set of cases involving leafleting and pamphleteering. For him, the Colorado statute—making it a crime to "knowingly approach another person within eight feet of such person . . . for the purpose of passing a leaflet or handbill to, displaying a sign to, or engaging in oral protest, education, or counseling with such other person in the public way or sidewalk area"—was manifestly unconstitutional. The majority, in contrast, emphasized that the statute was narrow and confined, leaving open ample channels of communication. Justice Kennedy was unimpressed. He began his twenty-nine-page dissent this way: "The Court's holding contradicts more than a half-century of well-established First Amendment principles." The Court, Kennedy said, was doing something for the first time—and that's presumptively suspect in the common-law constitutional tradition. "For the first time, the Court approves a law which bars a private citizen from passing a message, in a peaceful manner and on a profound moral issue, to a fellow citizen on a public sidewalk." He was outraged. "To say that one citizen can approach another to ask the time or the weather forecast or the directions to Main Street but not to initiate discussion on one of the most basic moral and political issues in all of contemporary discourse, a question touching profound ideas in philosophy and theology, is an astonishing view of the First Amendment." The Court's approach, he said, "is an affront to First Amendment teachings." "Teachings," of course, meant the Court's prior decisions.

To be sure, as elsewhere in the law, nuance counts. And Justice Kennedy, in particular, seems to have a "thumb on the scales" in First Amendment cases. He tends, strongly, to err on the side of promoting First Amendment values. Still and all, much of the Court's modern case law is squarely on the side of a libertarian approach to First Amendment issues.

In the abortion-speech case more specifically, however, Justice Kennedy seemed to be speaking in particular to the most influential of the common-law constitutionalists, Justice Sandra Day O'Connor. So frequently over the years they had voted together, including in some of the watershed moments when the Court faced thorny questions regarding abortion and school prayer. The two westerners, both Stanford alums, were kindred spirits. Both stood solidly on middle ground, in the spirit of Justice Lewis Powell, Jr. But in the late 1990s, the O'Connor–Kennedy voting relationship began to fray. And Justice Kennedy seemed to take umbrage at the growing separation.

Justice O'Connor had teamed up with someone new—an appointee of President Clinton. On several large issues (with federalism a notable exception), Justice O'Connor and Justice Stephen Breyer were solidly together. Their growing judicial kinship was evidenced most provocatively on partial-birth abortion, the most controversial social-issues case of recent years (*Stenburg v. Carhart* [2000]). Along with thirty other states, Nebraska had outlawed a particularly grisly abortion method, one carried out by delivery (partial or otherwise) of the fetus into the vagina before procedures too gruesome to describe in detail (but fully described in Justice Breyer's majority opinion and in Justice Thomas's dissent) were employed to terminate life. In the face of disapproval of the particular procedure (called D&X) by various medical authorities, the Court still overturned Nebraska's ban on this procedure. The states were to be severely limited in their regulation of specific medical procedures used in the abortion context. Justice Kennedy was especially dismayed. The decision departed from the "common law" of the Constitution. Specifically, Kennedy viewed the decision as inconsistent with the carefully wrought compromise opinion in *Planned Parenthood v. Casey,* the pivotal 1992 case reaffirming the Court's landmark decision in *Roe v. Wade* but permitting the states to impose regulations on the procedure, such as parental notification.

To Kennedy, O'Connor had betrayed the *Casey* compromise constructed by the O'Connor–Kennedy–Souter trio. But what lay behind the wounds, it seems, was a different calibration of common-law constitutionalism. The two centrists, O'Connor and Kennedy, were not marching to the beat of the same drummer on this watershed issue. To the contrary, Justice O'Connor was a step (or two) in front. She proved to be more of an innovator within the traditions of common-law constitutionalism.

*   *   *

She is the most influential and powerful woman in America. Growing up on the Lazy B ranch in Arizona, Sandra Day O'Connor developed a fiercely independent bent of mind. At home with cowboys or ambassadors, and the Court's most prominent member of the Washington social scene, Justice O'Connor is the Court's pivotal member. As she goes, more frequently than not, so goes the Court.

Coupled with her fierce independence, Justice O'Connor's background as a state court judge in Arizona, entrusted directly with the development of the common law in the manner described in Justice Scalia's *A Matter of Interpretation,* perhaps contributed to her greater flexibility in interpreting the Court's prior cases, and in particular in fashioning the *Casey* compromise on *Roe v. Wade.* She was accustomed to the common-law tradition of finding a better rule in the analysis of legal problems. In other arenas, she had shown a flexible willingness to rewrite statutes in order to save them. She was willing to step back when the Court entered new arenas and proceed with what seemed to other members of the Court extreme caution. She was flexible, as common-law creators tend to be. She positioned herself in the center and articulated a theory or principle in her own way. Most prominently in this respect, Justice O'Connor displayed the quality of judicial creativity on highly charged church-state issues as well as abortion, fashioning entirely new doctrine. The Court, as we will see, has struggled for consistency in its decisions under the Establishment Clause of the First Amendment prohibiting laws "respecting an establishment of religion." The Court's work over the years has been largely a search for coherent, consistent doctrine. Justice O'Connor proved highly creative in this sensitive area of church-state relations. She created a new concept or principle in the law: the idea of "endorsement." That is, in her view, a violation of the Establishment Clause occurs when government "endorses" religion or religious practice. What did this mean? O'Connor stated the idea at a high level of generality. Government could not make one's religious beliefs, or lack thereof, relevant to one's standing in the political community. To do so would effect an "endorsement" of religion (or, conversely, irreligion).

What about the nation's motto, "In God We Trust"? Is this an endorsement of religion? Surely it is, many would say. The nation, speaking through its government in a statute, says that it is placing its trust not in the people, or the Constitution framed by "We the People," but in God. Others would say the national motto is merely an acknowledgment of our history and tradition, not rising to the level of an endorsement.

Ultimately, we are left to guess as to the reach of the undefined "endorsement" principle. Tellingly, the endorsement test was not drawn from prior case law; it was, rather, Justice O'Connor's "take" on the values that undergird the Establishment Clause and the many cases over the decades interpreting the meaning of that pivotal part of the First Amendment. She was seeking, as she put it, to *clarify* the law. She set forth her view to this effect in a separate, concurring opinion upholding the practice of including a creche in a Christmastime display on city property in Pawtucket, Rhode Island. That is, her vote was a "majority" vote, but she wrote a separate opinion setting forth the different way that she examined the Establishment Clause issue in the case. From that modest beginning in a single case, with the Court struggling over the constitutionality of the creche, the concept of endorsement was incorporated into the body of First Amendment law. After all, her centrist vote was of critical importance on a closely divided Court. Her vote, and frequently that of Justice Anthony Kennedy, proved decisive.

And thus, a centrist, common-law constitutionalist from Arizona, with little prior judicial experience before arriving in Washington, became the Court's most powerful member. Her power from the middle has never been more evident than in the Court's recent affirmative action decisions, where, having previously joined majorities requiring strict scrutiny of racial preferences, she became the critical fifth vote on the Court for the proposition that diversity in the classroom is a compelling governmental interest that can withstand strict scrutiny analysis. Her path to power was simple. Step one: positioning herself at the Court's center—avoiding strict doctrines or rigid, bright-line principles and thus leaving some running room for later cases. That meant, necessarily, rejecting textualism. Step two: being ready and willing to create new law. She was, in short, farther along the common-law constitutionalism spectrum than Justice Kennedy.

In so doing, she moved farther away from the Scalia school, thus triggering some of Justice Scalia's sharpest condemnatory language. He found doctrinal flexibility to be aggravating. But it was not just the conservatives who were upset. At other critical times, as in the June 2000 partial-birth abortion case, she also left her fellow centrist Justice Kennedy suffering in dissent as she engaged in common-law creativity. Just as in the Establishment Clause arena, so too in abortion. Justice O'Connor crafted what became the law of the land. She had fashioned a concept—now governing the law of abortion—dubbed "undue burden." That is, the state may regulate, but not prohibit (the "core holding" of *Roe v. Wade*), pre-viability abortions so long as those regulatory controls do not constitute an "undue burden" on the woman's right to choose. The origins of O'Connor's test were entirely unclear. A doctrine by the same name, undue burden, existed in a completely unrelated arena: the law of the Commerce Clause. That sort of test, which asks, for example, whether states could impose airbags requirements and the like, seemed far afield from abortion.

Justice O'Connor never supplied a detailed explanation of the test's origins. She did proceed, as time went on, to elucidate what the phrase meant, using such terms as *substantial obstacle*. But this was legal jargon. It was an abstract notion, calling for judgment. The question, continually recurring in the abortion cases, is what constitutes an undue burden? No one knows in advance what the justice(s) will decide.

The result of a particular challenge—yes, it's an undue burden or no, it's not—depends entirely on judicial judgment. On the spectrum of decision-making, this is at the polar opposite of relying on the text and structure or history of the Constitution. What really decides the case is the reasoned judgment of the justice. This is upsetting to adherents of Justice Scalia's *A Matter of Interpretation*. To make matters worse for the textualists, that judgment of the justice(s) is not necessarily guided by prior law. This is the creative dimension of Justice O'Connor's common-law constitutionalism. Rather than looking to the wisdom of generations of judges, as a common-law judge would do in weaving the law of contract or tort, in the Justice O'Connor approach *it is the judgment of the then sitting justice that counts*. There is little, and perhaps no, highly developed body of law to guide the judge in his or her analysis. The judge herself is, rather, the reasoned arbiter of competing interests.

This process of judging tends naturally to be highly subjective. And a justice's use of subjective judgment in construing the Constitution maximizes the federal judiciary's power at the (potential) expense of the political branches (or the states).

This way of approaching the job of interpreting the Constitution alarms the Scalia school. To the textualist justice,

this judgment-oriented approach to constitutional interpretation represents raw judicial power, guided essentially
by the individual justice's individualistic sense of right and
wrong. To be sure, the justice may have eminently sound
judgment; indeed, the judge (or justice) may be widely
viewed as a person of great wisdom and high integrity. Her
views may be firmly rooted in widely shared moral and
ethical norms. But that process of judging is not one of law,
the Scalia school would say. To textualists, that approach
is nothing less than judicial power in control, displacing
democratic choices made through the political process.

Depending on the level (or degree) of judicial creativity,
this fashioning of common-law constitutional principles
leaves a moderate centrist like Justice Kennedy uneasy.
That seemed to be happening as the closely watched term
ending in June 2000 drew to its remarkable close. And so
it came to be that in the partial-birth abortion case, a critical juncture in constitutional interpretation, Justice
Kennedy was unwilling to engage in a creative form of
common-law constitutionalism.

Into Justice Kennedy's place stepped Justice Stephen
Breyer. Law professor, judge (indeed, chief judge of the
U.S. Court of Appeals in Boston), and public-policy wonk,
Justice Breyer had come into his own through a profes-
sorship at the Harvard Law School coupled with a stint in
public service as a senior staffer on Capitol Hill. Then-
Professor Breyer, on leave from his academic perch at Harvard, became a deregulatory champion on Senator
Edward Kennedy's staff during the 1970s. He had served,
ably, as Senator Kennedy's chief counsel during the Carter
years when Washington was filled with bipartisan zeal for
deregulation. Chief Counsel Breyer's principal accom-
plishment was putting the old Civil Aeronautics Board out
of business (as principal staff architect of the Airline

Deregulation Act of 1978), while winning friends and admirers on both sides of the aisle. Of most enduring political importance, soon-to-be Judge Breyer won the ardent respect of Utah Republican Senator Orrin Hatch, who was destined to be chairman of the Senate Judiciary Committee. Years later, Breyer's relationship with Senator Hatch and other Judiciary Committee Republicans assured his smooth confirmation to replace retiring Nixon appointee Harry Blackmun. Justice Blackmun, the passionate defender (and author) of *Roe v. Wade,* had outlasted Republican presidents and left his vacant seat to be filled by President Clinton. His successor, he was confident, would zealously defend his principal legacy, *Roe v. Wade.*

The academic Breyer has mounted the most comprehensive attack on Justice Scalia's approach. "Attack," though, overstates it, in view of Justice Breyer's easygoing style. Like Scalia, Breyer is likable, witty, and a powerful speaker. Impressive in oral arguments, he sounds reassuring and measured. He avoids, scrupulously, being argumentative. He declines, with great effectiveness, to join the textualist school and carries on by example a very different style of constitutional judging. He displays balance, moderation, care. "Why be doctrinaire, why be so rigid?" he seems to ask. Who can be so sure? Consider all the relevant materials that will be helpful in statutory (and constitutional) interpretation. Take the case law very seriously, and *stare decisis* does indeed count. Armed with a powerful intellect combined with a charming personality, Breyer carries on the philosophical fight more subtly than the irrepressible Scalia.

The justice from San Francisco (Stanford undergraduate, then Harvard Law) has growing influence within the Court. He arrived six years after Justice Scalia, long indeed in "Court time," and he remains (as of this writing) the Court's most junior member. But influence he has, abundantly, wrapped in a quieter, less flamboyant style than the larger-than-life master of the textualist school. Justice Breyer doesn't occupy the bully pulpit with either the zeal or the frequency of Justice Scalia. Nor does he write as memorably, or as quotably, as his textualist counterpart. But he does his work with enormous collegiality. He seems to enjoy joint appearances more than solo performances. Justice Scalia is a one-man show; Justice Breyer seems more at home on panels. Sharing podiums, participating with his colleagues—especially Justices O'Connor and Ruth Bader Ginsburg—seems to be his preferred venue. His individual message, as a result, is not quite so vivid. He is not the Scalia-style nightingale alone in the forest.

This spirit of collegiality pours over into Breyer's philosophy of judging. Veteran of Capitol Hill that he is, Justice Breyer seems acutely sensitive to letting Congress (as opposed to state legislatures) have its way. His opinions convey deep respect for the congressional process, and—relatedly—modesty as to the judicial capacity to figure out knotty problems with which Congress must wrestle. He is also sensitive to the practical demands of government, as seen in his separate opinion in the Paula Corbin Jones case. There, while disagreeing with President Clinton's argument that he should enjoy a temporary immunity from civil litigation, Justice Breyer expressed worries about the possibility of distracting litigation. Judges, he insisted, should be highly respectful of the presidency and its demands.

The reader will have already noted the irony here. The textualist school argues against judicial power while frequently striking down Congress's work product. Justice Breyer, in contrast, strives mightily to sustain what Congress has done; indeed, he will defer to Congress when his fellow "liberals" will not. So it was that he found himself in dissent when the Court, including his fellow Clinton administration appointee Ruth Bader Ginsburg, struck down a law aimed at preventing sexually explicit channels, like the Playboy Channel, having their visual or audio signal intruding ("bleeding") into home(s) of viewers who had not subscribed to such salacious stuff. Signal bleed, as it is called, was obviously a serious problem for parents concerned about their children. Drawing from First Amendment precedents, Justice Kennedy—the ardent First Amendment defender—combined with the Court's liberal members and, intriguingly, with Justice Thomas to invalidate the law on First Amendment grounds. The reason was not love of Playboy or Spice Channel material. Rather, the same result (protecting homes against unwanted signals) could have been achieved through less intrusive methods.

But to Justice Breyer, these were technical issues calling for judicial modesty and deference to Congress. Reaching across the usual philosophical lines, Justice Breyer authored the main dissenting opinion in the case, joined by his textualist nemesis Justice Scalia and Chief Justice Rehnquist (who, as the senior justice in the minority, would have made the tactical decision to assign the writing to Justice Breyer) and his philosophical friend, Sandra Day O'Connor. Breyer expressed the need for deference to Congress's judgment in seeking to shield children from unwanted adult-programming signals. He challenges Justice Kennedy's analysis for the majority: "I could not disagree more when the majority implies that the Government's independent interest in offering such protection—preventing, say, an eight-year-old child from watching virulent pornography without parental consent—might not be 'compelling.'" To Justice Breyer, Congress knows best.

In a similar vein, joining (as he increasingly does) with Justice O'Connor, Breyer has moved to the center on the issue of government aid to parochial schools. If Congress wants it, Congress can have it. The upshot, surprisingly, is that Justice Breyer has actually shifted from his earlier opposition to such aid; he had initially embraced a more hard-line separationist approach to Establishment Clause issues. He has since moved a long way—to a position of embracing Congress's bipartisan effort to provide computers and other learning materials to all schools, including private parochial schools. No rigid doctrines for Breyer. Leaving behind the unyielding separationism of the Court's most liberal justices (who were quite willing to invalidate Congress's handiwork), Justice Breyer has been willing to accommodate. Yet he would not embrace the more doctrinally pure approach of Justice Thomas, who wrote the main opinion upholding Congress's program of aid to parochial schools. Rather, Justice Breyer was in agreement with his frequent jurisprudential companion, Justice O'Connor, in a separate opinion (for the two of them only). The upshot is that a seemingly odd couple— Justices O'Connor and Breyer—now are the decisive votes in this sensitive area of First Amendment law.

There is one huge chasm, however, between Justice Breyer and O'Connor: the rights and prerogatives of the states. Justice Breyer's ideal of deference to Congress leads him, in sharp contrast to Justice O'Connor, to uphold federal statutes that intrude into traditional arenas of state regulation, and he is increasingly the voice of the four-member minority in this respect. Although on the losing side on this issue, Justice Breyer now serves as the pro–congressional-power franchise player.

History here is an unerring guide. Democratic presidents since FDR have never failed in nominating justices who welcome congressional assertions of power to regulate, as against the claims of the states. Congress may, in the Democratic nominees' perspective, step over the constitutional line when it comes to individual rights. That not infrequently happens. So it was in the Playboy Entertainment case that Justice Ginsburg aligned herself with the First Amendment challengers to Congress's effort to keep adult-fare signals from bleeding into nonsubscribers' homes. But for the two appointees of President Clinton, the states will lose when Congress sees fit to legislate in arenas of their traditional authority. Of the two the nimble Justice Breyer has proved the more influential.

Thus, on the subject of partial-birth abortion, it was altogether natural that the writing assignment fell to Justice Breyer (made by the senior justice in the majority, Justice Stevens) to write the deeply controversial majority opinion invalidating the state law prohibiting the procedure. No one else would so likely win the vote of Justice O'Connor (to the dismay of Justice Kennedy) on this wrenching subject. Justice Breyer knew how to put the winning combination together.

For the Supreme Court of the past two decades, abortion has been the most divisive, intractable issue. This, more than any other issue (including right-to-die questions, school prayer, and affirmative action), has moved ordinary people to take to the streets. For pro-choice forces, anxious to avoid further erosion of *Roe*'s triumph for autonomy rights, Justice Breyer has become the pivotal justice. On this subject he is now the Court's leader. And he has achieved this status quietly, without offering a formal response to Justice Scalia's articulation of textualism.

For all their influence, however, none of the five key justices is as intriguing and original as Clarence Thomas. His life story is well known. Born into poverty in Pin Point, Georgia, Thomas was rescued from a dysfunctional family by a loving grandfather, raised as a Roman Catholic (and after a period of Episcopalianism returned to the faith of his youth), educated at Holy Cross and Yale Law School. He is a black conservative, a combination that confounds many. But even to his detractors, his warmth and humanity are unquestioned, as movingly reflected by the recent adoption of his nephew, Mark, and his becoming, by his own description, a soccer mom. He is a person of deep emotion, occasionally moved to tears on the podium, only minutes later to astonish companions who don't know him well with a robust, booming laugh. He is a justice of few questions at oral argument but one brimming with ideas, willing at times to play the iconoclast. He is unyieldingly principled, and thus a hero to conservatives. He is in the pro-liberty camp, as long as a textual basis can be found for the right or liberty in question. Like Scalia, for example, he frequently sides with criminal defendants, *when* they are asserting a textually rooted right (such as the Fourth Amendment's protection against unreasonable searches and seizures and the Fifth Amendment's protection against compelled self-incrimination). But otherwise he is skeptical of judicial power, and thus refuses not to follow the language of the Constitution and the Bill of Rights; he will not "create the law." The clearest example is the death penalty, which is textually grounded in the Constitution, and thus to Justice Thomas the death penalty cannot be *per se* unconstitutional. Thomas, in short, is the polar opposite of the common-law constitutionalist.

On the other hand, the early canard that Justice Thomas is simply a Scalia clone is barely heard any longer as Thomas moves into his second decade of service. They are both textualists, and this brings them together on a wide variety of issues. Abortion, thus, is utterly without constitutional protection, save for a general protection against arbitrary, irrational restraints on liberty. But Thomas is more willing than Scalia to revisit seemingly settled issues. If the Court's decisions are wrong, then the doctrine in question should be reexamined. The task of the principled justice, in Thomas's view, is to get the right answer—years and even decades of wrong answers by the Court don't make it right. And there are no compromises; that's the stuff of politics, not law. This mind-set positions Thomas wholly apart from O'Connor, even though they frequently agree on a bottom line as to the proper result in a case.

The three remaining justices are the forlorn liberals: two Republican appointees, John Paul Stevens and David Souter, and Ruth Bader Ginsburg, appointed in 1993 by President Clinton. Stevens, a bowtie-wearing midwesterner, is warm and gracious, as befits his midwestern roots. Extremely smart and creative, Stevens, appointed by President Ford in the wake of Watergate and the resignation of President Nixon, began his service on the Court as a bit of an odd man out. He seemed to look at legal problems differently, more creatively. But in due course he hit his stride, and he has been unabashedly liberal in approach for the past two decades. He is an untiring supporter of abortion rights, uncompromising in defense of a separationist approach to church-state issues, inclined to support the rights of criminal defendants, unsparing in objections to the death penalty. In short, he is a dream justice by the standards of the *New York Times* editorial board and the cultural elite. Even better for Warren Court admirers, Stevens will use judicial power to achieve what he thinks is right and just.

The result is that Justice Stevens, even with his great talents, has largely been marginalized. Despite his intellect and energy, he has taken on the role of naysayer. But he is not alone. Fellow Republican David Souter, who had served as attorney general of New Hampshire and as a justice on that state's supreme court before a brief stint on the federal court of appeals in Boston, has utterly confounded those around President Bush who engineered his nomination. He has become, with very few exceptions, reliably liberal. He thus has likewise been in dissent on the big issues, unless, of course, Justice O'Connor (or, to a lesser extent, Justice Kennedy) swings to the liberal camp. A lifelong bachelor, Souter is a prodigious worker and leads an ascetic style of life. But he labors, in the context of the Rehnquist Court, on the margins, lacking great influence on his fellow justices. His quick transformation from a traditional conservative to a reliable liberal remains unexplained. Unlike Harry Blackmun, who seemed radicalized by the uproar over his majority opinion in *Roe v. Wade,* Justice Souter has had no dramatic experiences during his quiet, unremarkable tenure that would explain his complete about-face.

In contrast, Ruth Bader Ginsburg has proved the reliable liberal that President Clinton sought. Her liberal background as a feminist activist lawyer and professor was offputting to Attorney General Griffin Bell, who during President Carter's tenure passed over then renowned ACLU lawyer Ruth Ginsburg in her quest to become solicitor general. After his departure, Judge Bell's successor, Attorney General Ben Civiletti, was entirely comfortable pushing her nomination as a judge on the court where I was destined to serve, the D.C. circuit court. There, she amassed an enviable record. Bright and energetic, she was an intellectual leader of that high-powered court, and became friendly with Judge Robert Bork and Judge Scalia, her future Supreme Court colleague. Her influence in the circuit court was great, but it has not been matched during her first decade of service on the Supreme Court. Like Stevens and Souter, she is a predictable liberal who has yet to articulate an overarching, unifying approach to constitutional interpretation. And she has not shown the flexibility that has brought together the increasingly powerful axis of Justices O'Connor and Breyer. They, not the liberals, are the dominant day-to-day players, while the most original thinking emanates from the conservative icons. And, as we will see in various settings, none is as original as Clarence Thomas.

PART TWO

The Rights of "We the People"

Chapter Three

★

SHOUTING FIRE IN CROWDED THEATERS: THE FREEDOM OF SPEECH

WILLIAM KUNSTLER HAD DEDICATED HIS LIFE to defending radical causes. Now the free-speech rights of flag-burners had brought him to the Supreme Court. In a case coming out of Texas, the Court had decided a year earlier that desecrating the flag as part of a political protest was protected "speech" under the First Amendment (*Texas v. Johnson* [1989]). With the country predictably outraged, Congress promptly passed the Flag Protection Act of 1989, which was now under constitutional challenge in the High Court. Kunstler was the lead lawyer for an assembly of radicals who had engaged in acts of flag desecration. All five were sitting in the rear of the courtroom, waiting for their case, *U.S. v. Eichman* (1990), to be heard by the nine justices. Their legal position was simple. The Court had held in the Texas case that flag desecration was protected expression under the Free Speech Clause, and all the defendants had done was what the flag-burner in *Texas v. Johnson* had managed to accomplish in front of Dallas City Hall—to express their views about U.S. policies (or some political party) by burning or otherwise profaning the flag. This was, they argued, the Texas case all over again.

The courtroom was overflowing with observers anxious to see the argument. This was an important chapter in the Court's history. In *Johnson,* the Court had effectively nullified the flag-desecration statutes of forty-eight states. Would the Court now strike down a law of Congress protecting the flag? Especially one framed in response to *Johnson* that did not contain aspects of the Texas statute that the Court, by a vote of 5–4, had found objectionable? Given the close vote in *Johnson,* all it would take was a single switched vote among the five justices in the majority, and Old Glory would carry the day.

Kunstler didn't seem worried. He was relaxed, bantering away. The marshals were clearing the courtroom after a long ceremony admitting scores of lawyers to membership in the Supreme Court bar. For $100 and a certificate in good standing from one's home state bar, a lawyer with three years' experience may be admitted to practice before the High Court. Because Congress had placed a provision in the law that required constitutional challenges to be moved to the Supreme Court, bypassing the courts of appeals, a special sitting of the Court had been scheduled. Some clever lawyers thought they could secure great seats by moving a lawyer's admission to the bar. Under this approach, it would "cost" $100 for two seats inside the bar of the Court, a prime location. One of the splendid things about the Court, apart from its majestic marble architecture and dazzling staircases, is that the courtroom seats for members of the Supreme Court bar are near the podium where the advocates stand to make their arguments. These enterprising lawyers figured they would have the best of all worlds. Friends and family of the new admittees sat in the regular seats, ostensibly savoring the happy occasion of the swearing in but in reality attending a historic argument over the meaning of the First Amendment.

But the plans of the insider-lawyers were foiled. Oral arguments are open to the public on a first-come, first-served basis, and outside the Court are two waiting groups. One is for those who want to see the entire argument; the other is for those who want to catch a glimpse—up to three minutes' worth. On the day *U.S. v. Eichman* was to be heard, the lines were long, and Court administrators decided to make as much room as they could to accommodate the unusually large number of visitors. So immediately upon completion of the bar-admission ceremony, marshals appeared to clear the courtroom. To the lawyers' chagrin, $100 bought what it always had, not the best seats in the house for the argument.

The Supreme Court thus experienced the equivalent in baseball of a rain delay. The justices, already seated, got up and left as the shepherding of new attendees into the courtroom began. The lawyers set to argue the case, which was the only argument for the day, chatted as the new audience was ushered in. My task, as solicitor general, was to defend the constitutionality of the statute. Kunstler's role, in contrast, was to defend the First Amendment rights of his five clients to desecrate or burn the flag.

Kunstler was friendly, avuncular, joking away. He was a complete natural, I thought, totally without pretense. I had expected haughty condescension, but there was not a trace. His glasses were perched—characteristically for Kunstler—on his forehead. Kunstler's co-counsel asked whether I would like to meet their clients, the flag-burners. Unlike the hapless lawyers in the $100 seats, the five had not been required to get up and leave during the seating reshuffle. I was a little fidgety and welcomed the excuse to walk around. Plus, I was curious.

One in particular I was especially curious to meet: Dred Scott Tyler, a black radical and an artist with a work displayed in a Chicago museum that required the visitor to walk all over the flag. Tyler's work had inflamed then Senator Bob Dole, who took to the Senate floor to denounce this outrage and argue for the new federal law. I asked Kunstler whether he was going with us for the courtesy call on his clients. "Oh, no," Kunstler replied with a broad smile. "I'm much too conservative for those guys."

Chuckling about Kunstler's "conservatism," we made our way back to the flag-burners' row. They were easily spotted, all dressed in countercultural black. They huddled together quietly in the back row, just in front of the thick curtains draping the rear of the courtroom. Kunstler's co-counsel made a straightforward introduction: "Folks, I'd like you to meet the solicitor general, who's going to be arguing the case for the government this morning." To my surprise, the flag-burners seemed friendly. Smiles and handshakes went uneventfully, with a particularly broad, friendly smile from Dred Scott Tyler. I reached across the aisle to shake hands. The moment was very cordial. Then we came to the flag-burner sitting closest to the aisle. He kept his arms folded and glared straight ahead, not looking my way or even at his own lawyer. "I don't shake hands with the government," he declared. The impromptu meet-and-greet session came to an abrupt end.

The grumpy flag-burner had accurately identified the role. The solicitor general was there to represent the government. He had to defend the constitutionality of the law, not an easy task. The Bush administration had strongly supported the goal of protecting the flag but differed with many in Congress over what it would take to accomplish that noble goal (as we saw it). In testimony before Congress, my colleagues in the Justice Department had taken the position that the broad sweep of the Court's opinion in the Texas case meant that *only* a constitutional amendment would suffice to protect the flag. A statute would not be enough. But Congress opted in favor of a statute, and it was now up to the Supreme Court to determine whether the law passed First Amendment muster. For my part, as the solicitor general, I was duty-bound to defend the constitutionality of a law passed by Congress if reasonable arguments could be mounted on its behalf. Inside the SG's office we labeled the operative standard the "straight-face" test. If the lawyer could argue a legal position with a straight face, then as the government's lawyer in the Supreme Court you had a moral and legal duty to do your best to defend the government's legal position. Make the argument to the best of your ability and do so in good faith, even if in your heart you think it's bound to lose. That's the government advocate's duty, as opposed to the obligation of the justices. In contrast, the justices are morally bound to use their independent judgment and come to a view as to what the right answer is under the relevant law, including the Constitution. Their job requires interpretation. In this context, the issue revolved around the term *freedom of speech*. Did this First Amendment freedom encompass actions, such as flag-burning, intended to communicate an idea or opinion? Justice Oliver Wendell Holmes had made a classic statement to the effect that shouting "Fire!" in a crowded theater was not "speech" in the First Amendment sense. This draws a distinction between utterances with no value to society, coupled with potential grave harm, and those, however unpopular, that had some form of "value" in a democratic society. Where did flag-burning fit in the constellation of First Amendment values and concerns?

The justices were now ready, and with new faces in the audience, the advocates resumed their positions at the counsel table. We fell quiet as the justices filed in. As usual, their entrance was quick; with curtains parting suddenly, having entered from three separate staging areas behind the courtroom, the nine justices stood in front of their oversized chairs. Taking their lead from the justices, everyone remained standing as the marshal sounded the traditional oye: "Oye, oye, oye all persons having business before the Supreme Court of the United States are ordered to draw nigh, for the Court is now sitting." With the marshal's voice filling the courtroom, I surveyed the nine justices. The marshal completed the oye: "God save the United States and this honorable Court." My mind raced back to a scene a few months earlier at the University of Illinois, where I had participated in a moot court with students arguing a mock case as part of their law-school training. The presiding judge at the law-school festivities was none other than Justice Scalia, one of the members of the five-vote majority in *Texas v. Johnson*. During a question-and-answer session with the students, Justice Scalia spoke to them about the role of the judge, and in particular a judge's moral duty to be intellectually honest, to set aside as fully as humanly possible any prejudices and predilections. His reflection was this: The good judge must try to do the right thing, to reach his judgment dispassionately, as the facts and the law lead, as opposed to playing favorites and going with the judge's own desires or preferences. It was wrong to say, in effect, "I'm sympathetic to the plaintiff, so I'll vote for that side."

That effort—the challenge to be neutral and open-minded—requires constant self-discipline, and good judges strive to exercise the necessary self-restraint. In this way judges differ from elected officials, who can rightly pursue their own visions of the good and reward their friends and punish (or at least not give aid to) their political enemies. Not so with judges. I was reminded during the University of Illinois festivities of a comment in my early days as an appellate court judge by a more senior judge, Harry Edwards, whom President Carter appointed. "Ken, you know you're really a judge when you vote, in conscience, against the folks who appointed you." That was exactly right. When the judge honestly votes against the friends who put him on the bench, then the judge is reaching the goal of being genuinely disinterested and dispassionate—as a truly honorable judge should be.

The likelihood of Justice Scalia's changing his view about the constitutionality of flag-burning seemed slim, especially as I recalled his statement to law students in Illinois. "I never slept better than the night I voted in the flag-burning case," he told the students in the Land of Lincoln. This had come as sobering news to me at the time, looking ahead as I was to the argument in the Dred Scott Tyler case. Justice Scalia was telling the students he knew deep down that he had voted honestly. He had faithfully interpreted the Constitution as he conscientiously saw it, as opposed to reading his personal or political views of what was right and just into the Constitution. Flag-burning was anathema to Justice Scalia the person. As a patriotic citizen, the justice warmly embraced traditional American values of love of country and respect for its great symbols, above all the flag. But his oath was to the law, including the higher law of the Constitution. In Justice Scalia's view, the First Amendment's free-speech provision protects unpopular expressions of opinion. The text of the First Amendment—protecting "the freedom of speech"—protected communications, including actions that conveyed an idea or message. Communications of popular views obviously require little if any protection from the law. It was the unpopular voice, the radical expression of viewpoint, that needed protection against the will of society. It was Dred Scott Tyler, the radical artist, who needed refuge, not political candidates of mainstream parties. In contrast to routine political debate and name-calling, flag-burning was designed to shock and outrage Americans who loved their country.

This was, the Court had often said, the basic role of free speech: protecting the unpopular, even shocking, expression of views. Expression of opinion (and dissemination of information) in an open, robust way without fear of governmental censorship or sanction lies at the foundation of a democratic society. Freedom of speech ranks very high on the scale of constitutional concerns. Without "freedom of speech," a democratic society cannot exist.

Sure enough, the Court remained exactly where it had been in *Texas v. Johnson*. Flag-burning, the Court reiterated, was an expressive act, and it communicated a political message in an especially powerful way. That's what the First Amendment's protection of "the freedom of speech" was all about: the protection of messages, including those conveyed in symbolic forms. Looking back, I could see that Bill Kunstler was destined to win and that my arguments on behalf of the statute's constitutionality were bound to fail.

Of course I did not know how the case would go as I began my argument. Pitching my case to Justice Harry Blackmun, then in his waning years on the Court, I cited opinions that he had joined in his early days as a justice (then newly appointed by President Nixon), opinions suggesting that flag-burning could be outlawed by Congress or the states. But he had been in the majority in the Texas case, and quickly enough he saw what I was doing. Saying nothing, he looked down at the podium where I was fielding questions and trying to weave in my arguments. He had a slight, almost mischievous smile of amusement. Seeing that I was directing my argument to him, the octogenarian justice telegraphed a message without saying a word. "I'm not buying" was his unspoken message. The new law, passed by an earnest Congress trying to navigate around the broad language in *Texas v. Johnson*, was doomed. The statute was pronounced unconstitutional by the same 5–4 margin. No justice had shifted.

The Court remained as deeply divided over flag-burning as it had been the year before. Once again the usual philosophical lines among the justices broke down as the raw emotions triggered by flag desecration seemed to color the way the justices saw the constitutional issue. The ideal of judging is, again, to try hard to set aside one's own emotions and predilections. But it's easier said than done. Justice John Paul Stevens, during the course of my courtesy call on him as the incoming solicitor general, mused that the voting pattern in the Texas case was perhaps more a product of generational attitudes than anything else. That is, the older members of the Court (Justice Stevens himself included) had rallied around the principle that the singularity of the flag—as the symbol of the nation and its unity—warranted an exception to the general rule of First Amendment protection of symbolic speech. Justice Blackmun, it seemed, was the older-generation exception who proved the rule of First Amendment free speech. The prohibition against government censorship exists to protect the unpopular, and even extreme, opinion.

Flag-burning presents perhaps the most vexing test of the rights of society as against the interests of the individual in engaging in highly offensive "speech." The outpouring of emotion in the wake of the terrorist assaults on the World Trade Center and the Pentagon in September 2001 highlighted the unifying effect of the flag, particularly in times of crisis and war. In that light, that this sort of overwhelmingly offensive activity enjoys First Amendment protection attests to the strength of the free-speech principle. If the principle can survive in this setting, and it did twice (and once in the face of a popular congressional set of protections), then it is a powerful principle indeed. Its sweep is grand, protecting virtually all communications in modern life with few exceptions symbolized by Holmes's graphic example of shouting "Fire!" in a crowded theater.

It is not only a powerful principle but also one, thanks to the Court, that reaches deeply into and broadly throughout American life. We have come a long way from the early days of the Republic when Congress passed the patently unconstitutional Sedition Act, which criminally punished criticism of government officials.

By its terms, the First Amendment provides only that *Congress* shall make no law "abridging the freedom of speech." This limitation appears to mean that the states could do as they please with "the freedom of speech." But early in the twentieth century the Court said that the states, too, are bound by the First Amendment. This ruling meant that governments at all levels would have to obey what the Court ruled substantively about freedom of speech. Thus did the reach of the First Amendment go all the way down to the tiniest part of local government. At the same time as the Court obligated the states, it also began interpreting the freedom of speech as well as the related provisions guaranteeing the freedom of press and the rights of assembly and petition. In other words, the Court started to put flesh on some fairly bare bones—the words of the First Amendment itself.

Case by case, with a number of these decisions by the Warren Court, the trends—generally libertarian— emerged. The Court broadened the meaning of protected speech, finding, for example, that it was not only what the Court called "symbolic expression" or "expressive conduct." The Court also found that protected speech didn't have to be about politics and elections, as the founding generation had thought of it, but could be about many other things. Indeed, as the cases in their entirety show, they could be about almost everything. Thus, in the 1977 case of *Abood v. Detroit Board of Education,* the Burger

Court could fairly observe, "It is no doubt true that a central purpose of the First Amendment was to protect the free discussion of governmental affairs. But our cases have never suggested that expression about philosophical, social, artistic, economic, literary, or ethical matters—to take a nonexclusive list of labels—is not entitled to full First Amendment protection."

Around the margins of expression, the Court sometimes said no. In 2000, for example, the Rehnquist Court said that the First Amendment did not protect from government regulation nude dancing in a commercial establishment. It was not that this activity had no First Amendment protection as a form of expression, but it was sufficiently removed from core free-speech concerns that government could regulate it in the interest of public morality and decency.

Such cases as this duly noted, the Court's decades-long march has been toward greater protection for a wide array of expressive activity. Issues involving our system of self-government merit the highest level of protection, but the First Amendment's sweep is vast, encompassing the full range of human expression—save for a small category of patently antisocial speech or communication, such as "fighting words" and obscenity.

In the process, the Court demonstrated a deepening reliance on the principle of *equality*. That is, government should treat similarly situated individuals and groups alike. "Thou shalt not discriminate" is the moral underpinning of not only equal protection but also of free speech. Almost a Golden Rule of constitutional law now embodied in First Amendment jurisprudence is this: Do unto others as you would have them do unto you.

Equality has proved a powerful tool in deciding free-speech questions, a strongly unifying principle in the Rehnquist Court years. For example, the Court has considered whether certain disfavored voices or perspectives, while not being prohibited, may nonetheless be treated differently from other speech. Overwhelmingly, the Court has upheld the claims of those who have been excluded from "speaking" by well-meaning but mistake-prone government officials. (We explore these cases later in the chapter.) Equality principles have carried the day in these and other cases. The High Court often has had to overturn a contrary lower court judgment. Indeed, lower federal courts have been somewhat slow to understand equality's power.

One issue where equality's power has been especially evident involves speech with religious content. Government officials know enough to permit political or social groups to speak on an equal footing. It won't do to say that Naderites are in but conservative groups are out. But the harder question is whether religious voices may be excluded from a forum—a place for speaking—provided by a government trying to maintain church-state separation. How, in other words, does the ban on "establishment" of religion fit with the free-speech guarantee?

State and federal judges alike have struggled with what seemed to them an Establishment Clause–free speech riddle. Courts around the country tilted strongly toward keeping speech with religious content out of the public forum. Their reasoning has been grounded in the Establishment Clause's requirement of separation of church and state. The relevant words of the First Amendment are simple but not immediately self-evident: "Congress shall make no law . . . respecting an establishment of religion." Yet, time and again, the Supreme Court has disagreed with and overruled state and lower federal courts. Speech with religious content, the Court has held, is simply another category of speech; it cannot be favored or disfavored.

This development began in *Widmar v. Vincent,* a 1981

case decided during Warren Burger's tenure as chief justice. A student Christian group at the University of Missouri at Kansas City wanted to hold a Bible study on campus. Their position, in effect, was this: "We're just like scores of other student groups, each with its own identity and purpose. Don't treat us differently. We only want the same treatment—access to campus—as anyone else." The university balked, and then refused. The reason, the university said, was that to allow a religious student-organization to meet on campus would run afoul of the Establishment Clause. Advised by university counsel, officials claimed they had an interest of the highest order—what the law calls a "compelling interest." The interest was that of avoiding a potential violation of the Constitution. Free speech, including the closely related freedom to associate, collided with the First Amendment mandate that church and state be separated.

The case was pending before the Court while I was on a trip to the University of Missouri at the main campus in Columbia. I was serving at the time in the Reagan administration as counselor to Attorney General William French Smith and found myself on occasion being asked to comment on cases pending in the Supreme Court. During a campus radio interview, I was asked about the case arising on the sister campus in Kansas City and how I thought the Court would decide the matter.

Predicting case outcomes is perilous at best, but this time I managed to find the right answer. The key, I said to the interviewer, was equality and nondiscrimination. No law-abiding student group should be excluded from using campus facilities. The state university would in no sense be "establishing" religion by allowing student groups to assemble freely. I went on to say that the students' rights under the Free Exercise Clause, also part of the First Amendment, were in danger if the university officials insisted on excluding their group while allowing numerous other student organizations to meet on campus.

So it was that Justice Sandra Day O'Connor, newly on the Court, joined forces with Justice Lewis F. Powell, Jr., in a strong majority opinion condemning the university's effort to exclude the faith-based group. What UMKC had done in the name of separation of church and state was unconstitutional. Having opened its doors to a wide variety of groups, more than 100 in all, it could not refuse groups that wanted to meet to discuss religious topics. Religious speech, including prayer and Bible study, represent forms of protected speech. Groups engaging in such speech, said the Court, may not be excluded while other organizations are permitted to meet and "speak." With *Widmar* equality became, virtually overnight, the great organizing principle of freedom of speech.

The Court was shy of being unanimous by only one vote—Justice White's. Yet its message, although completely clear, didn't sink in. University and school administrators around the country did not change their ways. Harry Truman once said about presidential power: "I give orders, and nothing happens." As time went on, the justices displayed frustration that public officials—and lower courts—weren't getting the straightforward message: Treat all groups, and speakers, alike. Don't target religious groups and deprive them of equal opportunity to meet and speak. This simple rule embraced the nondiscrimination principle, which is so familiar in other contexts. Once government establishes a "forum," a place where speech and assembly can take place, then it may not discriminate against certain views or perspectives. This basic rule of fair play was obvious in the political and ideological arena.

The difficulty, of course, lay in the First Amendment's ban on "establishing" religion. Couldn't a university permit all groups on a nondiscriminatory basis to meet—save for religious ones? Doesn't the establishment ban mean that a university may, and perhaps must, exclude certain groups?

The answer was no. *Equality* trumped *separation of church and state,* in part because permitting a group to meet on campus does not somehow turn a university itself into a chapter of that group. The "speech" and "assembly" of a group, whether political, social, or religious, are activities of the students, not the university. This is individual choice, an act of religious liberty. This was the kind of distinction that a first-year law student is trained to draw.

Distinctions count, and thoughtful analysis is necessary in order to draw reasoned, sensible distinctions. Even so, lower courts kept coming up with the wrong answer. Long after *Widmar* had been settled, schools and communities across the country kept posting "Do Not Enter" signs in the way of those planning to engage in religious speech.

Illustrative of the problem was the case of *Lamb's Chapel v. Center Moriches,* decided by the Rehnquist Court in 1993. A Long Island school district, like UMKC a decade earlier, told leaders of an evangelical church in the community, Lamb's Chapel, that they could not use school facilities after hours to show a film series of lectures by the well-known Christian psychologist James Dobson. The series, titled "Turn Your Heart toward Home," focused from a Christian perspective on the traditional family and the importance of parental involvement in the rearing of children. In excluding Lamb's Chapel from using the facilities, the Long Island school officials made it plain that there was nothing wrong with the film series. No "obscenity" or "fighting words," well-established categories of "unprotected" speech, were to be found in the films; indeed, to many the films were inspiring and uplifting. But the officials said, in essence, "We can't allow Dobson's programs onto school property after hours because the film series is religious in content." Meanwhile, a wide variety of groups were permitted to make use of school facilities. To the school authorities, keeping out religious groups was what separation of church and state required.

It was the same discriminatory viewpoint all over again. Ten years after *Widmar,* the Court was now unanimous in striking down a school district's exclusionary policy. The equality principle had grown in strength, overpowering contrary interests. The Dobson film series fell entirely within the range of activities and programs that ought to be permitted as after-hours events by a school district. *Equality demanded that religious perspectives be treated the same as secular viewpoints.*

But equality has not been the sole organizing principle of the Supreme Court's interpretation of the Free Speech Clause. Consider the story of Scott Southworth, who wasn't moved by the equality principle at all. He just wanted to be left alone. This was the core value of individual autonomy, which likewise informs the free-speech principle, tugging at the idea of equality. As a student at the University of Wisconsin's Madison campus in the mid-1990s, Southworth objected to paying student fees to support left-wing student organizations with which he vehemently disagreed. This compelled financial support, he felt, violated his rights of free speech. He should not be forced to subsidize the speech of groups to which he objected. Probably only in places like Madison could coerced student-fees support organizations such as the International Socialist Organization. These young socialists advocated, as was their First Amendment right, the overthrow of the government and the abolition of capitalism. In their view, the need was for "revolution, not reform." The young socialists declared: "Reforms within the capitalist system cannot put an end to oppression and exploitation. Capitalism must be overthrown." This was all highly offensive to Scott Southworth and four of his fellow students. They wanted out of Wisconsin's system of compulsory financial support.

Like other state universities, the University of Wisconsin imposed a nonrefundable student fee. The amount was $165 per semester. Students were told, in effect, "Pay it or else." The money supported uncontroversial items such as student health services and athletic programs on a nondiscriminatory basis. The university had heard the message about equality. Virtually any group, religious or secular, could qualify for subsidy from student fees under the university's egalitarian approach.

This was the flip side of the free-speech coin. Southworth and his fellow students weren't complaining about discrimination of the kind faced by the students in the *Widmar* case. Instead, they objected to being forced to support ideological and political groups with which they disagreed.

The Madison students were complaining, in short, about *coercion*. Did the First Amendment, properly interpreted, include a freedom from the coercive influence of the state to support an ideological message?

The issue was complicated. Everyone understands that taxpayers cannot somehow opt out of supporting particular government programs they dislike. Quite apart from practical concerns, a taxpayer-veto system also runs into the principle of majority rule. We have elections decided by majority vote as opposed to demanding the impossible: unanimity or virtual consensus. In addition to free speech (and free-press) guarantees, the citizenry's protection against overbearing majoritarian rule lies in the *structure* of our national and state institutions.

Liberty, the founders believed, would be protected by, among other things, dividing Congress into two different houses, requiring bills to be presented to the president for approval (or veto, with the possibility of a super-majority override) before they become law, and providing for judicial review as to a law's constitutionality in the context of an actual "case or controversy."

The problem in the *Southworth* case was that the University of Wisconsin is not the government writ large. The university could readily provide what the federal or state government could not: an opt-out or check-off system. Allowing students to have a vote with respect to financial support for voluntary student organizations seems fair. But the school officials apparently wanted nothing of the sort, preferring equality of support along with coercion of would-be conscientious objectors.

Lower courts were sympathetic to the students' claims. Both a federal district court in Wisconsin and the federal appeals court in Chicago ruled in their favor. Coercion, those courts concluded, was constitutionally impermissible. As the lower courts saw the issue, the coercive fee system ran afoul of basic principles developed by the Supreme Court in its "freedom of speech" cases. In fact, the *equality principle* emerging in these very cases required, the lower courts believed, some kind of escape from an otherwise coercive regime.

The lower courts were influenced in particular by the Rehnquist Court's 1995 decision in *Rosenberger v. Rector.* In that case, involving the University of Virginia, the Court held—by a narrow margin—that a student newspaper with a Christian perspective could not be denied support from student fees collected under a system akin to the one at the University of Wisconsin. The principles from *Widmar* and *Lamb's Chapel* were controlling. For the lower courts in the Wisconsin case, the fact that Virginia had to fund all such groups, in the interest of equality, made the concern about Southworth's coercion all the more acute.

With special emphasis on the coercion issue, the Wisconsin students pointed to a Supreme Court case that, in their view, supported their exemption claims. The case (*Abood v. City of Detroit* [1977]) protected the right of a teacher to avoid paying fees to a union *to the extent that the fees subsidized the union's political activities*. The case arose out of a struggle between a teachers' union, certified as the exclusive bargaining representative for public school teachers in Detroit, and non-union teachers who were required, under the collective bargaining agreement, to pay a "service fee" to the union. The fee was levied in place of union dues. The idea was to prevent "free riders," with the non-union teachers receiving the union's services (such as negotiating higher wages and benefits) without paying for them. But the non-union teachers contended that they should not have to pay the service fee to the extent that it was devoted to the union's political efforts.

In the Detroit case, the Supreme Court was deeply divided over whether public-sector employees could be required, as a condition of employment, to be in a union shop. A narrow majority said they could be. But on the liberty-of-conscience issue the Court was unanimous. Appealing to fundamental principles of human liberty, the Court ruled in favor of the objecting teachers. Drawing from Thomas Jefferson's writings about liberty, the Court held broadly that the objecting teachers could not be required to pay any amount beyond that necessary to fund the core union dues. Electing pro-union candidates to public office exceeded the union's proper role in exacting dues. The union's task was to represent teachers in contract negotiations with the board of education and other labor-related activities.

Here, the Court engaged in line-drawing. Some union activities were lawful and appropriate, but teachers who wanted no part of the union's vision of the good society more broadly didn't have to pay for them. Years later, the Court drew a similar distinction in *Keller v. California* (1990). The case involved an "integrated" bar association to which all practicing lawyers in California were required to belong. The bar association could require lawyers to pay an annual fee, but it could not use the money to finance anything other than its efforts to regulate, discipline, and control the bar and seek improvements in the administration of justice. Supporting, for example, a nuclear-weapons freeze was a political activity that went well beyond the scope of what bar associations were organized to do. To be sure, opposing nuclear-weapons proliferation was a perfectly lawful undertaking, and the bar association was at liberty to engage in such lobbying if its members so chose (and state law so permitted). But objecting lawyers could not be made to pay for that kind of lobbying activity. As a result, the Court decided that some sort of rebate system or check-off system (which the Court left to the discretion of the California bar) was necessary.

Abood and *Keller* were especially relevant in the Wisconsin case, for in both cases the Court had unanimously embraced a vigorously libertarian vision of free speech. Freedom of speech included, the Court said, a freedom from coerced support of speech with which the individual disagrees. This spirit infused the Court's landmark 1943 decision in *West Virginia v. Barnette*, where in soaring language the Court held that children in public schools could not be required, against their conscience, to participate in a flag salute or Pledge of Allegiance ceremony. It was permissible for public schools to have such ceremonies, but freedom of conscience—what Justice Robert Jackson eloquently called the "freedom of the mind"—required government to allow an exception for those who didn't want to participate. This same libertarian sentiment guided the Court a generation later, in the mid-1970s, to uphold the right of a liberty-minded New Hampshire citizen to tape over the state's motto, "Live Free or Die," which had been stamped on his automobile license plate. The individual could not be forced, the Court held, to be the unwilling conveyor of an ideological message.

Scott Southworth and his fellow UW-Madison students relied on those well-established freedom-of-conscience cases, and the two lower courts in the Midwest sided with them. But a unanimous Supreme Court disagreed. Without retreating from its precedents condemning coercive-fee regimes, the High Court reached its "coercion-is-okay-here" conclusion based on the unique nature of a university. Colleges and universities exist to foster opportunities for students to pursue a wide variety of interests: social, political, and ideological. This is far different from unions and bar associations, which have a much more limited role. But at the same time, the Court agreed that the students had a legitimate interest: their desire not to be coerced into supporting certain groups. And that interest could not be dismissed out of hand. The answer to the constitutional issue the Madison students raised was: equality. If the university were truly even-handed, funding all groups on a completely equal basis, then this egalitarian approach would provide the objecting students with sufficient First Amendment relief. Although the students couldn't get (a portion of) their money back and would have to tolerate their contributions funding radical groups, the students were not left entirely without a remedy. To the contrary, they could insist that the university be genuinely open and even-handed in the financing of all student groups.

This was a significant step under the First Amendment.

The Court, speaking through its most ardent defender of free speech, Justice Kennedy, imported from other First Amendment cases (such as *Lamb's Chapel*) the principle of equality in the doctrinal form of "viewpoint neutrality." Government could not discriminate against speakers, or forced contributors, on the basis of viewpoint. The equality principle again had triumphed.

At the same time, the Wisconsin decision, although unanimous, exposed fault lines on the Court, sharply separating the Court's center from its four-member left wing. Justices O'Connor and Kennedy viewed the objecting Madison students' situation with great empathy. It would not do to slough off their claims as unimportant. To the contrary, concerns about coercion, as illustrated by the Detroit teachers'-union case and the California-bar case, were of a very high order. But thanks to the equality principle, they agreed, it was acceptable for Wisconsin to administer an otherwise unconstitutional regime.

This balanced, nuanced approach stood in stark contrast to that taken by the Court's four left-leaning justices. Speaking through Justice Souter, the liberals could scarcely hide their disdain for the Wisconsin students' claims. Universities cannot be compared to teachers' unions and bar associations. Students can be forced to pay for speech they don't like.

Still and all, this was intramural scuffling. The nine justices did agree on the bottom line: The university, being the kind of institution it is, could require students to pay for speech activities that they found objectionable.

But how far might coercion go? How far would the Court let it go? The Court answered this question in *Boy Scouts of America v. Dale,* which it handed down a few months after *Southworth* (and which we introduced in Chapter Two). James Dale, an assistant Scout leader enrolled at Rutgers University, became a student activist in a gay and lesbian students' organization. When news of Dale's on-campus role reached his Scout troop, he was expelled. His gay lifestyle, which he made public as a campus leader, was deemed incompatible with the Boy Scouts' dedication to the "morally straight" life, as embodied in the organization's famous oath.

Dale, whose Scout service had been exemplary, successfully argued that his expulsion violated New Jersey's public accommodations law, a broad antidiscrimination statute. But the victory in the left-leaning New Jersey supreme court was short-lived as the Supreme Court, speaking through Chief Justice Rehnquist, held in favor of the Scouts. Freedom to associate had great force, here protecting traditional views that were unpopular among the cultural elite who trumpeted the gay-rights agenda.

In the *Scouts* case, the Court (albeit by a narrow 5–4 majority) was uncompromisingly on the side of associational liberty. It stood against government regulation. It was willing to bear the inevitable criticism flowing from its taking the "wrong" side in the culture wars. At the same time, this was the cautious, prudent Court unwilling to rock the boat. It had a core idea—individual autonomy—and would not, as the Warren Court might well have, bring about a fundamental change in American traditions. Flag-burners could be tolerated easily enough; that was at the core of free expression. Trampling over venerable organizations such as the Boy Scouts would have been viewed in much of the country as unwarranted and unwise. Where the stakes were high, the Court would show restraint.

Chapter Four

★

Hard Money and Soft:
The First Amendment
and Politics

THE CASE UNDER CONSIDERATION was *Buckley v. Valeo,* and the Court was in a hurry. The nation would choose a president in the upcoming November 1976 elections. But landmark campaign-reform measures passed in 1971 and amended in 1974 raised a series of important constitutional questions. The law set limits on the amounts contributed to and spent by campaigns. It required full disclosure of political donations and provided for federal financing of presidential campaigns. It also created a new bureaucracy to police federal elections: the Federal Election Commission. For decades, Congress had relied on disclosure requirements, plus bribery laws, to deter campaign-finance abuses. But the abuses that marked the 1972 presidential election were too many and too corrupting for Congress to ignore.

The law came under attack as critics said that challengers would have a harder time defeating incumbents and that third parties would find it more difficult to be competitive. But here in the Court, the law's constitutionality—not its virtues or vices as public policy—was the issue. The core question before the Burger Court was whether Congress, consistent with the First Amendment, could regulate the amount of money devoted to political campaigns. An impressive army of plaintiffs had attacked the law as a violation of the First Amendment's Free Speech Clause. The law, they asserted, violated freedom of political speech and also the right of association, which the Warren Court had derived from the First Amendment in a 1958 civil rights case.

The justices had little time to reflect. With the election year under way, a decision in *Buckley v. Valeo* needed to come down quickly. The conference room of Warren Burger's Court was getting crowded. Justice William Brennan moved to preside. Chief Justice Burger had shown up briefly, said hello, and turned the proceedings over to the senior justice. The law clerks, I among them, were mute. The situation was unusual, likely unprecedented. None of us had ever heard of law clerks assembling in the conference room with any of the justices to conduct the Court's business. But here we were, with Justice Brennan calling us to order.

Among those in the room, only Justice Brennan held a presidential commission, duly confirmed by the Senate to serve for life (during "good behavior," in the words of the Constitution). Justice Brennan, with his legendary Irish charm and wit, had a way with people. But on this day in January 1976 he was all business. He started giving assignments as though he were a staff officer barking orders of the day to the troops. The Court's opinion had to be drafted expeditiously and each chambers had its work to do.

The lead plaintiff in the case was Senator James Buckley of New York, a future judge. Jim Buckley was a gracious, genteel New Englander, the older brother of William F. Buckley, Jr. (I was destined, years later, to be Jim's colleague on the U.S. Court of Appeals in Washington, D.C.) Thanks to the vagaries of New York politics, Jim had managed to squeak into the Senate as the Conservative Party candidate from the liberal state. On the other side, the lead defendant was an unelected officer of the Senate, Francis Valeo. He had no personal stake in the case. The landmark lawsuit had been filed against him in his official capacity.

Leading luminaries of the law debated the free-speech issues. Archibald Cox, the hero of Watergate, argued on behalf of Common Cause in support of the law. Something had to be done, he contended, about the corrupting influence of money in politics. This comprehensive law was the answer, and it was fully constitutional. Lloyd Cutler, destined to serve as counsel to Presidents Carter and Clinton, made a similar argument. This was, he argued, needed progressive legislation that would bring greater integrity to government and promote public confidence.

Among the many doubters was Edward Levi, the former president of the University of Chicago and recently installed reform attorney general under President Gerald Ford. A giant in the law, Levi was restoring order and integrity to a Justice Department badly buffeted during Watergate. Joining him on the brief was the solicitor general of the United States—and future judge and Supreme Court nominee—Robert Bork. The two "generals," Attorney General Levi and Solicitor General Bork, had taken the unprecedented action of joining together to file their own, separate brief raising a series of issues about the law's constitutionality. This expression of views by two senior officers of the Justice Department was not only notable in itself. It stood in contrast to the *official* brief defending the law submitted by Bork's office. In the Levi-Bork view, the law raised profound issues of both free speech and separation of powers. Political contributions and expenditures were at the heart of First Amendment protections, they argued, and the statute's far-reaching limitations curtailed that fundamental political liberty. In addition, the unusual method of appointing members of the Federal Election Commission (permitting the House and Senate each to appoint two of the six commissioners) raised serious issues under the Constitution, which reserves the appointment power to the president. The brief was gently worded, as a true "friend of the court" submission, but its message of disapproval was plain.

My own service as solicitor general was almost fifteen years away, but, if only dimly, I sensed that something extraordinary was happening. As we saw in the flag-burning case, it falls to the solicitor general—and his superior the attorney general—to defend statutes passed by Congress against constitutional challenge. Even if the Justice Department finds the law objectionable, the duty still exists to defend the law. (The only exceptions are where the law invades the prerogatives of the executive branch or where no reasonable arguments can be advanced in support of the measure.)

In the Buckley case, practical politics were likewise at stake, not just great constitutional issues. The law's challengers represented a broad swath of the political spectrum from left to right. While the lead plaintiff was Senator Jim Buckley, a conservative icon, the challengers included well-known figures on the political left. Financial supporters of insurgent campaigns, including wealthy backers of Eugene McCarthy's challenge to Lyndon B. Johnson in the 1968 Democratic primaries, assailed the law. In their view, the law's strictures would tend to freeze the status quo, leaving the political field to the two major parties. Insurgents needed to raise seed money rapidly but they also needed to provoke debate on their issues, not search endlessly for funds.

Could anyone seriously suggest that a wealthy liberal

on Park Avenue was somehow trying to corrupt Eugene McCarthy by generously supporting his anti-Vietnam, anti-LBJ campaign? The suggestion of corruption (or its "appearance") was untenable. Gene McCarthy was incorruptible, a man of rectitude and high principle. Maybe you disagreed with him, but you couldn't reasonably question his integrity. And to challenge an incumbent president whose policies you despised you needed a great deal of money.

A similar refrain echoed from the Libertarian and Conservative Parties. They believed that their already difficult financial challenges would be made even more so by the pro-incumbent approach embodied in the "reform" legislation—which, not incidentally, had been written by incumbents. Minor parties, like insurgent candidates within the existing party structure, needed the ability to tap into large resources. Taking on the "establishment" within any party, or outside the existing two-party structure, required a critical mass of funds quickly assembled.

Deep policy concerns about the future of American politics inevitably bled into the argument over constitutional doctrine. Did limits on political contributions and spending violate the First Amendment? Was money simply a necessary ingredient for First Amendment speech and for that reason deserving of constitutional protection? Was the newly constituted Federal Election Commission, with its six voting members equally divided among appointees by the president, the president pro tem of the Senate, and the Speaker of the House, lawfully structured? The issues were many, and difficult.

As usual, in *Buckley v. Valeo* the justices had convened shortly after the oral argument to decide the case. Now, a day later, the law clerks were sitting in the conference room awaiting orders. Each of us represented a different justice, so there were nine of us in all. I clerked for Chief

Justice Burger, and he had designated me to be at this session. I knew this room well. My own office, shared with my co-clerk Pete Rossiter from Chicago, was literally next door to the chambers containing the formal conference room. This room was largely off limits. The regular tours of the Court never entered the room. But as a member of the chief's professional family, I could enter so long as the justices were not in conference. I frequently passed through this center of Court decision-making on my way to see the chief in one of his two offices, which were separated by the conference room itself.

For his part, the chief was largely in dissent from the Court's tentative judgment. The Court majority was of the view that Congress could, consistent with the First Amendment, limit the amount an individual could *contribute* to a campaign (the familiar $1,000 limitation) but could not curtail the amount a candidate could *spend* on his campaign. Chief Justice Burger would have struck down the entire statute as an abridgement of First Amendment rights. But the chief volunteered to help produce on very short notice what everyone recognized would be a massive opinion. He would help fashion the majority opinion, and yet write a lengthy dissent.

By long tradition, the justices zealously guard the "conference." No law clerks are present, nor are any support personnel permitted in the large room. The justices decide the cases that have been argued during the week (typically Monday through Wednesday). The chief justice, speaking first, sets forth his views on the case under discussion. Each case is discussed separately. There are no elaborate records, no recordings, no transcripts. Each justice takes whatever notes he or she chooses. The chief keeps an official scorecard. This way the assignment of opinions can be carried out soon after the conference adjourns. The junior justice sits at the end of the table and heads to the door with two messengers stationed nearby if something is needed inside the room.

Buckley v. Valeo melded three explosive elements: politics, free speech, and money. For decades, Congress had relied on disclosure requirements, coupled with bribery laws, to combat the threat of corruption in political campaigns. But bribery laws are hard to enforce. A quarter century after *Buckley v. Valeo,* in the uproar over President Clinton's last-minute pardon of financier fugitive Marc Rich, for example, one criminal defense lawyer simply harrumphed "good luck" when asked if a criminal prosecution for bribery might eventually result. The criminal laws were, in the main, seen as woefully inadequate tools to accomplish the broader policy goal of public integrity.

Yet modern politics required enormous amounts of money. The 1960 presidential campaign had marked the advent of mass communications in presidential elections. To reach the voters, candidates needed television, and that required much more money than ever before. Public concern about abuses in the 1972 campaign drove the reform effort. Examples were legion and detailed in the court of appeals decision in *Buckley.* Dairy lobbyists got a meeting on price supports after pledging contributions totaling $2 million. Fund-raisers secured contributions by promising ambassadorships.

Congress's answer was bold and comprehensive. The government now would regulate all aspects of federal campaigns. There would be public financing of presidential campaigns while private funds would continue to underwrite congressional campaigns. But per-candidate contributions by a single individual could not exceed $1,000 per election cycle (including primaries), and total contributions to all candidates for federal office would be capped at $25,000. Limits also would be placed on expenditures. A presidential campaign could spend no more than $10 million on a candidate vying for his party's nomination. Each party also could not exceed $20 million in spending on behalf of its presidential candidate. Anticipating the Ross Perot–Steve Forbes phenomenon, Congress also devised a way to prevent a wealthy presidential candidate from spending unlimited sums of his own money on his campaign.

Everyone recognized the basic free-speech point— namely that political speech often costs money. In the heyday of the Warren Court, during the civil rights era, the landmark 1964 case of *New York Times v. Sullivan* involved an advertisement in the *Times* paid for by civil rights leaders. The ad was critical of a local police department in Montgomery, Alabama, and appealed for contributions. In *Sullivan,* the Warren Court understood that the presence of money in an activity scarcely meant the absence of constitutional rights. To see the matter in the context of political campaigns would mean that the First Amendment protected only those who spend very little, candidates who knock on doors and ring doorbells.

Faced with this comprehensive piece of legislation, the Burger Court recognized that political campaigning was at the core of speech protected by the First Amendment. It was unwilling to say that Congress could do anything it wanted in the interest of restoring the public's confidence, which had been badly shaken in the wake of the post-Watergate revelations. The Court was emphatic: There were constitutional limits to the reformers' regulatory reach.

Nonetheless, the Court did not simply overrule the court of appeals (which, again, had sustained the law in its entirety). Instead, it split the law down the middle, upholding the contribution limits ($1,000 per candidate per election cycle) and public financing of campaigns, but striking down the expenditure limits. Half the law was

good, half was bad (with disclosure requirements, long
upheld under existing case law, being readily sustained).
But what doctrine could make this Solomonic result sensible and reasonable? Why go only halfway rather than
strike down the limitations on expenditures as well, as
Chief Justice Burger would have done? After all, couldn't
an "expenditure" be viewed as simply the flip side of a
"contribution"? You can't spend what you don't have,
loans aside. Shouldn't contributions and expenditures rise
or fall together? If one activity (contributions) could be
regulated, why not the other (expenditures)? Or, vice
versa, if expenditures were sacrosanct because of the First
Amendment's protection of free speech, what was it about
a political contribution that allowed the government to
curtail it? Moses couldn't speak well, the Bible reports, so
Aaron became the person to handle public speaking. Similarly, why couldn't the wealthy but publicity shy, inartic-
ulate donor say to the candidate of his choice, "Here,
speak frequently and fervently, because I believe strongly
in what you are saying. But you do the talking, not me."

The Burger Court thus had to wrestle with a basic question: Did money contributions deserve less First Amendment protection than the man atop a soapbox? The court
of appeals had upheld the entire statute by drawing a fundamental distinction between money and speech. Money-
giving could be regulated, just as other "conduct"
containing elements of "speech" or "expression" could
be. The appellate court had taken refuge in a 1968 Warren Court case, *United States v. O'Brien*. There, an anti-
war protestor burned his draft card in public to express
his vehement disagreement with U.S. policy in Vietnam.
This act, he said, constituted "symbolic speech" (like flag-
burning). His conduct, in other words, conveyed a message. Burning his draft card gave additional force to the
idea. The upshot, the draft-card burner argued, was that

he could not be criminally prosecuted for destroying the draft card that the law required him to carry. The First Amendment protected him just as it did others who engaged in symbolic speech.

The Supreme Court, in one of Chief Justice Warren's last decisions before handing over the reins to his successor, Warren Burger, rejected O'Brien's approach. Although recognizing that the act of burning the card conveyed a political message, the Court held that the government had a legitimate interest in protecting the integrity of Selective Service registration cards, and that this official interest was unrelated to any governmental desire to limit free speech.

This approach—justifying governmental efforts to regulate conduct that contained an expressive (or "speech") element—quickly found its way into First Amendment law. The court of appeals in *Buckley* followed it. The campaign contribution to a candidate constituted "conduct," not pure speech, and Congress could appropriately regulate the "conduct" by placing limits on the amounts an individual could contribute.

The Supreme Court was unmoved. It was faulty logic, the Burger Court suggested, to transport a legal principle from one setting to another where it did not belong. Quickly distinguishing *O'Brien,* the Court unanimously embraced money as constitutionally protected speech. Again, paying the print shop to print a pamphlet or paying the advertising department at the *New York Times* did not deactivate the First Amendment, just as the Warren Court had concluded.

This was a pivotal point. The Court could have said, "Money is different, this is not pure speech." But the Court's past cases prevented that conclusion. The Warren Court veterans—Justices Brennan, Marshall, and White—had served on the Court in *New York Times v. Sullivan,* so they could not easily dismiss the First Amendment significance of the act of contributing to the candidate of one's choice. Money wasn't speech, *per se,* but it was close, when the purpose in giving money was to make possible the conveying of a political message.

But the Court did draw on the appeals court's thinking. The Burger Court concluded that a contribution, while protected by the First Amendment, could be limited because it was only an *indirect* form of expression. That is, the money was given by the donor to the political campaign to facilitate speech by someone else, not the contributor himself. Plus, the contribution simply manifested support for a candidate but didn't explain the grounds for that support. This, the Court reasoned, gave Congress greater running room to regulate the amount of the contribution. For the Court, there was a somewhat diluted First Amendment interest.

Freedom of association, however, proved different. The Court embraced the proposition that a political contribution reflected a form of political association protected by the First Amendment. Thus, the justices held that contribution limits represented a serious abridgement of associational liberty. The government should not be able to place limits on the amount of dues one pays—or charitable contributions one makes—to an association or organization. Arguably, the more one gives to the organization, the more one asserts a sense of kinship and community: "I feel strongly about this, so I'm giving $10,000, not just $1,000." The cause may be political, not just charitable or civic or religious in nature. Politics is at the core of the First Amendment's concern, more so than artistic or other forms of expressive or associational activity that also rightly lay claim to First Amendment protection.

The Court was thus left, on the liberty side of the equation, with weighty claims to constitutional protection. If the generous donor now feels that instead of giving $10,000 in annual charitable gifts to the local library foundation he should do something about the direction of the country and give the money to an insurgent candidate who promises to double the library's budget, who is to say no? Making choices about which causes one will support, and to what extent, is at the heart of individual liberty.

This was not an easy set of questions. Only if the government could come up with a strong reason for curbing individual liberty might it try to do so.

The Burger Court found one. The government, it said, had an interest in guarding against not only actual corruption but its appearance. Thus, large donations given to library foundations were good, but those given to political candidates looked bad. They appeared to "buy" the candidate or at least give the donor undue sway over the candidate on issues. This appearance of influence or control, in turn, was corrosive of public confidence in government. And that was enough to justify the law. This interest was so powerful that it outweighed the not insignificant First Amendment interest in making generous contributions.

This was a classic example of judicial balancing. Instead of finding a specific answer to the problem in the text, structure, or history of the Constitution, the Court was openly making a policy judgment. The Court was sitting as if it were a court of equity, listening to different sides and seeking to fashion a judgment that fairly accommodated the legitimate competing interests.

Under this approach, the law's expenditure limits were struck down. The limits meant that the total amount of political activity—political speech—had been capped by government. This, the Court stated, was a direct and significant diminution of First Amendment freedoms.

The Court found that with political expenditures, the dangers of corruption and the appearance of corruption were greatly diminished. Large contributions might suggest that a candidate was under the influence of a donor. Not so with expenditures. If contributions were limited but expenditures were not, then candidates could gather smaller contributions from more donors and build a war chest that would underwrite more speech. That was, as the Court saw matters, a First Amendment benefit.

The Court had split the reform initiative in two. Contributions could be limited, expenditures could not. Likewise, wealthy presidential candidates—and recently we have had two, Ross Perot and Steve Forbes—could spend to their hearts' content. To limit Perot's spending on his own "Ross for Boss" campaign, or Steve Forbes's effort to reassemble the core Reagan constituency, would not pass muster under the First Amendment. The restriction on freedom was too direct, too substantial, to pass muster in light of the attenuated government interest in avoiding the appearance of corruption.

The Supreme Court's surgery was complete. The result was by no means what Congress had envisioned in passing the far-reaching reforms. To the contrary, the Court sent back to Capitol Hill a law remarkably different from the one that had emerged from the post-Watergate debates. In dissent, Chief Justice Burger bewailed what the Court had done. Guided by a libertarian perspective that contributions, like expenditures, constituted protected First Amendment activity, the chief complained that the Court had come up with its own version of "reform." He warned, prophetically, that the election process was likely to be skewed by this muddled result.

The rest is unfolding political history. The Burger Court's watershed decision in *Buckley v. Valeo* ushered in a world of enormous energy and effort devoted to raising money both "hard" (contributions directly to campaigns subject to the $1,000 limit) and "soft" (unlimited contributions to a political party). Candidates complain about the ceaseless search for funds in what became permanent campaigns for dollars. No one is satisfied with the system, yet no enduring consensus has emerged for campaign finance "reform." (The much-ballyhooed McCain-Feingold legislation, signed into law in March 2002 by President Bush, is under comprehensive attack by a wide range of individuals and groups, from the ACLU to the Christian Coalition, and it very much remains to be seen what the eventual outcome in the Supreme Court will be in reviewing that 91-page complex set of bewildering campaign finance regulations.)

Years after *Buckley*, the Rehnquist Court had an opportunity to reconsider its analysis and chose to stay the course. At issue in *Nixon v. Shrink Missouri PAC* (2000) was a state statute modeled after the federal law the Court had rewritten in *Buckley*. Political campaigns in Missouri had given rise to some shady episodes. In particular, a candidate for state treasurer had received large contributions from a Missouri bank, and then upon his election chose the contributing bank as the state's. Missourians were upset, and a statewide referendum imposing contribution caps swept to a landslide victory.

A somewhat marginal candidate for statewide office, Zev David Fredman, assailed Missouri's contribution limits. In his view, the Court's First Amendment law had changed in the years since *Buckley* was handed down. The Court's personnel had undergone an almost complete change since 1976, with only William Rehnquist, now the chief justice, still sitting as the new century dawned. In the interim, in case after case, the Court had held in a variety of settings that government could not restrict speech in order to prevent some *speculative* harm to the public interest. Under this developing body of law, the harm had to be actual, a concrete social evil of real moment, to sustain a curb on speech.

Libertarians sided with Candidate Fredman. Missouri, they thought, was overreacting. There was no demonstrated, systemic evil that the state legislature was trying to prevent. The legislature had simply yielded to the publicity that attended a single or, at most, a handful of episodes where there was no proof of a *quid pro quo*. Fredman and his allies also argued, in a replay of *Buckley*, that challengers needed seed money. If a candidate was not the choice of the existing party apparatus, then it would be very hard for the non-Establishment candidate to muster the necessary resources to get on the ballot or to unseat the favored candidate. These arguments had failed in *Buckley*. Would the deficiencies of the post-*Buckley* system of campaign finance better their chances now? Might *Buckley* be overruled?

The Rehnquist Court, speaking through Justice David Souter, held fast to *Buckley*. No matter how strong the criticisms of the current system, the Court had spoken in 1976, and it would not change its mind. Justice Souter, speaking for a six-member majority, quoted from *Buckley*'s strong language condemning large donations to candidates: "[W]e spoke in *Buckley* of the perception of corruption 'inherent in a regime of large individual financial contributions' to candidates for public office as a source of concern 'almost equal' to *quid pro quo* improbity." Nothing had changed. "Leave the perception of impropriety unanswered, and the cynical assumption that large donors call the tune could jeopardize the willingness of voters to take part in democratic governance." *Buckley* was still the law of the land.

But how secure was the *Buckley* regime? Suggestions came from President Clinton's two appointees, Justices Ruth Ginsburg and Stephen Breyer, that embraced a very

different kind of rationale for regulating campaign finance. Their principle was *equality,* one of the big ideas
that move the Rehnquist Court. Leveling the playing field
was an important characteristic of campaign finance reform, they maintained, and the political branches should
be given ample room to decide how to handle the difficult
issues it presents. They embraced the idea that a donor's
contribution to a political campaign triggers the First
Amendment: "[A] decision to contribute money to a campaign is a matter of First Amendment concern—not because money is speech (it is not) but because it enables
speech." On the other hand, contribution limits reflect an
effort to "protect the integrity of the electoral process—
the means through which a free society democratically
translates political speech into concrete governmental action." Invoking the equality principle, they added: "Moreover, by limiting the size of the largest contributions, such
restrictions aim to democratize the influence that money
itself may bring upon the electoral process."

Ginsburg and Breyer would take a step in the law that
the *Buckley* Court rejected. The Burger Court in *Buckley*
dismissed the idea that consensus about equality could justify limits on contributions. This is a broad, recurring
question in the law. By definition, equality frequently tugs
at freedom. To ensure equality, freedom is curtailed. The
civil rights laws of the 1960s, for example, prevented re-
tail establishments, even small ones, from refusing to do
business with individuals on account of race or national
origin. Equality concerns trumped liberty interests.

But equality in politics is a different matter. The point of
running for office is to win it. And winning office often involves hard, thankless tasks. Even if one party has a
"lock" on a particular district, there will still be occasions—as when the seat is open—when the competition to
win the dominant party's nomination becomes intense. In

that setting, winning the money race may be necessary to win the seat. The demand for equality collides with the demand for an open marketplace for political competition.

The seed of an egalitarian approach to campaign finance has now been planted. If the idea grows, it would threaten the other half of *Buckley*'s holding, namely its invalidation of limits on expenditures, including those made by wealthy candidates from their own resources. The two Clinton appointees, Justices Ginsburg and Breyer, openly suggested a new, equality-driven approach: "[I]t might prove possible to reinterpret aspects of *Buckley* in light of the post-*Buckley* experience . . . making less absolute the contribution/expenditure line, particularly in respect to independently wealthy candidates whose expenditures might be considered contributions to their own campaigns."

Ironically, the two Clinton appointees were building on a stinging opinion in dissent written by Justice Anthony Kennedy. The First Amendment's leading defender chided the Court's opinion for its smugness and arrogance. Justice Souter, he said, had been "cavalier" with First Amendment issues, treating claims raised by Zev David Fredman with indifference. He then turned his attention to *Buckley v. Valeo*. In a scathing attack on the post-*Buckley* regime, Justice Kennedy lamented that "the compromise the Court invented in *Buckley* set the stage for a new kind of speech to enter the political system. It is covert speech. The Court has forced a substantial amount of political speech underground, as contributors and candidates devise ever more elaborate methods of avoiding contribution limits, limits which take no account of rising campaign costs." Kennedy bemoaned the fact that the current system, bad as it was, had not arisen from the deliberate Congressional choice but was, instead, a judicial invention: "[I]ts unhappy origins are in our earlier decree in *Buckley*." *Buckley*'s bifurcation between contributions and expenditures had been unsound. "The melancholy history of campaign finance in *Buckley*'s wake shows what can happen when we intervene in the dynamics of speech and expression by inventing an artificial scheme of our own."

Justice Kennedy stopped short of embracing the libertarian approach taken by Chief Justice Burger in his dissent in *Buckley* and now championed by Justices Scalia and Thomas in their dissent in *Shrink*. But he indicated he would overrule *Buckley* and return the issue to Congress and the states. Perhaps new reforms would be legislated and would pass muster under the First Amendment. For now, however, *Buckley* should be jettisoned. "[T]he existing distortion of speech caused by the half-way house we created in *Buckley* ought to be eliminated. The First Amendment ought to be allowed to take its own course without further obstruction from the artificial system we have imposed."

For their part, Justices Thomas and Scalia would restore the law to its libertarian, pre-*Buckley* condition. Political speech, they said, is at the core of First Amendment concern. The *Buckley* incursion into the most important arena of free speech had created a "most curious anomaly." Turning to Fredman's candidacy, the dissenters noted his compelling need for large donations. Fredman lacked the advantages of incumbency, name recognition, or personal wealth. He had "managed to attract the support of a relatively small number of dedicated supporters," but their potential support would be a crime under Missouri law. The upshot: The state prevented Fredman's message from reaching the voters. This was emphatically wrong under the First Amendment.

But the three dissenters fell short. *Buckley* had moved the Burger Court to the First Amendment "middle ground," and the Rehnquist Court in *Shrink* was unwilling to vacate that territory, troubled though it had proven to be. Even if all sides seemed disgruntled with *Buckley*'s mandated system, the Court (by a 6–3 margin) would remain in what it deemed the constitutional center.

Dimmer now was the libertarian vision that had animated the justices in *Buckley* to condemn overregulation. Political contributions now had a bad name. This was ironic. As Stanford Law School Dean Kathleen Sullivan wrote in the *New York Times,* "Contributions to candidates and parties today do not line anybody's pockets, as they did in the heyday of machines like Tammany Hall. Vigilant media and law enforcement now nip improper personal enrichment in the bud, as politicians involved in the savings and loan scandals found out to their detriment. Political money today instead goes directly into political advertising, a quintessential form of political speech."

But the Supreme Court wasn't convinced. The justices were determined to stay the course. The Burger Court had spoken in *Buckley;* the Rehnquist Court would not change direction.

Chapter Five

★

Religion in the Public Square

Bridget Mergens was not just another student at a large public high school. The vivacious sophomore at Westside High School in suburban Omaha, Nebraska, in 1987 wanted to start a Bible study group. Like other non-curricular organizations, her group would meet on school premises when regular classes weren't in session. Her group would exclude no one.

The school administration refused Bridget's request. A Bible study group meeting on campus, Bridget was told, would violate the constitutional separation of church and state. Bridget protested. She pointed to other student groups meeting on campus, such as the Chess Club. As she saw it, there was no basis for discriminating against a student group simply because it was faith-based. Guided by the school board's attorney, the Westside principal held firm.

Bridget decided to challenge her principal's decision in a federal lawsuit. As we'll soon see, she ultimately won her case in the Supreme Court. I had the privilege of arguing the case as solicitor general. I wanted the Court to get the answer right. In my view, Bridget should win.

Someone not familiar with our nation's church-and-state disputes might wonder why the idea of letting some public high-school students *meet on their own initiative* to study the Bible on campus could be controversial, much less a matter people would actually battle over in court. The explanation lies in our history, a history that involves the Warren Court in particular.

Religious liberty was, as one writer has called it, our first liberty. Nowhere in the original Constitution was there a provision supporting one church or another as the official one, as had been the practice in the Old World. Indeed, in a provision reflecting the nation's commitment to religious liberty, the Constitution explicitly prohibited a religious test for holding public office. Of course, a Bill of Rights was soon added to the original Constitution. And the First Amendment provides, in pertinent part, that "Congress shall make no law respecting an establishment of religion, or prohibiting the free exercise thereof."

Note the beginning words: "Congress shall make no law. . . ." Those who framed and ratified the First Amendment sought to limit only Congress, not the states. Congress was not to establish a national religion, nor was Congress to prohibit the free exercise of religion. But the states were free to do with religion as they wished. Some states still had official churches when the First Amendment was added, but by 1833 they had all been dismantled: The commitment to religious liberty proved too great to allow their continuation for very long. This commitment, however, was not understood to command the elimination of religion from public life. To the contrary, religion was widely seen, even by nonbelievers such as Jefferson, as necessary to the maintenance of a good society. Thus, as the nineteenth century wore on, religious activities and observances were commonly found in, and even sponsored by, government agencies, including public schools.

This was not to remain. In the twentieth century, as the nation's demographics began to change, pressure grew to eliminate or alter certain of these activities and observances. Some states and localities made changes on their own initiative. In other instances lawsuits were filed, and eventually cases wended their way to the Supreme Court. In 1940, the Court held that the First Amendment's religion clause, like its free-speech provisions, applies not just to Congress but also to the states. On the strength of that holding, the Court was able to consider *Minersville v. Gobitis* (1940). It was a poignant case. Two children whose family were Jehovah's Witnesses were expelled from the public schools of Minersville, Pennsylvania, because, being Witnesses who believed they should not bow down to a graven image, they had refused to salute and pledge allegiance to the U.S. flag—a daily routine required by the school board. The children's father sued, claiming that the state had violated the First Amendment's free-exercise provision by compelling his children's participation in the salute-and-pledge ceremony—against what their faith told them. By a vote of 8–1, the Court rejected the family's claim.

Only three years later, however, the Court, in one of its most celebrated cases, *West Virginia State Board of Education v. Barnette,* completely switched positions. The West Virginia board, having duly absorbed the Court's teaching in the *Gobitis* decision, mandated a daily flag salute in the schools, expulsion from school being the penalty for nonsaluting children and criminal prosecution the vulnerability for their parents. A Jehovah's Witness, Walter Barnette, objected to the flag salute on the same grounds as the Gobitis family had done in the earlier case. The federal court in West Virginia took it upon itself not to enforce *Gobitis* and told the school board that it could not impose its new mandate.

This was extraordinary. Federal district courts are duty-bound to obey the Supreme Court, whether they agree or not. Otherwise, the system of law would break down.

But this proved to be harmless error. For on appeal, the Supreme Court, by a vote of 6–3, agreed with the contrarian district court and (with largely the same membership) overruled its own decision in *Gobitis*. The Court attached less weight to *stare decisis* than to its obligation to answer the constitutional question correctly. Though *Barnette* was argued in terms of free exercise, the majority opinion by Justice Robert Jackson, who'd been appointed by FDR, took a broader First Amendment position that no one could be forced to salute the flag. Freedom of the mind, wrote Jackson, is what all Americans, schoolchildren included, have as a matter of constitutional right.

Gobitis and *Barnette* were the Court's initial First Amendment journeys into the public schools. Then came one of the Court's most important decisions of the twentieth century. In 1947, the Court declined to condemn as unconstitutional the use of public funds to defray the costs of transporting pupils to church-related schools. The vote in *Everson v. Board of Education* was 5–4, but all nine justices agreed with the sweeping interpretation of the First Amendment advanced in the Court's opinion written by Justice Black, who was soon to be a mainstay of the Warren Court. Although upholding the bus-transportation program, *Everson* effectively denied the idea that religion has public value in a democracy. Citing the nation's founding history, Justice Black declared that the First Amendment does not allow laws that aid one religion, help all religions, or prefer one religion over another. Government, in sum, must be absolutely *neutral* toward religion. The

First Amendment, Black explained, was intended to erect a wall of separation between church and state. The wall— a metaphor taken from a letter Thomas Jefferson, as president, had written to the Danbury Baptists in 1802—must be kept high and impregnable.

This ruling set the tone for the decades to follow, and it was this separationist wall that Bridget Mergens ran into many years later. Its blueprint was sketched in *Everson,* and over the years the Court built it up—high and impregnable. Briefly, we turn to how it happened.

In 1948, the Court in *McCollum v. Board of Education* adhered to *Everson* in a case involving public schools. Specifically, it struck down an Illinois school board's released-time program under which teachers from any religious group wishing to participate were allowed to offer religious instruction in the school for one hour each week. Justice Black wrote the Court's opinion, and only Justice Stanley Reed (an FDR appointee) dissented. An avowed atheist had challenged the released-time program, which the state did not fund but whose teachers it approved and supervised. *McCollum* marked the Court's first-ever invalidation of a state practice as an establishment of religion. Justice Black reaffirmed *Everson* by rejecting the school board's argument that the First Amendment, properly understood, forbids only government preference of one religion over another. Justice Reed, challenging the Court's understanding of First Amendment history, criticized the Court's reliance on Jefferson's wall metaphor: A rule of law should not be drawn from a figure of speech, he complained. But his view was swept away in the rising separationist tide.

In 1952, the Court in *Zorach v. Clauson* declined by a vote of 6–3 to strike down a released-time program from New York City. Here the religious instruction for public-school students was provided *off campus,* and the teachers in the program were not approved by the state. These facts distinguished the case, in the majority's view, from *McCollum*. Notably, in neither case were students compelled to participate in the programs at issue—the lesson of *Barnette* had been absorbed. But in *McCollum* the students had a right not to participate in the program; to exercise this right, they had to act affirmatively by asking to be excused. In *Zorach* the students had a right to participate; to exercise this right, they simply signed up. Thus, in *Zorach,* the burden of decision-making fell not upon non-participants but upon those taking the trouble to opt in to the program—a choice, in the Court's view, that was not coerced by the state.

It was also in 1952 that the Court turned away a taxpayer complaining about Bible reading in a public school, ruling that as a mere taxpayer he had no standing to bring such a case. Ten years later, however, the Court, with Earl Warren in his ninth year as chief justice, decided a case brought by plaintiffs with a true interest at stake: parents, as it turned out, of children in the New Hyde Park, New York, public schools. The state board of regents had composed a brief, nondenominational prayer for daily use in New York's schools. "Almighty God," it went, "we acknowledge our dependence upon Thee, and we beg Thy blessings upon us, our parents, our teachers and our Country." The parents said that the prayer was an unconstitutional establishment of religion. The Court, with Justice Black applying the hard separationist doctrine he had announced in *Everson,* agreed by a vote of 6–1. *Engel v. Vitale* was the case, and it was followed the next year by *Abington v. Schempp,* an 8–1 decision. In his opinion for the Court, Justice Tom Clark extended *Engel* by striking down state-sponsored Bible readings and the saying of the Lord's Prayer in public schools.

In neither *Engel* nor *Schempp* was student participation

required. Consistent with the teaching of *Barnette* (the flag-salute case), students could be excused. But this fact did not affect the Court's judgment: Public schools may not sponsor things religious.

The Warren Court's School Prayer Decisions, as they are called, set off a political and cultural firestorm. At the time, they were widely seen as a misguided attempt, at best, to remove God from the classroom. Of course, there were not a few—including many of religious conviction— who saw the decisions as blessings in disguise, since state-ordained prayers tended to be watered down, mere exercises in civil religion that, in various faith communities, did not satisfy the requisites of genuine prayer. But the dominant public response was one of strong objection to what the Court had done. Prayers over public-address systems persisted in many public schools for many years, and constitutional amendments to overrule the decisions were often suggested, though none was ever formally proposed by Congress, much less ratified.

The Warren Court became the Burger Court, but the Court's view of religion and the public schools did not change. In 1980, the Court was asked to decide a case that well illustrated the public's continuing discontent with the School Prayer Decisions. Kentucky had passed a law requiring its schools to post a copy of the Ten Commandments. It was as if Kentucky had this thought: If the Supreme Court won't allow school prayer or Bible reading, how can it not permit us merely to display a copy of the source of so much law in the West, the tablets Moses brought down from Mount Sinai? But in *Stone v. Graham*, the Court, adhering to *Engel* and to *Abington*, held firm against even this appearance of religion in public schools. The separationist viewpoint was now deep-seated in the Court's outlook.

In 1985, the Burger Court reviewed *Wallace v. Jaffree*, a

case from Alabama. That state, like a number of others, had passed a law authorizing its schools to set aside a moment of silence in which students might meditate or even pray. If anyone still thought that the School Prayer Decisions might be reconsidered by the Burger Court, that idea was laid to rest in *Jaffree*. Stability reigned. By a vote of 6–3, the justices adhered to separationist doctrine in holding the Alabama law unconstitutional. Dissenting at length, William Rehnquist (still an associate justice) took sharp issue with *Everson*'s view of history. Rehnquist discerned in the founding history different principles from those that previous Court majorities had accepted. He concluded that the First Amendment does not forbid government from preferring religion over nonreligion, and that government may aid religion, so long as it does not favor one religion over another.

Shortly thereafter, Rehnquist moved to the Court's center seat as chief justice. Soon enough, it seemed that he might have the votes to permit religion, at least to some extent, to return to the public schools. Antonin Scalia had taken the seat Rehnquist vacated when he became chief, and Anthony Kennedy in 1988 had replaced Justice Powell. In 1990, David Souter took Justice Brennan's place, and the next year Clarence Thomas succeeded Justice Marshall. All of the new justices were appointed by Republican presidents committed to the philosophy of judicial restraint. Presumably, they were all judicial conservatives. Two of the departing justices—Brennan and Marshall—were, unequivocally, judicial liberals. On Religion Clause questions, they had consistently cast separationist votes.

Nothing changed. Notwithstanding these shifts in the Court's membership, the Rehnquist Court accepted and even extended the teachings of the School Prayer Decisions. This surprising development came in the waning months of the Bush administration. Stability had trumped restoration of traditional understanding of the constitutional order.

Specifically, in the 1992 case of *Lee v. Weisman,* the Rehnquist Court ruled unconstitutional a prayer included in a public-school graduation ceremony. The principle of *stare decisis* carried the day. As the case was proceeding to the Court for argument and decision, I thought it would prove to be terribly important for the country and its traditions, and so the solicitor general's office entered the case on behalf of the school board. Since I felt strongly about the issue, I decided to argue the case personally. In my argument, I emphasized the voluntary nature of the ceremony. Just as portions of the audience might disagree with the graduation speaker's remarks, so too the noncoercive nature of the graduation ceremony itself shielded the prayer, I thought, from a successful First Amendment challenge.

In particular, the background of the case, I thought, would win the Court's sympathies. For years, the middle and high schools of Providence, Rhode Island, had invited local members of the clergy to deliver invocation and benedictions as part of their schools graduation ceremonies. Following this tradition, the principal of Nathan Bishop Middle School invited Rabbi Leslie Gutterman of Temple Beth El to offer the prayers at his school's 1989 graduation ceremony. Four days before the event, Daniel Weisman, whose eighth-grade daughter Deborah was in the graduating class, sought a federal court order to prevent the prayer from being uttered at the ceremony. The motion was denied, but Weisman continued his case, seeking a decision that would prevent any more graduation prayers. Weisman won in district court, the court of appeals, and then the Supreme Court, the last by a vote of 5–4.

This apparently was not the outcome when the justices first cast their votes. As we discussed in Chapter Four, in *Buckley v. Valeo,* the justices meet in the private conference to vote in the same week they hear the oral argument in a given case. If the chief justice votes with the majority, he then assigns the task of writing the Court's opinion to one of the justices who voted with him. If the chief is in the minority, the most senior justice in the majority assigns the opinion-writing duty to a justice on his side. According to news reports, when the justices met in conference after the oral argument in *Weisman,* they voted 5–4 in favor of the school, not the parents. This majority included Chief Justice Rehnquist and Justices White, Scalia, Kennedy, and Thomas. Rehnquist then assigned the job of writing the opinion for the Court to Kennedy. Sometime afterward, however, Kennedy switched sides—thus flipping the outcome in the case. He did write the Court's opinion, but it was one totally different from the opinion he had been assigned.

I must confess my own surprise at this turn of events. I thought the Court would find something wrong not with the Providence policy, but with the doctrine rooted in *Everson* it had long used to review establishment-ban questions. Indeed, as solicitor general, I asked the Court in *Weisman* to reconsider this doctrine, for if it meant the Providence policy was unconstitutional, which surely it was not, then the doctrine must be wrong. But the Court did not see the policy as I did and it left the *Everson* doctrine intact. "This case does not require us to revisit . . . difficult [First Amendment] questions," wrote Kennedy. "We can decide the case without reconsidering [our] general constitutional framework. . . . Thus we do not accept the invitation of petitioners and amicus the United States to reconsider our case law."

I was taken aback. Kennedy, a Reagan appointee, wrote

from a sweepingly separationist perspective. His opinion read like one from the Warren Court. "History," he said, "was not enough to justify an inherently religious practice in a public school setting," even one—as the Nathan Bishop Middle School's had been when Rabbi Gutterman offered his prayers—sensitive to the feelings of those of different faiths or of none at all. Nor did the fact of voluntary attendance at the ceremony impress Kennedy, who dismissed the idea of voluntariness as entirely formalistic and technical. "It was sophistry," he said, "to suggest that graduates objecting to the prayers and their families would simply absent themselves from the ceremonies for that reason, since most graduates do want to be with their peers in these formal, final sessions."

The Kennedy majority seemed most troubled by the involvement of the state, in the form of the public-school authorities, in securing and even framing the terms of the prayers. School principals issued the invitations to Providence clergy, and they provided the clergy with guidelines that encouraged the articulation of inclusive and nondivisive prayers. For the Kennedy majority, this fact appeared to decide the case, for it made *Weisman* akin to *Engel v. Vitale,* the original school-prayer case, where the New York Board of Education actually wrote the prayer used in the state's public schools. Like New York thirty years earlier, Providence, in the Court's view, had violated the First Amendment's establishment ban.

For the four dissenters, tradition and history were the preferred tools of interpreting the Constitution. In their view, both those tools supported prayers at ceremonial occasions. Providence, they said, had done nothing that could not be found in other parts of the country. The majority, as the dissenters saw it, had engaged in psychobabble by finding coercion in an entirely voluntary ceremony quite different from the ordinary day-to-day classroom setting of a public school. A graduation ceremony was a one-time-only event, with no suggestion of indoctrination; it was more like an invocation at an inauguration or the opening of a legislative session.

But the dissenters' protests fell short. Stability reigned— just as it would eight years later in the next school-prayer case, *Santa Fe Independent School District v. Doe*. Here, the issue was the constitutionality of student-led and student-initiated prayers before a high-school football game. By a vote of 6–3, with Justice Stevens writing, the Court condemned the prayers as unconstitutional. Even though the decision to pray and the words prayed would be the students', the prayer nonetheless was authorized by a government policy and took place on government property at government-sponsored school-related events. It would "force" those in the stands to participate in an act of worship. This was impermissible under separationist doctrine. In dissent, Chief Justice Rehnquist said the majority opinion bristles with hostility to all things religious in public life.

The story of religion and the public schools from over the past half century is the same. To repeat, the public schools may not sponsor religious activities. There is an important footnote to this story, however, and it involves Bridget Mergens, the student at Westside High School in Omaha. The footnote shows, again, the unifying force of the principle of equality. Equality can trump the separationist principle.

The background of the *Mergens* case begins in the early 1980s. At that time, Congress grew concerned about reports of public schools stepping in to halt religious expressions or activities of students that could not reasonably be construed as sponsored or coerced by government. Congress saw, moreover, that two federal courts of appeals had ruled that student religious groups could not, consistent with the First Amendment's establishment ban, meet on school premises during noninstructional time. In short, some schools and some courts had made the High Court's separationist doctrine even harder. In my own view those courts were wrong, swept away by an unduly rigid approach to church-state relationships in the context of schools. Nor was I alone in this sentiment. Congress, disagreeing with the lower courts' view of the establishment ban, passed a law that it believed was consistent with the Supreme Court's rulings. Congress hoped that the law would make the schools more willing to accommodate the truly free exercise of religion by students. To do so, Congress tapped into the equality principle.

More specifically, Congress found the principle for this new law in one of the Supreme Court's own decisions, *Widmar v. Vincent* (1981), which we examined in Chapter Three, which discussed freedom of speech. At issue there, as we saw, was a state-university regulation prohibiting student use of campus facilities for religious meetings. The Court, by a vote of 8–1, struck down the regulation on free-speech grounds, declining to address the establishment and free exercise issues in the case. *The idea, again, was one of equality:* The university had opened its campus facilities to the use of numerous student groups and it could not single out for exclusion a faith-based organization.

Congress saw in the university case a broad, equal-access principle that if properly applied could open public schools to student-led religious activities. Not surprisingly, the law, enacted in 1984, was styled the Equal Access Act. It provides that high schools receiving federal funds that allow a single noncurricular, student-led group to meet on campus must extend this same right to any other such groups—even religious ones. Everyone is to enjoy equal access, and no one may be discriminated against on account of religion.

Congress found middle ground. It did so by reframing the issue of religion and the public schools in terms of the enduring principle of equality and then extending the reach of this principle to high-school students. Republicans and Democrats might disagree on school prayer, but they were united in rejecting the exclusion of religious groups from a forum to which all other high-school students had access. Equality was the unifying banner under which almost everyone could march.

Alas, in the years after the act was passed, some ardent separationists were found in the ranks of public-school administrators. Some of these administrators were in Omaha, at the Westside High School attended by Bridget Mergens. She was distressed when school officials, turning down her request, suggested that she take her group to the church located across the street from the school, or to some other church. Bridget's lawsuit claimed that Westside High School had violated the Equal Access Act by refusing to allow her group to meet on school premises. The school board responded by challenging the law itself, on two grounds. First, it said, Congress surely would not have intended to intrude so deeply into the traditional discretion of local school boards by passing such a law. Second, it argued that if Congress did have such an intent, then the law violated the First Amendment's establishment ban.

Preparing for the oral argument, I was increasingly convinced that neither argument had any merit whatever. And sure enough, neither argument gave the Court the slightest pause. Congress, it said, had clearly intended to cast its anti-exclusionary net broadly. Responding to broadening suggestions by Senator Patrick Leahy of Vermont, a liberal Democrat, Congress had moved the statutory trigger all

the way down to one: If a high school let one noncurricular group meet on campus, it had to let any other eligible
group meet there too. (The only way to evade the law,
then, was not to let any student group meet.) The key element in determining whether a group should be allowed
to meet, the Court emphasized, was voluntariness. So long
as students *on their own initiative* had formed their group,
whatever it might be, the school could not object to their
meeting on campus.

Only Justice Stevens dissented. In his view, Congress really hadn't intended to intrude so deeply into the affairs of
a public high school. His point was exceptionally weak,
since Congress was absolutely clear on the subject. Thus,
by a vote of 8–1, the Court in *Westside v. Mergens* reaffirmed what Congress had legislated: equality as a principle in matters involving religion and the public schools.
Bridget had won. The victory was savored by others who
followed Bridget's example, however, since by the time the
Court issued its ruling, Bridget had long since graduated.

The principle of equality enjoyed the overwhelming
support of the American people. That it did so was in part
a result of the Warren Court and in particular its decisions
outlawing segregation and racial discrimination, but in
part also a result of the increasing racial and ethnic diversity of the nation and of—last but hardly least—the egalitarian beat of the free market. The market prized ability
and performance, not inherited (or government-granted)
position. Allow competition; don't arbitrarily exclude a
competitor (including a Bible study club) from the marketplace.

More than a decade after *Mergens,* the nation still is
very wedded to equality as a unifying value. So is the
Court. And its commitment is manifested in numerous
areas of constitutional law, not just religion. But *Mergens*
showed the special appeal of equality, for on matters of re-

ligion and the public schools the Court had stuck, starting with *Engel,* and would stick, through *Santa Fe,* to a hard separationist position. In *Mergens,* however, a law framing an issue of religion and the schools in terms of equality roundly defeated establishment concerns. Not only was equality a unifying principle, its power over other, potentially competing principles was undeniable.

Chapter Six

★

Parochial Schools and Public Money: The Neutrality Principle

Lisa Savoy is an articulate, determined educator. She works tirelessly in the inner-city schools of Washington, D.C., cajoling, urging the students to try hard to succeed. In charge of academic programs, Lisa was my liaison at Anacostia Senior High School, a large public school in the heart of one of Washington's inner-city neighborhoods. Upon leaving the Independent Counsel's Office in the autumn of 1999, I volunteered to help out at the school. Then serving as assistant principal, Lisa guided me to assist in a program that brings law students into the D.C. public schools to teach, as part of the regular curriculum, a course in constitutional law.

My idea was to help bring resources into the school. I would assist the law student–teachers in the class, bring in other speakers, and arrange occasional field trips, especially to the Supreme Court. Lisa Savoy showed me that my idea was incomplete. Don't just bring resources in, she indicated, but help find or create opportunities for the students outside of school and away from their daily neighborhood and home environments.

Lisa Savoy's broader message was this: Large inner-city

high schools can be challenging for students wanting to learn. This is the principal reason why many inner-city parents want a different way. I saw this firsthand in Wisconsin when I served (in the mid-1990s) on the legal team for then Governor Tommy Thompson to defend the Milwaukee school-choice program. Under the program, needy parents who meet certain financial criteria receive vouchers they can use to send their children to private schools, including religious and parochial schools. The program came under immediate attack in the courts. I was delighted to jump into the fray to help defend the Milwaukee program. I felt strongly that poor parents should have the chance to guide their children to better schools. I also felt that, properly interpreted, the Establishment Clause should not stand in the way of these kids having better schools. The challenge in Wisconsin was the Supreme Court's elaborate body of case law concerning various programs of aid to religious schools. We eventually won the Wisconsin case, and the program has remained in effect over the past few years, benefiting thousands of needy Milwaukee families. But the victory was difficult and uncertain as a result of the confusion surrounding the Supreme Court's teachings on government aid to parochial schools.

For decades, the Supreme Court has developed an inconsistent body of law involving state aid to parochial and church-related schools. Its struggle tells us much about the Court and the challenges modern justices have faced in coping with one of the most divisive issues in American life. For years the Court simply seemed inadequate to the task. The Court's center (first Justice Powell, then Justice O'Connor) struggled to identify a principled approach that would safeguard the constitutionally required separation of church and state and yet not be unduly rigid and doctrinaire. After all, religious schools were schools. They were accredited by the states to carry out a basic public function, the education of the young. These were schools, not monasteries or seminaries, engaged in education.

Nothing in law or tradition requires that all such human services be rendered by the state or, in the private sector, by purely secular entities. By way of example, St. Jude's is a children's *hospital*, not a Sunday school or catechism class. In recent years we have seen politicians in both major political parties endorse using faith-based institutions to deliver social services. During the 2000 presidential campaign in particular, both Al Gore and George W. Bush pushed for an expansion of this policy idea, and as president, George W. Bush created in the White House an office dedicated to advancing the concept, the Office of Faith-Based and Community Institutions. The reason is simple: Faith-based organizations tend to get results.

The idea is hardly new. Religious orders and churches have long operated hospitals for the sick and the needy and provided education for both children and college-age kids. For years it was not thought strange, much less unconstitutional, for government to provide financial assistance to these organizations in their role as human-service providers. Helping a Catholic hospital with a government-research grant was never deemed, for obvious reasons, as somehow equivalent to paying the priest's salary for conducting mass.

But for the Supreme Court, aid to schools (as opposed to colleges or hospitals) has proved impossible to handle sensibly. Especially during the 1970s and 1980s, the Court tacked in one direction and then another. The justices gave the appearance of a Court just making up the rules as it went along.

In recent years, the Court has tried hard to be more consistent and predictable in this important area of the law. Indeed, in 1997, the Rehnquist Court reversed a major

Burger Court precedent from the mid-1980s forbidding federally funded special-needs teachers from carrying on their work on public school premises, and in 2000 it decided a case, *Mitchell v. Helms,* that promises to make it easier for a state to aid religious schools and other faith-based institutions. The upshot is that, even as the hard separationist doctrine of *Everson* remains alive when the Court reviews questions regarding religion and the public schools, that is definitely not the case when it takes up issues involving aid to religious schools. A dichotomy exists: Greater leeway is permitted in the setting of aid to *parochial* schools than in the arena of religious activity in *public* schools.

The story of the justices' involvement in this area of American life begins with the Warren Court. The Court under Earl Warren was asked to address the constitutionality of public aid to religious schools just once—in the 1968 case of *Board of Education v. Allen.* Twenty-one years had passed since the Court last reviewed an issue of this kind, in the landmark *Everson* case. Notwithstanding its separationist doctrine, the Court in *Everson* had *upheld* state funding of the cost of transporting pupils to their schools, whether public or religious. Then, in *Allen,* the Warren Court, which had assailed the settled practices of state-sponsored school prayer and Bible readings in the School Prayer Decisions, upheld a New York state law requiring local schools to lend textbooks free of charge to students in grades seven to twelve, including those attending religious schools. These books were entirely secular in content. A contrary decision striking down the lending arrangement might have been condemned as discriminatory against children in religious schools. With Justice White writing the majority opinion, the Warren Court brushed aside the *Everson* argument that the high wall of separation required a hands-off policy, that the state should not be in the business of subsidizing education in church-related schools. Basic economics effectively made the separationist point, pressed in separate dissents by Justices Black, Douglas, and Fortas. Funds freed from costly textbook purchases for secular courses could be employed to pursue the religious mission of the schools.

But *Allen* hardly settled matters, and soon enough the Court, now under Warren Burger, was facing a variety of issues involving aid to religious schools. Indeed, the Burger Court—not the Warren Court—became the first to hold that some forms of aid are unconstitutional.

In 1971, the Burger Court decided a case that has since been the subject of withering critiques, even by the justices themselves—*Lemon v. Kurtzman*. At issue were state laws of Pennsylvania and Rhode Island that supported instructors teaching secular subjects in church-related elementary and secondary schools. The Court held the laws unconstitutional in an opinion written by Chief Justice Burger, the first of several notable ones he wrote in the church-state area. (His predecessor, Earl Warren, wrote no important opinions in this area.) *Lemon*'s significance lies in its legal doctrine, specifically its three-part inquiry for determining whether a government action passes muster under the First Amendment. The Court presented this test—the "*Lemon* test"—as a codification of rules found in its cases dating back to *Everson*. The test poses three questions about a challenged program: (1) Does it have a primary purpose of aiding religion? (2) Does it have the primary effect of aiding religion? and (3) Does it cause an excessive entanglement of state officers and functions with church authorities and functions? To avoid condemnation, a challenged program must pass all three parts.

By devising this three-part test, the Court tried to meet its professional challenge—to fashion a standard that would yield up consistent, predictable results grounded in the language and history of a particular part of the Constitution, here the First Amendment's ban on establishment of religion. In various branches of law, the Court seeks to fashion its rulings in a way that inspires confidence that the process, even if the reader disagrees with the result, is based on principled legal reasoning.

Chief Justice Burger authored the *Lemon* decision shortly before I came on board as his law clerk. To my thinking, the decision was a disaster. Never hostile to religion, the chief had managed to fashion a test that was deadly in its application, killing government programs that seemed to have little to do with helping religion. Millions of schoolchildren were being educated in parochial (and other private) schools. Legislators believed they should make sure that schoolchildren, whether in public or private schools, had access to certain educational tools. But application of the *Lemon* test often forbade that even-handed result; the government, under *Lemon*'s strictures, could not fund efforts to help kids in church-related schools. All too often, the Court concluded that various programs of *direct* aid to schools had the "primary effect" of aiding religion.

This seemed both harsh and counterintuitive. In particular, needy schoolkids in inner-city parochial schools, while otherwise receiving a splendid education, were being denied educational resources that would enable them to develop their skills and talents. That seemed to me then, and still does, wrongheaded.

In two key cases, a plurality (three justices) led by Justice Powell departed from the textbooks-are-okay precedent (*Allen*) and embarked on a new constitutional course. Two systems of government financial assistance to schools in the form of nontextbook instructional materials and aids were struck down. With the Court otherwise sharply divided between the anti-aid Jeffersonians (the Court's then liberal wing) and the pro-aid accommodationists (the Court's then conservatives), the justices in the middle came up with an entirely new approach to resolving church-state questions: The issue was, the Powell plurality opined, whether aid was "substantial."

This was all newly minted. Nothing in the earlier cases had focused on the "substantial" (or not) nature of the aid. The question was not the quantity of the aid, but whether the government assistance was secular, non-ideological, and available generally to schoolchildren wherever they were being educated. That had been the Warren Court's approach in the *Allen* case justifying the provision of textbooks to parochial schoolkids.

The Court struggled for years with doctrinal consistency in this area. Increasingly, it was openly apologizing for its work product. No one could tell in advance what the Court, with its shifting majorities, would uphold. Under the Court's decisions, textbooks were okay but maps were not. The distinctions seemed increasingly fine, to the point of being illusory. As then Justice Rehnquist scornfully noted in one opinion, if textbooks were okay but maps were not, how would the Court resolve the issue of a book of maps?

Consistency proved elusive year after year, and results from case to case seemed arbitrary. Even the principal tool in the justices' toolbox, the *Lemon* test, proved too pliable. It had failed to yield predictable results, and the justices battled over its application in a variety of settings—not just in aid to parochial schools.

A controversial 1983 case made the point well. Nebraska, like other states, had an official chaplain for the legislature, paid for by state funds. In *Marsh v. Chambers,* this long-standing practice was challenged as a violation of the First Amendment. But there was a major problem with this constitutional attack: The U.S. Congress itself had chaplains. In fact, the very Congress that wrote the Bill of Rights had appointed the first chaplains, thus initiating a tradition unbroken over two centuries. That tradition clearly supported the constitutionality of the practice, an outcome just as clearly at odds with the Court's separationist doctrine.

As a method of interpreting the Constitution, history and tradition loom large for the justices. Time and again, the Court considers past arrangements and practices. And if a practice enjoyed the approval of the founding generation, especially of the early Congresses, that historic grounding is viewed by virtually all justices as going far toward establishing its constitutionality. The assumption is that James Madison and his contemporaries well understood the reach of the Constitution, and that it would be presumptuous to invalidate practices the founders themselves approved.

The centrists in the early-to-mid-1980s, led by the aging Justice Powell and the newly appointed Justice O'Connor, reached for this history to decide the *Marsh v. Chambers* case in favor of the chaplains. If the practice of legislative chaplains was sanctioned (indeed inaugurated) by the very Congress that framed the Establishment Clause and succeeding Congresses to the present day had embraced it, then the practice could not be invalidated.

Even so, with history so monolithically in favor of the practice, the Court could not achieve the unanimity (or even near-unanimity) that it had often found in applying the principle. Within the Court was a sharp clash of competing views. Justice Brennan, battling to save *Everson*'s doctrine, assailed Chief Justice Burger's history-laden opinion. History, Justice Brennan and his fellow liberals opined, was only one of the various tools the Court uses in constitutional analysis. History did not foreclose other approaches, since even the founding generation could be wrong. It could be morally wrong, as the original Constitution was in its indirect sanctioning of slavery, or it could be legally wrong, as the Federalist-dominated Congress was in 1798 when it passed the Alien and Sedition Acts, which in effect forbade criticism of high government officials.

In particular, Justice Brennan—who would have invalidated the practice of state-paid chaplains—criticized Chief Justice Burger's majority opinion for failing to consider more recent developments in constitutional doctrine. Invoking the three-part *Lemon* test, Justice Brennan concluded that the state may not pay for chaplains.

As Brennan explained, Nebraska's chaplaincy failed all three parts of the *Lemon* test. First, it did not have a primarily secular purpose. If the legislature's goal was to give an air of solemnity and dignity to the proceedings (which would be a permissible, nonreligious purpose), prayer was entirely unnecessary. Other ceremonies would achieve that purpose, including a recitation of the Pledge of Allegiance, readings from the Constitution or Bill of Rights, and the like. Nor—the second part of the *Lemon* test—did the chaplaincy have primarily a secular effect. Prayer was at the heart of religious observance, and an ordained clergyman delivering prayers in a formal legislative setting could only be viewed as having the effect of advancing religion. Finally, a state's employment of a paid chaplain "excessively entangled" the government with the religious community. Issues inevitably emerged as to which chaplain to choose from which faith community, what the chaplain's duties should be, and so on. All of this in Brennan's view brought church and state into too close a relationship.

The intriguing point about the Court's internal debate over the chaplaincy question is that the majority in *Marsh v. Chambers* chose not to respond to the dissent. Ordinarily, a dissenting opinion causes the five or more justices in the majority to set forth replies and rebuttals, if only in one or more footnotes. The majority's response typically moves the dissenters to refine their objections. The two sides go back and forth in a written dialogue among the justices—all behind the scenes and unknown to the public—that then finds expression in the set of opinions formally released by the Court.

In *Marsh,* history seemed sufficient to the Burger Court majority to justify dispensing with the usual judicial conversation. The majority had history on its side, and that was enough. No further commentary or analysis was needed. The majority and the dissent simply talked past each other. The majority used history, and the dissent used the *Lemon* test. The choice of tools determined the outcome. History had the votes; the judicially created "*Lemon* test" fell short.

Marsh sharply illustrated the divisions over church and state within the Burger Court. In that Court's final year, the justices began searching for a new approach, particularly on school-aid cases. Often the Court's center moved to a position rooted in earlier principles and carried the justices back to a more predictable set of rules. While carefully avoiding an outright overruling of earlier cases, the Court found a different mode of analysis.

With one faction remaining ardently separationist, the Court's center began to emphasize *neutrality,* a principle closely related to the pivotal concept of equality. Like equality, neutrality was one of the large, unifying ideas around which the Court could rally. The issue now became: Does government treat religious institutions and secular (state) institutions in the same manner? Does it, in providing secular assistance, regard public schools and religious schools on the same terms? If government is indeed neutral, under this theory, then there is no Establishment Clause problem.

The neutrality principle was not developed overnight. To the contrary, over a number of years, the Court worked its way through a series of cases raising numerous church-state questions. From this examination of a variety of patterns, constitutional rules slowly emerged, term by term. Facts drove, or at least heavily shaped, the law. This was the lawyer's craft.

The degree to which the sheer facts in a case influence the Court's decision-making is often neglected, even by full-time observers of the Court's work. The Court's concern for the facts is not surprising, since it is a lawyers' Court, not one of politicians. Politicians make policy in the less rigorous setting of the executive branch or Congress. In these venues, debate about what is good for society—whether tax cuts, on the one hand, or budget-deficit reduction on the other—occurs in mainly general terms. "No tax cuts for the top 1 percent," or "free small businesses from the heavy hand of government regulation" are familiar examples from the political arena. Not so in the Supreme Court. The justices focus closely on the specific facts of the case.

Congress typically graces legislation with a "preamble" or its equivalent. Those opening provisions of a law will set forth findings in general terms. The substance then follows.

The Court's work is much different. Nuances count. The Court's rigorous focus on the facts leads to a decision, then another, and eventually a body of law is produced. This is exactly what happened with the issue of aid to religious schools.

The Court, in effect, jettisoned (or ignored) much of its more recent doctrine and returned to what it saw as first principles. The analysis, in short, was this: Government assists a host of activities, some of which are undertaken by religious organizations. Congress (or other levels of government) should be able to finance those activities, as long as the activities are secular and the government aid is being provided neutrally and across the board.

A breakthrough came in the waning days of the Burger Court when, in 1986, it addressed *Witters v. Washington,* a case involving a blind student who wanted to use state-provided vocational education funds to attend a Bible college to prepare for the ministry. Authorities in Washington state refused. Train for some secular vocation, they helpfully suggested, and the state will gladly provide assistance, but the state cannot pay for a person to become a minister or church worker, as that would violate the Establishment Clause.

The Supreme Court disagreed, unanimously. The program in question—and this fact the Court deemed critical—provided aid to *the student himself,* who then used the assistance as he saw fit to prepare for a vocation of his choosing. This was *not* a government payment to the Inland Empire School of the Bible, where the blind student was training for the ministry; it was, to the contrary, aid paid directly to the student, who then decided for himself, without state encouragement or direction, what he would study. As the Court saw the case, the fact that the student wished to become a minister should not have concerned the state. Choice of vocation—religious or secular—was entirely that of the student.

This set of facts guided the Court to embrace neutrality as a core principle. The state should not have directed the blind student into a particular vocational path. Rather, it should simply have provided assistance, neutrally, to a category of persons, blind adults, who were seeking vocational training. Applied this way, neutrality is a form of *equality.*

Neutrality is at stake in the bitterly fought contest over government programs, such as the Milwaukee and Cleveland voucher programs, that enable schoolchildren from poor families to attend private, often church-related schools. In Milwaukee's program, the state provides payments (in the form of "vouchers") to qualifying families, who then choose where they will use the vouchers. The state gives no guidance, direction, or even a hint about what school—religious or secular—is right for any child. The family chooses. The state's money simply follows the *family's choice* for the child. Voucher programs extend the neutrality principle in the *Witters* case to children in grades kindergarten through twelve. The Court is preparing to resolve that question in the closely watched Cleveland case, argued on February 20, 2002.

All in all, the Court has permitted Congress more flexibility in recent years to provide assistance to religious schools. The Court, led again by the centrists—Justices O'Connor and Kennedy—has emphasized the need for neutrality in school-aid programs. A neutral program, one that allows aid to all schools regardless of their private or church-related nature, seeks to foster and improve education, but neither supports nor attacks religion. No hint has been detected in these congressional programs of a financial bailout for financially struggling religious schools, a feature that doomed a New York program of aid in an opinion authored early on in the Burger Court by Justice Powell.

The pivotal year for the Rehnquist Court was 1997, when it upheld a federal aid-to-education program established during the Great Society of President Lyndon Johnson. Under a statute passed thirty years earlier, Congress authorized federal funding—on a neutral basis—for remedial educational services provided by public school personnel on the premises of religious schools. This kind of program had been struck down by the Burger Court in 1985. But the Rehnquist Court took a different view. The

Court rejected the Powell plurality's prohibition on "substantial aid to the educational function" of the schools. That was no longer the law, the Court held. In the intervening years, a whole host of decisions, including the blind-student case (*Witters*), had eroded the premise of the Powell approach.

The Rehnquist Court had found new ground. It had shifted from a strictly separationist perspective and become more tolerant about government aid to religious schools—as long as the aid is distributed on the basis of "criteria that neither favor nor disfavor religion" and in a form that does not lead to "government inculcation of religious beliefs" or "excessive entanglement." The Court confirmed this approach in the spring of 2000, when it decided that a federal school-aid program under which states and localities lend materials and equipment to both public and private schools does not violate the Establishment Clause. Here again, the Court overruled prior decisions, either in whole or in part. In doing so, the majority showed little concern about the value of stability and "staying the course." It seemed, rather, to be focused on clearing out some of the confused precedents of the Burger Court.

As in so many arenas, the Court had engaged in a multi-year careful refining of its own precedents. Trial and error, the methodology of common-law judges slowly developing an elaborate body of law, was the same method at work in constitutional law.

All the while, as the religion cases continue to press for the Court's resolution, the marshal begins the Court's daily sessions with the traditional cry, invoking God's blessing: "God save the United States, and this Honorable Court." Looking on from his permanent seat high above the justices, a marble Moses holds forever the Ten Commandments. Notwithstanding the Warren and Burger

Courts' drive toward separation, religious tradition continues to find its way into public life, as demonstrated by the outpouring of religious sentiment and patriotism in the wake of the terrorist attacks of September 11, 2001. For its part, the Rehnquist Court seems increasingly comfortable with those traditions. Moderation and flexibility have replaced doctrinal rigidity.

Chapter Seven

★

THE CONSTITUTIONAL "RIGHT" OF PRIVACY: ABORTION AND BEYOND

JOE BIDEN WAS ON A MISSION. As I was sitting in the witness chair, the chairman of the Senate Judiciary Committee was justifying, after the fact, his successful assault two years earlier on the Supreme Court nomination of Robert Bork. Judge Bork was, at the time of his nomination in 1987, singularly qualified to serve on the Supreme Court. He had served, with great distinction, as a judge on the D.C. Circuit, as solicitor general, and as a professor of law at the Yale Law School. But Chairman Biden skillfully engineered Judge Bork's defeat.

It was now 1989, and I was a convenient vehicle for Biden to make his points. He was looking to history to justify himself. My role, as President George Bush's nominee for solicitor general, was fundamentally to listen to what the chairman had to say and then, if there was a need, to respond. Confirmation hearings are not infrequently opportunities for the senators doing the "questioning" to be "heard." It is, in truth, "the senators' 'hearing.'"

This exchange, however, was a genuine give-and-take. The subject was "liberty." More precisely, the question was whether the Constitution's protection of liberty (as contained in the Fifth Amendment and the Fourteenth Amendment in the Due Process Clause, which prohibit a deprivation of "liberty . . . without due process of law") carried with it real, enforceable "rights," not just a guarantee that the government will provide basic procedures, such as notifying an individual of the government's proposed action in a timely manner and affording the person an opportunity to be heard, such as at a trial.

I had thought about this long and hard, first as a law clerk, then in my work for Attorney General Smith, and, above all, as a judge (and Judge Bork's colleague) on the D.C. Circuit. My view as to the meaning of "liberty," as protected by the Due Process Clause, was guided by history and tradition. It had long been settled that due process of law meant that certain liberties of the people, for example, the right to marry, merited constitutional protection.

To that extent, I agreed with Chairman Biden. And that sliver of agreement was all that was needed for him to win his point about the concept of liberty. Not a word was mentioned about abortion generally or *Roe v. Wade* specifically. All I needed to say to the chairman in the context of a lengthy colloquy over the meaning of this provision was, modestly, "I believe in the concept of 'substantive' due process." That "concession" was seen, rightly or wrongly, as separating me from my much-admired friend and judicial colleague, Bob Bork. Judge Bork was skeptical of that notion of due process. The phrase more naturally meant procedural protections, such as a fair opportunity to be heard before being deprived of liberty or property. Judge Bork, as we will see, resisted expanding the idea of due process to include protections, say, of family life, such as how to educate one's children. I bowed to history, and the century-old interpretation of the

Due Process Clause as protecting various unenumerated liberties.

Confirmation thus assured, I was relieved, yet sorrowful for what had happened to Judge Bork's nomination. The defeat of Bob Bork still hovered over the halls of the Senate.

In a case destined to loom large in Judge Bork's 1987 confirmation hearings, the Warren Court in 1965 struck down a Connecticut law that outlawed contraceptives. The case was *Griswold v. Connecticut.* The Court held that the law unconstitutionally intruded on *married persons'* rights to marital privacy. Eight years later, relying on the principles in *Griswold,* the Burger Court in *Roe v. Wade* declared that the Constitution's protection of privacy encompasses a woman's right to abortion. The decision invalidated virtually every state abortion law and ignited a firestorm of controversy that continues still today. Indeed, few decisions in the modern history of the Court rank higher than *Roe* on the controversy meter— not even *Bush v. Gore.* At a minimum, very few decisions have so deeply affected the Court, or our politics, especially in the selection and confirmation of judges.

Since *Roe,* the Court has declined to press the logic of personal privacy to create a broad right to individual autonomy so as to encompass, for example, homosexuality or a right to assisted suicide. The Court also has declined to make abortion an absolute right and has approved numerous regulations of abortion, such as parental notification provisions. Yet when the Court was explicitly asked to overrule *Roe*—as, in my capacity as solicitor general, I did ask in the 1992 case of *Planned Parenthood v. Casey*—the Court adamantly refused. *Roe,* which built— wrongly, I believe—on *Griswold,* remains the law of the land.

Abortion is a big story, one of the biggest of our time.

As a constitutional matter, the issue in *Roe* concerned "liberty." That was also the issue in the earlier *Griswold* case and, many years later, in the cases on homosexuality and assisted suicide. These cases, in sum, all involve the same idea: liberty as protected by the Due Process Clause. That is why, in trying to understand what the Court did in *Roe* and subsequent abortion cases, it's important also to consider the modern series of liberty cases starting with the Warren Court's marquee decision, *Griswold*. Today's Court, if it had been asked to decide *Roe* as an initial matter, likely would have come out the other way. *Roe,* though, is on the books, and once rooted it's proven hard to eradicate and to return abortion policy, like assisted suicide, to the states. But what the Rehnquist Court clearly is unwilling to do is use the reasoning and logic of *Roe v. Wade* in deciding other divisive issues involving the concept of liberty.

This is emphatically not a Court anxious to announce some new constitutional right that pitches the nation into another lengthy and bitter debate over the decision's consequences and legitimacy. A case making a "liberty" claim invokes the Fifth Amendment, which says, again, that the federal government may not deprive anyone of liberty without due process of law, or the Fourteenth Amendment, which imposes the same obligation upon the states. The question for the Court in a case of this kind is to determine the meaning of the term *liberty*. The justices don't simply (or at least they shouldn't) define liberty any way they want; they aren't legislators or members of the executive branch. Because the justices are judges, their role is quite different. When called upon to decide whether a federal or state law is constitutional, they are being asked to decide whether the law at issue is at odds with our highest law, the Constitution. That is why, in explaining a constitutional decision to the world, the Court is obligated to justify its result by citing the part of the Constitution at issue and engaging in legal reasoning as to its meaning and how it should be applied. What will not do is to make a political appeal such as "the American people want...". That's politics, not law.

A basic criticism of the Warren Court was that it scanted the task of legal reasoning, offering too little or even none at all. The Court under Chief Justice Warren, it was often said, acted not as judges but as reformers, moved by what the Yale Law School's Alexander Bickel called the idea of progress. Making things better, moving society forward, doing the right thing—this was what the Warren Court appeared to be up to, and this was what it shouldn't have been doing.

Roe v. Wade was decided in 1973, four years after Earl Warren stepped down. But to many observers it seemed like just the kind of decision the Warren Court would have rendered. The justices were asked to decide the constitutionality of a state law largely outlawing abortion. In striking down the law, the Court, with Justice Blackmun writing for the majority, held that a woman's liberty interest was greater than the government's interest in the life in the womb. The Court declared that the Constitution included a right of privacy broad enough to protect a woman's right to choose an abortion up to the point (very late in the second trimester if not the beginning of the third) when the unborn could live outside the womb— what is known as viability. States could still prohibit abortions, but only those, in effect, in the third trimester of a pregnancy, and even then subject to the health and safety of the mother.

However you might judge the outcome in *Roe,* and I do not admire that outcome, the Court's opinion suffered from a grave deficiency in legal reasoning. Even to observers who liked the pro-choice result, the Court's opinion seemed more like legislation than adjudication—a blast from the Warren Court past. The Court reached its conclusion, that pre-viability abortions may not be prohibited, by consulting history and citing precedents. As we have seen, history and precedent are two of the principal tools the Court uses in deciding constitutional issues. But the problem in *Roe* was that the particular tools the Court used couldn't do what the Court wanted. The history Justice Blackmun surveyed at length—the history of abortion regulation—was inconclusive. And the main case Justice Blackmun invoked, *Griswold v. Connecticut,* did not provide a basis for the new constitutional right he announced.

Griswold, again, was the case striking down what Justice Potter Stewart called an "uncommonly silly" law, a Connecticut statute prohibiting physicians from providing contraceptives to married couples. The law was not only antiquated but obviously intruded into the marital relationship. That was the critical fact in the case. The issue was not whether unmarried persons could buy contraceptives but whether married persons could under the care of their physician. More precisely, it was whether doctors could be criminally prosecuted for providing, or prescribing, contraceptives to married individuals. How was such a law deemed unconstitutional? Because the Court, looking to history, found that marriage had enjoyed legal protection for centuries. There was thus a "liberty interest" at stake—the liberty that married couples by law had long enjoyed. It was a liberty that the Constitution (specifically, the Due Process Clause of the Fourteenth Amendment) protected, and Connecticut had violated it with its anti-contraception prohibition.

In *Roe,* the Court expanded the liberty protected in *Griswold* to include the new right to an abortion. The obvious problem with this extension was that *Griswold* directly involved the marriage relationship while *Roe* did not, and while marriage had been protected by law for centuries, the "right to choose" had not. *Griswold* was, as lawyers and judges say, distinguishable. Its reasoning did not readily answer all questions as to reproductive freedom specifically or bodily autonomy more generally.

The dissenting justices, led by the legendary football hero Justice White (appointed by President Kennedy), were quick to point all of this out. The Court, the dissenters complained, had invented rights not found in American law or in the history and traditions of the American people. Nothing in the concept of liberty prevented the states, if they wished, to outlaw abortion. States were as free, constitutionally speaking, to do with abortion as they were to do with myriad social-policy matters. The states mandated compulsory education and compulsory health vaccinations, for example, and enacted statutory rape laws. They prohibited euthanasia. That being so, states could also regulate, and even outlaw, abortion.

What separated the justices was not a policy disagreement but a disagreement over legal reasoning of a kind often seen when the Court decides some of the most controversial cases on its docket. While the majority was less precise in its approach, the dissenters were clear about how a case like *Roe* should be decided. For the dissenters, constitutional liberty was defined as the right or prerogative of the individual to carry on activities or to enjoy human relationships that historically had been protected by law (such as the common law or statutes) in clearly articulated ways. The common law elaborated by courts over decades and even centuries might provide protections. Or protection might be provided by laws enacted by state legislatures, ordinances by city councils, and the like. Or, in the absence of relevant common or statutory law, the liberty might be protected less formally—in the history and traditions of the American people. These are, in short, culturally based protections. The dissenters thus would be willing to protect a liberty claim even if it did not enjoy specific legal rooting.

Taking this approach, the dissenters charged that abortion did not enjoy constitutional protection because the "right to choose" had never been firmly established in either common law or in legislation. Nor did history or tradition provide protection for the abortion decision. To the contrary, abortion was mainly forbidden by the majority of states, enforced by the criminal law. What is striking about the dissents in *Roe* is that they foreshadowed the approach that would prevail in later cases in which the Court *refused* to extend the protection of liberty in new contexts—homosexual conduct and assisted suicide—conduct argued to involve fundamental liberties like the "right" to abortion. But before the Court engaged those issues it had more abortion cases to decide. Here, as in other areas during the Burger Court years, Justice Lewis Powell became the justice to watch in these cases.

Having joined the majority in *Roe,* Powell was a pivotal member of narrow majorities that rejected efforts to extend *Roe*'s logic. For Powell, the Constitution protected the abortion liberty, but this "right" did not prevent government from making basic policy choices, including ones that might be deemed pro-life. Powell-led majorities concluded, for example, that Congress and the states could discriminate against abortion by refusing to finance it. Justice Blackmun, *Roe*'s author, was exceedingly displeased with the Court's refusal to establish an absolute, or near-absolute, abortion right. Blackmun, together with Justices Brennan and Marshall, found himself in dissent in most of the post-*Roe* abortion cases. For example, the Court upheld various restrictions, such as waiting periods before the abortion could be performed.

But would the Court overrule *Roe*? Just as Richard

Nixon in 1968 had vowed to change the direction of the Court, so too did Ronald Reagan in 1980. Both used, albeit twelve years apart, similar language in describing the kind of judges they would appoint: "strict constructionists," judges who would interpret the law and not make it up. And both implied that certain decisions ought to be overruled. Nixon attacked the Warren Court's criminal law cases, *Miranda v. Arizona* in particular. Reagan was concerned about the Burger Court's most celebrated case, *Roe v. Wade.* Indeed, to Reaganites, *Roe* symbolized the excesses of a federal judiciary that both Reagan and the elder President Bush sought to change through their judicial appointments. And the future of *Roe* itself turned out to be the abiding social-issue question of not just the Reagan presidency but also of that of President Bush (the first). Both administrations regarded *Roe,* as a matter of constitutional law, as indefensible. As counselor to Attorney General Smith, I favored the Justice Department taking a principled, firm position: *Roe v. Wade* was wrongly decided; it had improperly thrust the federal judiciary into fashioning social policy entrusted to the states; and it should not be permitted to stand. Thus matters stood at the dawn of the Reagan administration.

In 1981, Justice Potter Stewart, who had joined the majority in *Roe,* retired. The idea of appointing Robert Bork was immediately born. Bork, a Yale Law professor who had served as solicitor general under President Nixon, was the leading candidate to replace Stewart. In the Justice Department, where I was working at the time, Bob Bork was far and away our first choice. But the president wouldn't name him. Reagan had promised during the campaign to appoint the first woman to the Court, and he wanted to fulfill that promise now. So he asked us to find qualified women who shared his judicial philosophy. Sandra Day O'Connor topped our list. The president nominated her, and she was easily confirmed. The biggest issue in the confirmation was from the political right—whether Justice O'Connor was "sound" as to the legitimacy of *Roe v. Wade*. The question was skirted. O'Connor showed an impressive familiarity with the issues, but refused, rightly, to take a position on a matter that was certain to come before her.

By my reckoning, Bork could have been counted upon to vote to overrule *Roe*. But even with the less-easy-to-peg O'Connor sitting instead, it was apparent that there was no longer a majority willing to approach new claims of "liberty" as the freewheeling *Roe* majority had in 1973.

The proof came in 1986 when the Court, in *Bowers v. Hardwick*, was asked whether a Georgia law outlawing consensual homosexual sodomy was constitutional. In order to strike down the law, of course, the Court would have to declare that category of sexual activity to be a new constitutional liberty. The Court refused in an opinion written by Justice White, who had dissented in *Roe*. Using the same legal reasoning as in his *Roe* dissent, White, joined by Justices Powell and O'Connor, canvassed the laws of all fifty states in order to discern whether consensual homosexual sodomy had been accorded legal protection. He found it had not. In fact, most states had outlawed the behavior. The Court thus had no basis for declaring that the Constitution protected consensual homosexual relationships. In *Griswold,* of course, just the opposite had been true. For in the rich history, including the common law, showing that the marital relationship had been protected in law, the Court found solid grounds for striking down the state law barring contraceptives for married couples.

In *Bowers,* the Court was unsparing in its criticism of the methodology employed by the majority in *Roe*. The Court, Justice White warned, was at its greatest peril when it sought to provide constitutional shelter for liberty claims lacking demonstrable approval in law or the traditions of the people.

When *Bowers* was decided, President Reagan's decision to pass over Judge Bork seemed to have made no difference insofar as *Roe*'s future was concerned. *Bowers* showed that the Court had already shifted, thanks to Powell and O'Connor, to a more traditional, anti-*Roe* methodology. The more methodical, lawyerly judges were in the ascendancy. Of particular concern to pro-choice groups was the Court's dismissive attitude to the position Justice Blackmun advanced in dissent. At long last, Justice Blackmun put together an intellectually coherent defense of constitutional libertarianism broad enough to encompass abortion and homosexual rights. He emphasized, in particular, the Court's precedents supporting individual freedom concerning intimate, personal decisions. But the Court brushed aside Blackmun's new, improved argument.

So it was that *Roe* seemed doomed. It was only a matter of time. Or of perhaps one new appointment to the Court. And when Justice Powell, who had joined the majority in *Roe* but now had converted to the anti-*Roe* methodology, stepped down in 1987, it appeared that the Court soon would be overruling one of its most disputed decisions ever.

President Reagan put gender and ethnic politics aside and in the waning years of his presidency, picked Robert Bork to fill Powell's seat. At long last, the pivotal choice of Robert Bork had been made. Winning confirmation, however, proved illusive. As a result of the 1986 elections, Democrats controlled the Senate, and Democratic Senator Joe Biden was now chairman of the Senate Judiciary Committee. The Democrats were thus better positioned to defeat Bork than they would have been in 1981 or, for that matter, in 1986 (when Chief Justice Burger stepped down), when Republicans controlled the Senate. Nor was it in Judge Bork's favor that the justice he would replace was Lewis Powell, regarded, rightly, as a justice squarely in the ideological center. Judge Bork's rigorous, well-developed philosophy of judging put him unambiguously to the right of the centrist Powell. Clearly an adherent of the textualist school and a restrained interpretation of judicial power, Judge Bork was an outspoken critic of *Griswold;* in his view, the Court should enforce only those rights found in the Constitution and its history. In short, there was little doubt that if Judge Bork were confirmed, he would shift the balance of the Court to the right. Pro-choice forces in particular viewed his prospect with alarm. Not by happenstance did Senator Edward Kennedy, a Democrat from Massachusetts, on the day President Reagan nominated Judge Bork stand in the Senate to denounce the selection as though it were something out of the Dark Ages. Senator Kennedy drew a wild caricature of Bob Bork as someone who would return America to an era when women ruined or lost their lives as a result of back-alley abortions. Kennedy knew full well that reversing *Roe v. Wade* would simply return the issue, like countless others, to the states. This was demagoguery.

The demonization worked, although in fairness Judge Bork's performance in the closely watched confirmation hearings did not win over the hearts and minds of the American people. The Senate rejected by the vote of 58–42 one of the most qualified individuals ever selected for the High Court. But the Senate did more than defeat Robert Bork. It forced President Reagan to name someone more to the Democratic-controlled Senate's liking, which is to say someone less to the right than Bork, someone less likely to shift the Court's balance. Anthony Kennedy was the eventual choice. His record on the Ninth Circuit was one of caution and circumspection. On the High Court, his caution was manifested when the Court, in *Planned Parenthood v. Casey* (1992), confronted the question of whether *Roe v. Wade* should be overruled.

The question in *Casey* arose in the context of a constitutional challenge to Pennsylvania's abortion regulations, including a waiting period before the abortion procedure could be performed. Planned Parenthood wanted the regulations declared unconstitutional, a violation of the abortion liberty declared in *Roe*. The Commonwealth of Pennsylvania, under Democratic Governor Bob Casey, vigorously defended them. Various friends of the Court, including the United States, which I represented as the solicitor general, argued not only in defense of the regulations but also for the overruling of *Roe* itself. The time was ripe, in my judgment, for the Court to reconsider *Roe*. My argument was this: *Roe v. Wade* was not grounded in the text or history of the Constitution. The traditions of law and medical practice did not sanction nontherapeutic abortions. The Court had ignored the limited role of courts by divining a sweeping right of "privacy"—in the sense of individual autonomy—that invalidated state efforts (if states so chose) to protect the sanctity of life.

I had miscalculated. To be sure, the Court upheld all but one of Pennsylvania's challenged regulations. But the Rehnquist Court pointedly declined to overrule *Roe*. Justice Kennedy, joined by Justice O'Connor and a third justice named by a Republican president, David Souter, wrote a plurality opinion expressing reservations about the reasoning employed by the Court in *Roe*. The plurality opinion said that *Roe*'s reasoning was weak. It intimated that its authors, had they been on the Court in 1973, would not have joined the majority, but the justices would not now vote to overrule *Roe*. The reason was stability, they explained. The principle of *stare decisis* loomed large in their analysis. Law needs to be predictable. An abiding institutional respect for prior decisions creates, in effect, a presumption of correctness.

Much of what the plurality said was true—if the law at issue is a law passed by Congress. Once the Supreme Court interprets a federal statute, that's the end of the matter. The Court, for reasons of ensuring stability in the law, won't return to that particular issue. This is the principle of *stare decisis* in its most powerful form. In contrast, Congress may overturn a High Court interpretation of one of its laws simply by passing a new law. But Congress has no such ability in the case of a constitutional decision. Thus, in the case of abortion, Congress is powerless to override *Roe*'s judgment that the Constitution includes the abortion liberty. A law passed by Congress cannot undo *Roe*. Only a constitutional amendment, which requires action by the states, could do that. Or, to put it more precisely, only a constitutional amendment or a ruling by the Court itself could do that.

In my judgment, the Court ought to be more willing to reassess its prior constitutional decisions, for two reasons. First, there is the sheer difficulty of correcting a wrong decision by constitutional amendment. A supermajority of the states—some three-quarters in all—is necessary to ratify an amendment. Second, the Court itself is unelected yet enjoys broad power to issue rules that affect the culture. Given this power, the Court is in the position—as no one else is—to correct its own erroneous readings of the Constitution. *Plessy v. Ferguson,* the infamous 1896 decision upholding the concept of separate but equal treatment of individuals along racial lines, should have been overruled long before the Court's action a half century later in *Brown v. Board of Education.*

In previous eras, the Court has been more than willing—eager, even—to overrule its own constitutional holdings. The New Deal Court (after the failed Court-packing plan) in particular did not let arguments about the sanctity of precedent or the importance of stability in the law deter it from reversing recent decisions. The Court came to the view that previous Courts had been wrong, substituting as they had their own judgments for the views of duly elected legislatures and Congress. There were no visible signs of anguished hand-wringing or soul-searching by the New Deal Court as it chopped away at what it deemed wrong constitutional decisions.

But the Supreme Court in 1992, in *Planned Parenthood v. Casey,* did not see its role that way. The three justices (O'Connor, Kennedy, and Souter) set forth an intricate theory of the value of precedent in constitutional law. Their theory was novel. It centered on public expectations, not on the internal strength of the precedent itself in law and logic. This was an overtly political and cultural approach toward constitutional interpretation. Constitutional principles, the justices explained, had become embodied in everyday social arrangements. *Roe v. Wade* had been on the books for almost a generation, and millions of individuals had come to rely on it. Given this reality, it would require a compelling reason to overrule the case. But, they concluded, no such reason had been advanced. Anticipating the objection that their approach would carve wrong constitutional decisions into stone, the justices articulated a new rationale for *Roe* by drawing on cases decided before *Roe.* This body of case law provided a *plausible* basis for *Roe,* said the justices, even though they might not have agreed with it had they been sitting in the *Roe* litigation in the first instance.

Still, the three-justice plurality could not dispel the lingering sense that *Roe* was wrong, and that they felt it was wrongly decided. No other Court, nor indeed any other justice, had ever suggested that a prior decision interpreting the Constitution might be wrong but that broader, prudential interests in continuity and settled expectations counseled in favor of sticking with precedent.

History had taken a decisive turn. Judge Bork, the consensus Republican choice for the Court throughout the 1980s, would never have embraced such an unorthodox approach toward interpreting the Constitution. This was creative, prudential reasoning, not constitutional analysis. It was judicial statecraft. The O'Connor-Kennedy-Souter troika was overtly appealing to public perceptions and (possibly) public opinion. The center of the Court was unwilling to subject the Court to the sustained attack pro-*Roe* forces would surely initiate. The Court would be demonized; anti-*Roe* justices would surely be savaged in the nation's editorial pages. Instead, the three were willing to withstand the vigorous criticisms of *Roe*'s opponents, including partisans of the presidents (Reagan and Bush) who had appointed them.

The anti-*Roe* dissenters had an opinion-writing field day (as dissenters are wont to do). But it was to no avail. Mention was made of *Plessy v. Ferguson,* which ratified segregation. It, too, had been deeply rooted. It, too, was enshrined in settled expectations. But segregation was constitutionally wrong. The "separate but equal" rationalization had been a fig leaf to cover over the profound violation of the Constitution—the fact that the government, in implementing segregation, singled out individuals on grounds of race in order to separate them. This was not only morally offensive, but legally indefensible. The Court understood this in *Brown v. Board of Education,* and did the right thing by overruling *Plessy.* Why not here as well?

The *Casey* plurality's middle-of-the-road approach was widely seen as at best feckless, and at worst an abdication of a solemn judicial obligation to be principled in coming to judgment. This appeared to be a willful search for the least controversial middle ground. Under the troika's apparent worldview, the Court should avoid divisive controversies to the fullest extent possible, or at least avoid making bad matters worse by changing course. Justices, it appears, should be mindful of public attitudes, and tack the judicial course accordingly.

Abortion proved unique. As we'll see, the centrists' approach toward *Roe v. Wade* was not employed elsewhere. In other areas of law, especially federalism, O'Connor and Kennedy provided the pivotal votes to steer an anti-Washington, pro-states approach. (We will focus on this in Chapter Thirteen, "The Rehnquist Court and the Federal Republic.") On race, O'Connor and Kennedy held sway, aggressively overturning precedents, as we will see in Chapter Eight, "Counting by Race." They were firm and resolute on *Bush v. Gore*. As for the junior member of the troika, Souter soon encamped in the Court's left wing, railed against the centrist-conservative majority's approach in a variety of areas, and showed no interest in the genteel approach to *stare decisis* that he vigorously espoused in *Casey*. The troika came together to preserve *Roe v. Wade*, then vanished.

The middle-of-the-road approach did not, in the end, portend a revival of *Roe*'s discredited methodology. The "right to die" and assisted suicide cases of the 1990s made that clear. Liberty, as a pivotal constitutional word, was sufficiently broad to protect the "right to choose," divined in *Roe v. Wade*. But it was not broad enough to include a right to terminate one's own life (or that of a loved one). There would be no overarching libertarian, autonomy-centered approach to the concept of liberty.

The Court first grappled with this question in the case of Nancy Beth Cruzan, which I argued as solicitor general. It was an unspeakably sad case. Following a tragic car wreck, Nancy declined into the netherworld of a persistent vegetative state. The prognosis was hopeless. She would continue to breathe, to have cycles of waking and sleep, but she would never resume normal everyday life.

As the years went by, Nancy's family grew more and more distraught. Having determined that her life should be ended, they requested the medical provider, a Missouri state facility providing permanent care at no expense to the family, to terminate Nancy's nutrition and hydration. Already in effect, and not in dispute, was a Do Not Resuscitate protocol—Nancy was not to be resuscitated in the event of cardiac or respiratory arrest.

The distinction between the two procedures—the requested termination of food and drink on the one hand, and the DNR order on the other—was seen by the state medical facility in Missouri as fundamentally important, morally and professionally. To starve the patient would violate basic precepts of professional ethics. Depriving the patient of food and drink would constitute a killing. In contrast, refraining from using life-saving measures in the event of a cardiac or respiratory arrest was viewed as entirely different. That would allow death to occur naturally. Nancy's family was turned down.

Relying expressly on *Roe v. Wade*'s reasoning, Nancy's parents filed suit in Missouri state court seeking an order that would force the state medical-care provider to terminate Nancy's feeding. The matter wended its way through the Missouri state courts and arrived at the Supreme Court, with the two sides sharply divided. At issue, as in *Roe v. Wade*, was the meaning of "liberty." Did it encompass the right of a family member to decide whether to terminate Nancy's life? *Roe*'s logic suggested as much, so long as the surrogate decision-maker was guided by a genuine desire to seek the "best interests" of the patient, who languished unable to decide for herself. Nancy's mother and father were convinced: Nancy would not want to continue life in her current state.

The Court fragmented sharply, just as it had in the abortion controversy years before. But here the forces espousing a broad, privacy-informed approach to the concept of liberty fell short. Over strenuous dissents, Justices O'Connor and Kennedy combined with Chief Justice Rehnquist and Justices White and Scalia to reject the family's claim. The analysis on both sides echoed the debate in *Roe v. Wade*, with the majority of justices reaching out to existing, established sources of law to determine whether the claimed interest (termination of life) enjoyed protection in common-law decisions or in statutes. The claim failed. No common-law decision or statutes could be identified as pointing squarely toward protection of surrogate decision-making in matters of life and death.

The *Cruzan* majority showed considerable deference to Missouri's vigorously asserted interest in protecting life. In particular, throughout its law (both statutory and judge-made), Missouri had embraced strongly pro-life positions. It frowned severely on suicide (including imposing criminal sanctions for those who assist in its commission). Missouri specifically sought to guard against, for example, the malevolent terminating of life of an elderly relative. The Court let Missouri keep its demanding rule that required "clear and convincing" evidence of the patient's intent before allowing a surrogate decision-maker to take the life-ending step of terminating food and drink.

The *Cruzan* Court thus steered clear of controversy. Instead of imposing one approach on all the states—the command model of *Roe*, which had proved so sharply divisive—the Court permitted the states to try different approaches. The *Cruzan* model, one of restraint and caution, was more comfortable for the Rehnquist Court.

Another element was at work. The Court was mindful of the delicacy of life-termination issues as they intersected with law. Nancy Cruzan was resuscitated by emergency rescue personnel using state-of-the-art procedures. Tragically, the rescue unit arrived on the scene only after Nancy had been lying facedown in a pool of water. She had stopped breathing. She had been brought back from the very brink of death, but with virtually no discernible brain activity.

Her situation was vexing at moral and religious levels. How could even loving family members make a decision about life and death, at least where the patient would be allowed to die through failure to feed and hydrate? In Nancy Cruzan's case, it was clear that she would have experienced pain had she been allowed to die. As one nurse testified at the state proceeding, depriving an animal of food and drink would result in a criminal prosecution. Other members of the medical staff said they would resign, in conscience, rather than be party to depriving Nancy of food and water.

These images of life, death, and forced dying troubled the Court. *Roe v. Wade* had taught a bitter lesson. It was the better part of wisdom for the Court to be cautious.

Roe v. Wade, coupled with the fury unleashed by the Bork nomination, also taught presidents a lesson: Avoid a *Roe*-centered controversy in choosing justices for the High Court. Just as the Court shouldn't boldly enter a field of controversial and divisive social policy as it did in *Roe,* so, too, presidents might want to avoid a Bork-type nomination that might convulse the nation. No more "impact" appointments, unless a president were willing to take on a divisive, costly fight. This cautious approach led to nomination of the uncontroversial Anthony Kennedy, to the choice of David Souter by President Bush, and to the selections of Justices Ruth Ginsburg and Stephen Breyer by President Clinton.

Roe had transformed High Court nominations into a bloody battleground. The response was to put on the

Court slightly right-of-center (the mistaken perception of the soon predictably liberal Souter) or mildly left-of-center (Ginsburg and Breyer) nominees, thereby avoiding costly battles that would distract the attention of the nation (and the Senate). The risk-averse president will thus nominate individuals who can be steered through the confirmation process with a minimum of controversy.

"Impact" appointments, such as that of Justice Clarence Thomas, would come only at a political price. Judge Thomas, who had chaired the EEOC under President Reagan, was considered well worth the battle. His nomination would mark a genuine turning point since Justice Thurgood Marshall's seat would be occupied by an African American of a polar-opposite judicial philosophy. The nomination proved bitterly divisive, especially in the wake of allegations mounted by Thomas's former colleague at the EEOC, Anita Hill. The rancorous hearings culminated in a narrow 52–48 vote in favor of confirmation.

The Thomas appointment, though, was the exception that proved the rule in the Reagan-Bush-Clinton administrations. To preserve presidential strength for other battles, the strategy would be to nominate comfortably "mainstream" judges.

Chastened by the *Roe*-caused turmoil, complete with annual marches of protest and counterprotest directed at the Court, "mainstream" justices had also learned a bitter lesson. The Court must not, as it had in the Warren Court era, get out in front of the country. Don't drive the agenda of social policy. The Court had done so in the abortion arena. Little did the *Roe* Court expect that a firestorm, never to abate, would be unleashed. Not even the dissenters had predicted that.

Given the *Roe*-induced caution of today's Court, the century's final set of significant decisions under the "liberty" concept were predictable as the Court gave short shrift to aggressive decisions by lower courts invalidating state-imposed bans on physician-assisted suicide. All nine justices joined in these decisions, albeit in different opinions setting forth various rationales. But on this all justices agreed: States could prohibit physician-assisted suicide. The Court would not step in and freeze the legislative debate. To the contrary, the justices would allow the process of debate—and state-by-state experimentation—to proceed, with the Court (potentially) stepping in only to avoid extreme or extravagant results. That was the tried-and-true process abruptly halted—in the abortion arena—by *Roe v. Wade.*

The Court thus closed the century paying tribute, in effect, to a fundamental tenet of the judicial philosophy of Oliver Wendell Holmes, Jr. Early in the century, when the Supreme Court had been overturning Progressive-era reforms in case after case, Justice Holmes was in vigorous dissent. His objections to the Court's invalidation of those reform measures were grounded not in his own social philosophy. Quite the contrary. Justice Holmes, a survivor of three wounds during the Civil War, was given over to Social Darwinist thinking. Since only the fittest would survive, it was folly for Congress or state legislatures to interfere with the unfolding of the natural order of life. But Justice Holmes was equally convinced that, as an unelected judge, he should not impose his philosophical views on the people's elected representatives. Other than to protect certain rights (such as free speech) set forth in the Bill of Rights, the unelected judiciary should not interfere with policy choices by Congress and state legislatures. This, then, was the philosophy of judicial restraint.

With the unanimous upholding of state anti-euthanasia laws, the Court closed the twentieth century with the same spirit that animated Holmes's great dissents at the dawn of the 1900s. The Court would not overturn *Roe,* but the *Roe* methodology would not be carried over to other fields of social policy. Thus, the Court rebuffed the efforts of grandparents to override the judgment of a custodial parent as to visitation rights. The Court was unwilling to establish a new set of rights on behalf of grandparents or other members of an extended family. The Court, with Justice O'Connor writing the lead opinion for a plurality of the justices, held that the state statute at issue, which permitted courts broadly to fashion visitation rights over parental objections, was unconstitutional as applied to the specific circumstances at issue—a loving mother determining that her late husband's parents should not be able to visit their grandchildren freely. The grandparents' lawsuit against the children's mother to enforce their "rights" under state law would fall short.

Restraint, more than two decades after *Roe*, seemed finally to be the order of the day. But *Roe* itself would survive, a tribute to the Rehnquist Court's determination to stay the course. Even attorney general John Ashcroft, a reliable conservative, testified at his confirmation hearings that *Roe* was "settled law." And in 2003, for the first time in recent history, the Court relied on the *Roe* methodology when it held unconstitutional a Texas law barring homosexual sodomy, thereby overruling its earlier decision in *Bowers v. Hardwick*. *Roe*, the single most controversial decision of the last generation, has been preserved. It remains to be seen whether it will actually be expanded.

Chapter Eight

★

COUNTING BY RACE I: THE AFFIRMATIVE ACTION CONTROVERSY

THE ONE AND ONLY TIME I WAS OVERRULED by the president (George Bush) during my tenure as solicitor general was in a desegregation case. The issue was whether the Mississippi higher-education system had taken sufficient steps to dismantle its old, dual system of segregated state-supported colleges and universities. Supporting private plaintiffs who had filed the original lawsuit in Mississippi, the Civil Rights Division had taken the position that more needed to be done, from Ole Miss to Mississippi State to Jackson State and the other institutions in the state system. For its part, Mississippi's lawyers argued that the prior race-based system of admissions (whites only at some schools) was ended when the state announced a policy of race-neutral admissions. Candidates could apply to any institution, whether white or historically black, and be considered on their merits, not on the basis of race.

Our view at the Justice Department was that more indeed needed to be done. We argued back and forth about what "more" was, including whether any institutions would need to be closed down. The practical result of a dual (or segregated) system is, of course, excess capacity. Too many schools were built in order to have two systems of education. To remedy segregation (to "dismantle" the old dual system), some institutions would likely either be closed or have their mission substantially modified, say, switching from a four-year institution to a community (or "junior") college.

And therein lay the seeds of serious disagreement. The African-American challengers in the litigation felt strongly that one important remedy for the long history of unlawful segregation was to channel more funds into the historically black institutions, such as Jackson State and Mississippi Valley State. I disagreed. The underlying issue was unlawful segregation, drawing lines on the ground of race and channeling students into particular institutions by virtue of race. The victims of this unconstitutional policy were, under my thinking, the individual students. Institutions, on the other hand, had no rights to "equal" treatment.

My position was viewed with alarm throughout much of the African-American higher-education community. Eventually, the president himself stepped in. Responding to the direct appeal of a number of presidents of historically black institutions, the president overruled my position and directed me to change the government's position in the Supreme Court. This was awkward, to be sure, but not terribly embarrassing. The president, after all, was the ultimate decision-maker as to what would be the position of the United States in the Supreme Court. In some quarters that view would be mildly controversial, since the president would be intruding into the "independence" of the solicitor general. My view was different. In our system, the president is ultimately responsible for the actions of the executive branch, including the Justice Department.

What President Bush was doing was based on his judgment and conscience, and I respected both his opinion and his rightful prerogative as the chief executive. As solicitor general, in contrast, I was an "inferior" or "subordinate" officer in the executive branch. If I could not in conscience abide by the president's judgment, then I should resign.

This was not, happily, a resignation kind of issue. I accepted the president's overruling and oversaw preparation of our second brief (the "Reply" brief) to modify our earlier position. The second brief made it clear that the government was in no wise suggesting that predominantly black institutions should be closed.

This did not go unnoticed. My oral argument in the Mississippi case had gone reasonably well, and I was about to wrap up my presentation and sit down. Justice Scalia, never one to miss an opportunity to have a little fun, picked up both briefs we had filed and asked, with a puckish grin, "Now which of these two briefs reflects the position of the United States?" He knew full well, especially since there had been a fair amount of publicity about the president overruling the solicitor general in a case about race and desegregation. I smiled right back, and simply said: "Oh, Justice Scalia, the position of the United States is set forth in the Reply brief." I sat down quickly. The justices well knew that I had been taken to the presidential woodshed, and the Court, in good humor, would not let that go unnoticed.

Race: This is the enduring issue in American life, including important matters that come to the attention of the nation's highest court.

Gunnar Myrdal, the Swedish sociologist, called it the American dilemma. The O. J. Simpson trial, as the 1990s unfolded, starkly reminded the world of the severe fault lines infecting race relations in the United States. The O. J. drama in Los Angeles had been foreshadowed by the Rodney King beating, triggering rioting seen around the world.

These race-driven events demonstrated that unhealed

wounds lived on 130 years after the Civil War and almost a half century after the deep-seated tradition of segregation was condemned by the Supreme Court in the landmark case of *Brown v. Board of Education.*

The issue in that case, decided in the early days of the Warren Court, was the constitutionality of racially segregated public schools, found throughout the South and in some other parts of the country as well. The Court came down emphatically against segregated schools, condemning them as violating the Fourteenth Amendment's guarantee of the equal protection of the laws. To reach this decision, the Warren Court, as we mentioned earlier, overruled *Plessy v. Ferguson,* the 1896 case that had provided the legal basis for state-sponsored segregation. So much for *stare decisis,* the value given to precedent. It had, in contrast to abortion and *Miranda,* as we shall soon see, no weight in the highly charged context of affirmative action.

Chief Justice Earl Warren had taken his seat on the Court not long before *Brown* was rendered. Warren, as chief justice, was able to bring and hold the entire Court together in an opinion that he read from the bench. *Brown* proved to be one of Warren's, and indeed the Court's, greatest achievements. It not only reversed *Plessy* and condemned school segregation but also launched the Court's assault on government-imposed segregation more generally. In a series of cases decided in *Brown*'s wake, the Court invalidated segregation in public parks, beaches and recreation facilities, and public transportation. Each time, the Court issued a memorandum opinion in which it simply cited *Brown* as the basis for its new judgment. Where racial segregation took place wasn't the issue for the Court; that it occurred at all was the problem.

Brown ratified the civil rights movement in its work even as it inspired the movement to go forth and do more. The Court—and much of the country—could not deny the compelling moral argument of civil rights. It was the message of equality, the great unifying principle of so much of the Court's work, as we saw in the earlier chapters on religion. In 1957, Congress enacted the first of several statutes designed to protect civil rights against racial discrimination. The two most important came in the Johnson administration: the Civil Rights Act of 1964 and the Voting Rights Act of 1965. Taken together, they extended the principle of nondiscrimination throughout the public sector and into much of the private sector.

Challenges to the civil rights laws made their way to the High Court, which showed restraint (another unifying principle) by deferring to the political branches. Congress had the power, the Court held, to regulate even local eating establishments and small motels, and in particular to require local restaurants and other "public accommodations" to be open to individuals of all races. This was the spirit of John Marshall living on, vindicating national power—ultimately the power of Congress to guide the country's destiny. In the same spirit, the Court concluded that Congress could require states with records of race discrimination in voting to eradicate any measure that had been used to exclude blacks from the voting booth. Thus did the Court condemn the poll tax and literacy tests. In addition, the Warren Court held that Congress enjoyed the power to require offending states to submit for Justice Department review any proposed change, no matter how modest, in voting and election procedures.

Happily for the country, the justices were unanimous on these matters. Equality triumphed. And the justices remained unanimous in two highly important race cases decided in 1971 by the Burger Court. Indeed, Chief Justice Burger wrote the Court's opinion in both cases. In the first, the Court issued a ringing endorsement of a district judge's sweeping busing order in Charlotte, North Carolina. The order was destined to remain in place (in some measure) for an entire generation. The case also provided the model for similarly sweeping busing orders around the country. In the second case, the Court broadened the 1964 Civil Rights Act's definition of prohibited discrimination in employment. A power company in North Carolina had required a high-school diploma for entry-level jobs. Fewer black than white applicants could meet this requirement. The Court ruled that the 1964 law prohibits not only overt discrimination but practices "fair in form but discriminatory in operation." Only if such practices could be demonstrably tied to job performance would they be legal.

But the moral and legal choices soon became more difficult. Eliminating discriminatory barriers was seen, in many quarters, as not enough. To get beyond racism, it was said, race had to be taken into account. This translated into a fundamental moral and legal dilemma: Was it right to consider race in determining the allocation of limited job or educational or other opportunities? Was "affirmative action" that preferred minorities on account of their race indeed lawful?

Two justices led the way in crafting the Court's answers: Justices Lewis F. Powell, Jr., and Sandra Day O'Connor. Indeed, Powell's concurring opinion in the landmark 1978 case of *Bakke v. Board of Regents* remains important—and controversial—still today. As for Justice O'Connor, her opinions for the Court in cases involving public contracts and voting constitute a large part of the current law on race.

Bakke, in particular, has long been the flagship case in race-related admissions issues. The facts of the case were troubling. Allan Bakke, a white applicant, applied for admission to the University of California (Davis) Medical School. There were 100 places in what would have been his class. Sixteen of these were set aside for minority applicants. Allan Bakke was rejected. On paper, he was more qualified than those admitted under the university's set-aside program, which insulated minority applicants from comparison with those competing for the eighty-four other seats. Bakke sued, contending that the medical school's two-track system discriminated against him on grounds of race.

When the case arrived in the Supreme Court, the outcome was entirely in doubt. Philosophical lines, so clear in *Brown* and in the decisions upholding the constitutionality of the landmark civil rights legislation of the 1960s, were now blurred. William O. Douglas, an FDR appointee and one of the Court's most outspoken liberals, had railed against race-based affirmative action in his dissent from the Court's denial of *certiorari* in a 1974 case raising the same issue Allan Bakke later did. The reliable friend of liberty and author of an anti-establishment book titled *Points of Rebellion,* Douglas wrote that students should be admitted on the basis of "individual attributes," not the "capricious and irrelevant factor" of race. But Douglas was no longer on the Court, having been forced to step down in 1975, the victim of crippling strokes. President Ford quickly replaced him with John Paul Stevens, a bow-tie-wearing midwesterner who had been a judge on the U.S. Court of Appeals for the Seventh Circuit. What would the five appointees of President Nixon and Ford—enough to make a majority—do? The future of affirmative action in higher education was now in the hands of the Burger Court.

The *Bakke* case revealed a Court not only far from unanimous; it was as deeply divided on affirmative action as the country itself. The Burger Court invalidated the Davis program and ordered Bakke admitted. But the Court went on to say that Davis and institutions of higher education generally may take race into account in admitting students. There were different majorities—the narrowest possible—for each of these conclusions. Four justices—Justice Potter Stewart, Chief Justice Burger, Justice (and future chief justice) Rehnquist, and Justice Stevens—sided with Bakke. Four others—Justices William Brennan, Byron White, Thurgood Marshall, and Harry Blackmun—said the set-aside program was legal. The crucial opinion was Justice Lewis Powell's. Powell agreed with the first group of four and thus provided the fifth vote necessary to strike down the program and order Bakke's admission. But Powell also agreed with the second group of four that a university may take race into account in choosing applicants.

To complicate things still further, Powell disagreed with the pro–affirmative action group in two ways. First, he was unwilling to endorse what the four justices would uphold: a two-track admissions system, one for nonminorities and the other for minorities. Instead, for Powell, a school must use a unitary admissions system that puts all applications in one basket, so to speak. Second, whereas this foursome said race may be taken into account to remedy societal discrimination, Powell justified consideration of race on a different ground: to achieve educational diversity.

Powell's opinion was the work of a lawyer laboring hard to find middle ground. He avoided abstract principles. He noted the inherent sensitivity of any line-drawing on the basis of race. He cited cases showing why the judiciary should be deeply skeptical when government makes distinctions grounded in race. If a public agency wishes to do that, he said, it must have a very good explanation, since it is best if government does its business in a racially neutral fashion. Powell was willing to let government, in this case a state medical school's admissions office, take race into account because education was different from all other areas, including employment, where race-based decisions can be deeply problematic. What makes higher education different, he said, is the First Amendment freedom to make judgments about the educational mission, including the kind of student body a college or university chooses to have. Thus, a university may choose to create a diverse student body on the theory that such a student body will promote an educational environment of most benefit to all students. Diversity, for Powell, encompassed multiple diversities—of geographical and cultural backgrounds, races and ethnicities, and unique academic, athletic, or artistic talents. Diversity, for him, was not merely racial diversity.

Powell searched for a plausible example to make his case, and like the careful lawyer he was and the influential school-board chairman (in Richmond) he had once been, he invoked the admissions policy of one of the nation's top schools, Harvard University. Harvard, he said, had sought to ensure diversity in each class by taking into account what might be called nonracial diversity factors—geography, for example. An applicant from Montana might have a leg up on yet another smart applicant from the Northeast. But now, Powell noted, Harvard also took into account race and ethnicity. Minority students, Powell said, can contribute something white students cannot offer.

There were limits, however. Having sanctioned the use of race in the admissions process, Powell did not want race to become the *sole* factor in deciding which students actually got in. Here again, his instinct was that of the careful lawyer seeking a way to avoid a constitutional problem. Powell's solution was to say that race may be *a* factor, a plus in a student's file. But *how much* that plus might count was unclear. Powell simply said that the weight given to race, like that given to the other nonracial diversity factors, could vary from year to year depending on the mix both of the student body and the applicants for the incoming class.

Powell's middle way was not without its weaknesses, as the four pro–affirmative action justices were quick to point out. There is no difference, they said, between setting aside a predetermined number of places for minorities and using minority status as a positive factor to be considered in evaluating applications. In other words, a school could achieve the same results as Davis simply by following the kind of admissions policy Powell had endorsed. Either way, race would be given the same weight.

Powell was unpersuaded; he believed there was a big difference in what he proposed: The rights of someone like Allan Bakke would be better protected in a unitary admissions system rather than one, like Davis's, that was in part racially exclusionary and set up a quota for a certain number of minorities. Still, a unitary system that took race into account was one that compromised the principle of race neutrality. The principle "Don't assign children to schools on the basis of race" had, of course, been at the core of *Brown*.

Notwithstanding the weaknesses of his position, Powell's triumph was evident. Even though he spoke only for himself, Justice Powell had managed to find the position that decided the case for a deeply fractured Court and, as a result, set the critical rule for affirmative action in higher education for years to come. Colleges, universities, and graduate and professional schools were largely supportive of his opinion. Not until the nineties would its weaknesses be challenged in litigation in Texas, Michigan, and elsewhere.

Meanwhile, divisions on the Burger Court as to the issue of race sharpened. Unanimity was lost. Equality as a unifying principle could not bring the increasingly warring justices together. To the contrary, the Court's deep ambivalence toward affirmative action mirrored a deeply divided nation. In *Fullilove v. Klutznick* (1980), a divided Court upheld, by a 6–3 vote, a 10 percent set-aside passed by Congress to benefit minority contractors on federally funded public-works projects. On its face, the program seemed flatly inconsistent with *Bakke;* a specified percentage of federal public-works projects had been carved out and reserved *exclusively* for minority-owned businesses. In his plurality opinion, Chief Justice Burger failed to set forth a coherent justification for Congress's foray into affirmative action. The chief's opinion brimmed with language emphasizing the great respect owed to Congress, the novelty of the issue, and the virtues of judicial restraint. As his former law clerk on the threshold of joining the Justice Department in the incoming Reagan administration, I knew that the chief's approach was inadequate as a standard to guide future cases. It was, truth be told, a muddled opinion, but it was guided by the unifying principle of deference—the judiciary should not stand in the way of Congress's judgment. This was, at bottom, a punt. The chief, whom I loved and respected, had authored an intellectually lazy opinion that would not stand the test of time.

Tellingly, the principal critique of Chief Justice Burger's deference-to-Congress approach came from Justice Powell. The pivotal justice in *Bakke* said that the Court's conclusion was correct, but that greater attention to legal reasoning and analysis was needed. More careful lawyering was called for. As Powell saw it, simply repeating the mantra of "defer to Congress" wasn't sufficient. He was right.

Ironically, Justice Powell's observation was the abiding critique of the Warren Court, which had championed specific results without doing the hard work of the legal craft: explaining in rigorous fashion why the Court was resolving the issue the way it did. Here the Burger Court was

wandering about directionless. It seized upon large principles, such as judicial restraint, but the legal reasoning
seemed thin and unconvincing. The unpredictability and
fragility of the Court's approach to affirmative action was
apparent in the position of the justice who early on was
the Burger Court's wild card, Justice Stevens. Soon to align
himself solidly on the left and thereafter to be, steadfastly,
one of the Court's most liberal members, Stevens was still
relatively new on the Court. But not a strain of liberalism
was evident in his dissent. Justice Stevens railed against
the congressional set-aside as unconstitutional. Showing
the same hostility Justice Powell had toward the set-aside
in *Bakke*, Justice Stevens made it clear that if Congress
sought to legislate in the delicate arena of race relations, it
had to move cautiously. In the case at hand, as Justice
Stevens saw it, Congress had simply pulled the 10 percent
set-aside figure out of the air. There had been no committee hearings, no elaborate legislative findings seeking to
justify the program. The set-aside, as he saw it, was simply born on the floor of the House of Representatives. It
was an act of legislative will, essentially unconsidered and
undebated, when great care was needed.

The approaches of Justices Powell and Stevens foreshadowed the more analytical approach taken by majorities in future cases. These were lawyers, not politicians.
They were more careful and rigorous in analysis. Lawyerly
style aside, however, divisions on the Court deepened, and
Justice Stevens soon moved squarely to the pro–affirmative action camp, joining Justices Brennan, Marshall, and
Blackmun. He did so with no explanation whatever of his
about-face. He moved, silently, to the left—and remained
there.

As Justice Stevens veered leftward (and thus diminished
his importance), a new justice emerged to play the central
role in shaping the Court's approach in race cases: Justice

O'Connor. Appointed by President Reagan in 1981, she served alongside Powell for six years. Two years after Powell stepped down, in a case coming out of Powell's beloved Richmond, she took control of the law of affirmative action. At issue was the constitutionality of an ordinance passed by the City of Richmond in 1983. This ordinance, patterned in key respects after the federal public-works set-aside sustained in the 1980 *Fullilove* case, specified that 30 percent of all public works were to be subcontracted to minority-owned businesses. The city council justified the ordinance mainly by citing a statistical disparity: that in the previous five years a paltry two-thirds of 1 percent of city construction contracts had been awarded to minority-owned businesses, yet minorities constituted more than half of Richmond's population. The council settled on the particular percentage of contracts to be routed to minority businesses by picking one more or less halfway between two-thirds of 1 percent and 50 percent. As for the minority groups eligible for the set-aside business, the council designated the same ones Congress had when it passed the federal set-aside sustained in *Fullilove*. These were: blacks, Hispanics, Asians, and Eskimos or Aleuts. That made no sense. At last report, Richmond boasted an Eskimo and Aleut population of zero (or just about). As if more were needed, these businesses could be located anywhere in the country; the ordinance did not make eligible only local or state businesses. A business *not* owned by one of these designated (and rather far-flung) minorities had sued the city, claiming that the ordinance violated the Fourteenth Amendment's guarantee of the equal protection of the laws.

The Court in *Croson v. City of Richmond* voted 6–3 to strike down the Richmond ordinance. The outcome illustrated the profound difference wrought by changes in the Court's composition, for two of those who had joined the majority in *Fullilove* were no longer on the Court—Chief Justice Burger and Justice Powell—and all three justices named by President Reagan were in the majority— O'Connor, joined by Justices Scalia and Kennedy. O'Connor's opinion for the Court, moreover, displayed a deep concern for legal doctrine, and rigor—not found in previous majority opinions—in affirmative-action cases. The looseness of *Fullilove* was a thing of the past. Ronald Reagan's appointees had changed the law of affirmative action.

The Court's race jurisprudence had left some basic questions unresolved. The Court long ago had agreed that in reviewing an equal-protection challenge to a state-sponsored racial classification it should use a test known as "strict scrutiny." This is, as the name suggests, the most demanding test possible. Under a strict-scrutiny standard, unless the racial classification in question has been *narrowly tailored* to achieve a *compelling state interest,* it is unconstitutional. Obviously, none of the racial classifications of the Jim Crow era—ones that invidiously discriminated against blacks—could survive this test.

But the Court had not resolved whether racial classifications designed to *help* blacks, so-called benign classifications that were preferential toward African Americans, should be subjected, when challenged, to the same test. A minority of four justices had argued in *Bakke* that racial preferences, because they were benign, should instead be subjected to a less demanding (and generally permissive) test. But that position had never commanded a majority. In *Croson,* a majority—speaking through Justice O'Connor—finally emerged to say that racial preferences must indeed be examined under strict scrutiny.

The significance of the case lay in its unambiguous (and far-reaching) rule: The Equal Protection Clause is the same for all persons, regardless of race. Because no racial classification has ever satisfied strict scrutiny, this doctrine implied a clear threat to racial preferences wherever they existed. The Constitution, in this context at least, was all but color-blind.

Applying her rigorous approach, Justice O'Connor found the Richmond set-aside wanting in terms of both "compelling interest" and "narrow tailoring." She suggested, importantly, that *remedying discrimination* was the only interest that the Court could deem "compelling." Anything short of that would fail the strict-scrutiny standard. Richmond had failed to demonstrate that there was such discrimination to be remedied. O'Connor brushed aside the statistical disparity: You could not infer discrimination simply from that. Even if the disparity were discrimination, the set-aside itself was not a narrowly tailored remedy, she said. The city council didn't consider race-neutral means of increasing minority participation in city contracting; indeed, it settled on the 30 percent set-aside without pondering other options. Nor had the city council provided means by which those administering the set-aside could learn whether its beneficiaries had actually suffered discrimination on the part of the city or prime contractors. Finally, said O'Connor, because the remedy was available to businesses far removed from Richmond, there could be some odd results. A successful black, Hispanic, or Asian entrepreneur from another part of the nation could enjoy an absolute preference over other citizens (in Richmond) based solely on race.

O'Connor, in short, had cut the poorly crafted Richmond program to pieces. An earlier Court would likely have been less demanding and far more indulgent. But the Rehnquist Court, with O'Connor in the lead, was proving different. It was not only deciding cases but, in that process, framing doctrine that could guide the lower courts—doctrine that clearly threatened racial preferences. The Rehnquist Court was, at least in this context, strenuously evenhanded in applying the equality principle.

A year after *Croson,* the Court seemed suddenly, and strangely, to backtrack. In *Metro Broadcasting v. Federal Communications Commission* (1990), it upheld racial preferences used by the commission in the grant and transfer of broadcast licenses. Soon enough the Court, with Justice O'Connor writing, would reverse *Metro Broadcasting.* But the case powerfully illustrated Justice Stevens's movement to the left. In *Bakke,* as we saw, Stevens had voted to strike down Davis medical school's racially preferential admissions program. But now, in the context of broadcasting, Stevens abandoned that position to join the foursome in *Bakke* who voted to sustain a similar program, thus producing the slim majority that sided with the FCC. This new (and, as it turned out, fleeting) majority said that the FCC's preferences were benign in character and thus shouldn't be subjected to the same strict-scrutiny review as the old-fashioned, invidious ones. The majority insisted on applying the more relaxed standard of intermediate scrutiny. In dissent, O'Connor insisted that there is no such thing as a "benign" racial classification, and that all racial classifications must satisfy strict scrutiny.

Metro Broadcasting was written by Justice Brennan. It was to be his last opinion in a remarkable tenure that started in 1957, when he was appointed by President Eisenhower. This veteran holdover from the Warren Court was replaced by David Souter. A year later Thurgood Marshall would step down, and Clarence Thomas took his seat. President Bush made both appointments.

These two changes in the Court's composition suggested that *Metro Broadcasting* would be short-lived. After all, two judicial liberals had been replaced by two judicial conservatives, or so it seemed.

As it happened, David Souter soon enough began to vote in a fashion not unlike Justice Brennan. Justice Thomas, however, bore out the hopes of his patron, casting votes almost exactly opposite to Marshall's. The subsequent changes in the Court's composition did not alter the single-vote but all-important shift to the right, insofar as race cases are concerned. Ruth Bader Ginsburg took Justice Blackmun's seat in 1993, and Stephen Breyer replaced Justice White in 1994.

So it was that in 1995 Justice Thomas's vote made the difference in the watershed case of *Adarand v. Peña*. The case involved a federal program authorizing a racial preference in subcontracting on highway projects. Adarand, a white-owned construction company, mounted an equal-protection challenge, losing in lower courts applying the more relaxed standard of *Metro Broadcasting*. In her opinion for the Court in *Adarand,* however, Justice O'Connor flatly overruled *Metro Broadcasting*. In the process, she reaffirmed and extended the legal doctrine she had announced in *Croson,* making clear that any race-based measure used by any government, federal or state, must be subjected to the most demanding standard of review, strict scrutiny.

As the year 2000 closed, it had become clear that the Rehnquist Court had resorted, at least for a time, to remaining quiet on issues of affirmative action. But even then, the Court's next encounter with the issue was brewing. Arguably the biggest case in recent years was *Hopwood v. University of Texas,* an equal-protection challenge to the race-based admissions policy used by the University of Texas Law School. The U.S. Court of Appeals for the Fifth Circuit not only struck down the policy but held that the diversity rationale advanced by the school—consistent with Justice Powell's opinion in *Bakke*—could not suffice as a compelling interest under strict scrutiny. Remarkably, the Supreme Court in 1997 declined to review the Fifth Circuit's decision. But the Court took up the issue of diversity in higher education half a decade later, in the context of the University of Michigan's law school and undergraduate admissions programs. In *Grutter v. Bollinger*, a sharply divided Court upheld the use of race as a plus factor to achieve diversity in the classroom. Not surprisingly, Justice O'Connor was at the forefront, writing the opinion for the Court. As if to make clear who the guiding forces were in shaping the Court's affirmative action jurisprudence over the past quarter century, Justice O'Connor relied heavily on Justice Powell's opinion in *Bakke*, and in that respect the Court's holding in *Grutter*, for all the fanfare it surely will receive, is quite consistent with the Court's earlier cases. But the importance of *Grutter* should not be underestimated, for a majority of the Court expressly held that "student body diversity is a compelling state interest that can justify the use of race in university admissions."

Still, the Court's holding should be viewed as limited, for, in a companion case, *Gratz v. Bollinger*, the Court invalidated the Michigan undergraduate affirmative action program by a 6–3 margin. That program assigned twenty points to applicants based solely on their minority status, and the Court found such a program too crude to survive strict scrutiny. Taken together, these cases stand for the proposition that schools may use racial classifications to achieve classroom diversity, but must be very careful in doing so.

Justice O'Connor was in charge. Like Lewis Powell before her, she controlled the law of affirmative action. And consistent with her jurisprudence in other areas of the law, there would be no absolutes. She would not categorically bar the consideration of race. But she would not categorically allow it either. Great care and careful tailoring would be required of the state.

Chapter Nine

★

Counting by Race II:
Gerrymandering and Voting

As with affirmative action, the 1990s also brought greater clarity to the law of race and voting. The great decisions of the 1960s upholding Congress's power as exercised in the Voting Rights Act had given way to a series of halting, tentative decisions suggesting, once again, uncertainty on the part of the Court. And uncertainty carried with it lack of consensus.

The new battleground was congressional redistricting. In the wake of the 1990 Census, states covered by the provisions of the Voting Rights Act requiring advance clearance by the Justice Department of changes in election law and procedures began the process of submitting their new congressional districting plans to the Justice Department for review. The Justice Department's Civil Rights Division asked forthrightly for the first time whether the plans created appropriate opportunities for African-American candidates to be elected to seats in the House of Representatives.

This was ironic. The Justice Department under Ronald Reagan had worked hard to promote the ideal of racial neutrality in government decision-making. But under President George Bush (the elder), policy changed. Led by a delightful, charming New York lawyer, John Dunne, the Bush I Justice Department pushed the race envelope. It demanded, in effect, set-aside districts. It did so through its aggressive interpretation of the Voting Rights Act. As Dunne saw it, the Voting Rights Act *required* covered states to maximize the opportunity for African Americans to elect a minority representative through creative, case-sensitive line-drawing of district lines.

I had serious doubts about all this. But Attorney General Dick Thornburgh supported the Civil Rights Division's race-conscious policies, and given the organization of the Justice Department, it was not within my power to call a halt to it. Unless the legal issue was one involving an appeal from a lower federal court to a court of appeals or an effort to seek review in the Supreme Court, the call was not for the solicitor general to make.

The issue was not unfamiliar to me, though, even if the responsibility belonged to others in the Justice Department. In the early 1970s I had served as a law clerk on the old Fifth Circuit (a court of appeals whose jurisdiction at the time ranged from Florida to Texas). We saw from time to time questionable election practices coming out of the Deep South. I understood full well that race could play a decidedly negative role in elections, including practices designed to manipulate the process unfavorably to blacks— practices that Congress tried to outlaw. I had written a law-review article that argued in favor of federal courts having the power, when necessary to vindicate voting rights, to actually overrule an election and order a new one.

This Justice Department approach raised squarely a question of "benign" or "inclusive" line-drawing on grounds of race. It was the *Bakke* issue—whether lines can be established on grounds of race in order to be more in-

Reno (1993) was born. It challenged the gerrymander as race based. Drawing on principles articulated by Justice Powell in *Bakke* and developed through the burgeoning case law on race, the plaintiffs maintained that the gerrymander was an unconstitutional deprivation of the equal protection of the laws. This was line-drawing by race in order to ensure the election of an African-American representative. As traditional liberals, Shaw and Shimm shared the sentiments of outrage expressed by Warren Court veteran Justice Douglas in the *DeFunis* case shortly before his retirement. Race had become a cutting-edge issue in elections.

The judiciary was in an awkward position. Traditionally, federal courts had taken a hands-off approach to gerrymander-based challenges. To the victor go the spoils, and if those in charge of redistricting reconfigured boundary lines so as to maximize the electoral opportunities of the party in power, so be it. There was nothing the courts could, or should, do.

This was, in Justice Felix Frankfurter's formulation in *Colegrove v. Green* (1946), a "political thicket" he had warned the Warren Court not to enter. Standards would be extraordinarily hard for the courts to articulate in response to charges that district lines were improperly drawn or that legislative districts were malapportioned. But the Warren Court had been untroubled. Ploughing under well-settled law, the Court under Chief Justice Warren held in a series of decisions that the Constitution's demand of "equal protection" required a standard of "one-person, one-vote." No overrepresentation of rural districts, the norm in many states, would be allowed. The Constitution, as understood by the High Court under Earl Warren, demanded equality. This was the mandate even though history and tradition had protected such malapportioned schemes as necessary to carry out another vision

clusive of minorities—applied to the setting of congressional redistricting. The Supreme Court had never faced this issue. It was a Republican-controlled Civil Rights Division that had brought the issue to the fore through the demand for black-controlled districts.

The initial battle in this new debate took place in North Carolina. Due to its population growth during the prior decade, North Carolina was entitled to an additional House seat. The state legislature agreed upon a redistricting plan. But the Civil Rights Division then rejected the plan during the Justice Department pre-clearance process. The division decided that a new district, the North Carolina Twelfth, could be created in such a manner as to facilitate the election of the state's first elected black member of the House since Reconstruction. North Carolina resisted, but the Justice Department held firm. The Civil Rights Division advanced a proposed district that would satisfy the traditional criteria used by legislatures in drawing district lines, including such factors as compactness, contiguity, and respect for traditional political boundaries (such as county and city lines).

The Justice Department's computer-generated plan neglected to consider another traditional criterion: protecting the incumbent members. Under the plan, incumbent protection would have been compromised, since at least one sitting member of the state's congressional delegation would likely have lost his seat. This outcome was unacceptable to the power brokers in Raleigh. They drew up their own plan in an attempt to satisfy all parties. Yet this state-sponsored plan, also computer generated, spawned a course of litigation that continued for a decade. The reason was obvious on the face of the plan: The minority-favored district was a bizarrely shaped oddity that differed widely from its eleven counterparts across the state.

Robinson Everett, a professor at the Duke Law School,

initiated the legal challenge in the early 1990s. Offended by what he considered a blatant, race-based gerrymander, this former judge, who had been appointed chief judge of the United States Court of Appeals for Military Review by President Carter, broached the subject with another professor at the law school, Melvin Shimm. (Both were professors of mine when I attended the Duke Law School from 1970 to 1973.) Soon Ruth Shaw, widow of a Duke sociology professor, was on board. Shaw and Shimm lived in Durham. Neither was a southerner. Shaw hailed from Minnesota, Shimm from New York City. Both were educated outside the South. Both were Democrats. Shimm, in fact, had been a dues-paying member of the NAACP.

They had lost their congressman in the wake of the early 1990s redistricting. Now, suddenly, their representative was a gentleman named Mel Watt. Congressman Watt wasn't from Durham either. He hailed from Charlotte, located more than 150 miles southwest, down Interstate 85. Charlotte was almost on the South Carolina border, close to the North Carolina mountains. Durham, by contrast, was in the northern Piedmont, not far from the Virginia line. It was in the middle of the Research Triangle, a booming educational and research juggernaut. Tobacco had long been in decline, and "research and development" was thriving, carried out by three major universities within a thirty-mile radius. Charlotte was growing too, but it was a major financial center, one of the largest money centers outside of Wall Street.

The district lines fashioned by the incumbent-conscious North Carolina legislature were odd in the extreme. The district tore asunder traditional political boundaries, snaking along the narrow corridors of Interstate 85 as it moved southwest from the Research Triangle to the predominantly African-American neighborhoods of Charlotte. Robinson Everett, Ruth Shaw, and Mel Shimm not

only felt disenfranchised, they were outraged at the grotesque, bizarre shape of the Twelfth District. It crept along Interstate 85 from Durham to Charlotte, taking in predominantly black neighborhoods along the way. As one wag put it at the time, "If you're driving down Interstate 85 with your car doors open, you'll kill half the constituents."

To Robinson Everett, this was profoundly wrong. Not only was the gerrymander race-based, but Durham's sense of community had been compromised. The member of Congress representing Durham had always been attuned to community interests and needs, but that no longer was true.

When American Airlines inaugurated trans-Atlantic service from Raleigh-Durham to London in 1992, public officials and aspirants to public office turned out at the regional airport to celebrate. But Durham's new congressman, Mel Watt, was a no-show. He didn't seem to bother much about this part of his district. His base was Charlotte, and the black community more specifically. Airline service to London was a huge irrelevancy to the world of the black Piedmont situated along the great interstate highway. So on this notable occasion, the congressman stayed in Charlotte while the Research Triangle celebrated the thought of flying direct to London.

Gerrymandering had operated to exclude Shaw and Shimm. Their congressman was one in name only. From their perspective, the congressman never wrote, never visited, and, from appearances, simply didn't care. Shaw and Shimm, like many others, felt that the redistricting plan had abandoned them. And the sole reason for the abandonment, as they saw it, was race.

They went to court. With Ruth Shaw as lead plaintiff and with the Clinton administration embracing and defending the Bush-inspired policies, the case of *Shaw v.*

of the public interest—to ensure that all geographic areas and economic interests enjoyed representation in the electoral process (in the same fashion as the malapportioned United States Senate with each state, regardless of population, allotted two senators).

Although it represented an aggressive intrusion into the world of brass-knuckles politics, the one-person, one-vote standard was at least race neutral. The only matters of interest in the equal-protection analysis were raw population numbers. Each state's electoral district should represent virtually the same number of individuals.

The race issue, however, severely complicated the role of the federal courts in redistricting. The judiciary, now deep in the political thicket, was faced with fresh issues raised by the ostensibly benign use of race to remedy discrimination at the ballot box. To many voters, however, the newly drawn lines represented a dream come true: election of the first African-American congressman since Reconstruction. In view of the history of racially polarized voting in the state, only a specially configured district, drawn so as to create a substantial black majority, would "ensure" the election of an African American. Even under that race-based approach, white majorities in the other eleven districts would still be able to elect eleven of the twelve members in the delegation. Thus the traditional power structures wouldn't be disturbed that much; indeed, in contrast to the Justice Department's approach, every incumbent would be protected under the state's plan.

That being said, oddly shaped districts set off alarm bells. Political gerrymandering was one thing, so long as the constitutional rule (created by the Warren Court) of one-person, one-vote was scrupulously honored. The district might look odd, or even bizarre, but if the voting power of each district in the state (or subsidiary jurisdiction) was mathematically equal, then there was no injury for the courts to worry about.

But as Ruth Shaw and Mel Shimm saw things, the use of race as a criterion changed the rules. Gerrymandering to protect (or enhance) a political party's position of ascendancy was one thing. Racial gerrymandering was quite another.

That was the hook for the Shaw litigation. Complaints about irregularly shaped districts, without more, would not stir the federal judiciary to action. But race-based gerrymandering would, or at least might. The seeming oddity was that the complaints about race-based line-drawing came from white voters. Indeed, the complaint sounded similar to white complaints—such as Allan Bakke's—about minority preferences in higher education.

But there was a fundamental difference between Ruth Shaw and Allan Bakke. Bakke was out on the street. He had been denied admission to a medical school that had only a limited number of seats in each class. Shaw, however, had not been denied access to the ballot box. She could still vote. This contrast in circumstances suggested the uniqueness of voting and elections.

There was another difference as well. The UC Davis Medical School opened in 1968. It had no history of racial discrimination. There was nothing for it to remedy. This could not be said of North Carolina in the conduct of elections and the regulation of voting. Like other southern states, North Carolina, notwithstanding its thriving economy and vaunted higher-educational institutions, still suffered from a history of racial discrimination in voting. This was part of a broader pattern of discrimination in education and employment opportunities. Indeed, it was North Carolina that had generated the case affirming court-ordered busing to achieve racial balance—*Swann v. Charlotte-Mecklenberg* (1971)—and the case broadening the employment discrimination provisions of the 1964 Civil Rights Act—*Griggs v. Duke Power* (1971). Both decisions arose from racist practices in public-school education and private employment.

The Court was vexed. The issue, again, was fundamentally different from *Bakke* because Shaw could still vote. In addition, this was a case where line-drawing was absolutely necessary. In no other way could district lines be fixed. In that line-drawing process, race-related data were inevitably present. The Court had previously said, echoing Justice Powell's opinion in *Bakke,* that such demographics could be taken into account in drawing district lines. Cohesive communities could be torn asunder, if the legislature so chose, in view of the traditional, virtually total discretion enjoyed by states and localities in this arena. The enduring message from the Warren Court seemed to be: Abide by one-person, one-vote, and the federal judiciary will not interfere with the electoral process, with one exception—if there seems to be an effort to "dilute" the effectiveness of a cohesive minority community that might otherwise enjoy "success" in the voting process. Success meant the election of a member of that minority group.

The Court's underlying assumption was this: Blacks will vote for blacks if given the choice, whereas whites will only vote for whites. There would be, in short, race-conscious voting. Voting data tended to support this unhappy assumption. In some localities there was a history of racially polarized voting coupled with steps taken by those in power to diminish the effect of the rising levels of black voting. Courts had struck down, as unconstitutional attempts to split the minority vote, at-large districts in which voters choose, say, all five members of a city council or county board of supervisors. Drawing five separate districts, in contrast, would enable a minority-dominated community within a city or county to elect a candidate from that community, instead of facing the tidal-wave effect of city-wide, or county-wide, voting.

The result was a huge riddle. North Carolina was recognizing the lack of success enjoyed by blacks in congressional races and trying to change that. Yet there was an appearance of excess, of using extreme measures to satisfy the Justice Department's demand that a "safe" district be created (a "majority minority" district consisting of a majority of African-American voters). There had been another, less extreme way of creating such a district without running roughshod over traditional districting principles. But the district that could have been proposed, with no extremes in line-drawing, would have pitted two incumbents against one another, and the state legislature seemed determined that no incumbent should lose his or her seat.

At a more theoretical level, at issue in the districting controversy was the moral definition of community. "Who is my neighbor" is a moral and religious question. "Neighbor" historically has meant much more than a physical or geographic relationship; it has meant more than cultural or racial connectedness. The term has conveyed a sense of the universality of human relationships, of the basic human dignity of each person and the respect each is owed. Thus, we are to seek the welfare and well-being not only of those who look, speak, and act as we do (the clan or tribe) but also of those whose appearances and ways seem very different from our own.

In that more philosophic or religious sense, racial gerrymandering seemed odd. Not only were "we the American people" not getting beyond race, we were openly embracing it and creating specially drawn districts reserved for African Americans, Latinos, or possibly other (theoretically any racial or ethnic-minority) groups.

Political scientists expressed worries about such self-consciously "reserved" seats. A "majority minority" district was to be created for the explicit purpose of facilitating the election of a minority representative. This suggested that the "set-aside" representative was being selected to represent "minority" interests. This seemed different from Democrats claiming to be "disenfranchised" when a Republican was elected, or vice versa. After all, a representative, while belonging to a political party, nonetheless represents all of the district's residents, not just the 50 percent–plus portion of those who voted for him.

This concept of a universal representative—one belonging to the entire district—was well established in practical politics. Thus, for years, members of Congress have mailed newsletters not only to district residents who are members of their own party, but to all residents in the district. After all, the representative might very well succeed in appealing across party lines and thus broaden his or her base of support. The dynamics of representation seemed different in set-aside districts—especially those drawn in contorted ways to further minimize the importance of political communities. Still, these districts were yielding the election of more minorities, a goal encouraged by the Justice Department in its enforcement of the Voting Rights Act.

In the 1993 *Shaw* case, the Court struggled with this set of issues. The burden of resolving these questions fell once again to Justice O'Connor—just as in the affirmative-action arena. She took a traditional lawyerly tack by repairing to the Court's previous decisions, its body of precedent. Nothing, in her judgment, was "directly on point"—that is, no prior decision of the Court was "controlling" in the sense that it pointed to how *Shaw* should be decided. But O'Connor found a close cousin, a civil rights case from the 1960s. She returned, ironically, to the days of the Warren Court.

Here O'Connor made a move well understood by judges. If there is no case "directly on point," as is often true, there still may be a comparable or analogous case. And the old case might provide at least a starting point for thinking about how the new case should be decided.

The prior case selected by Justice O'Connor was *Gomillion v. Lightfoot* (1960). There, the Alabama legislature, at the behest of the city fathers in Tuskegee, Alabama, responded to the growing enfranchisement of black citizens in Tuskegee by redrawing its long-standing boundary lines. Whereas Tuskegee used to be neatly rectangular in shape, it now had boundaries that were anything but rectangular: nooks, crannies, peninsulas, spikes, and other strange lines characterized the new Tuskegee. But the point of the remapping was clear. Comfortably situated inside the new city boundaries was the entire white citizenry. Now outside these boundaries was virtually the city's entire black population.

The Supreme Court, speaking through Justice Felix Frankfurter, invalidated this exclusionary action. The only possible intent, the Court found, in Alabama's drawing these particularly strange boundary lines was to cast the black citizenry outside the city's boundaries. This was a manifest act of race-based disenfranchisement, executed just as blacks were beginning to show political progress. This racially driven line-drawing, the Court held, ran afoul of the Fifteenth Amendment, which protects the right to vote from racial discrimination.

Gomillion was, in the context of voting, *Brown v. Board of Education* all over again. In practical effect, African Americans were being removed from the community and relegated to second-rate status as residents of the unincorporated portions of the county, which had fewer services and civic amenities. Black schoolchildren experienced much the same circumstances when they were required to enroll in their own schools, ostensibly equal to "white" schools yet inferior to them. The line-drawing was so blatant that Justice Frankfurter, in an opinion that was uncharacteristically short for him, dismissed the effort as transparently racist.

Gomillion was the case that Justice O'Connor, speaking for a five-member majority in 1993, relied upon in the *Shaw* case. The Tuskegee decision, she wrote, meant that the federal courts have jurisdiction over efforts to draw political boundary lines. In particular, the use of race was simply too sensitive to warrant a judicial "hands off" approach. Drawing a broader principle from the egregious setting of the Tuskegee experience, O'Connor echoed Justice Powell's sentiments in *Bakke,* by emphasizing that race-based line-drawing, because of its acute sensitivity, had to be done carefully and cautiously.

Thus, in Justice O'Connor's view, Ruth Shaw's case had to be heard. It would not do to dismiss the case, as the lower courts had, simply because the complaining white voters were still allowed access to the ballot box. *Gomillion* stood for the proposition that any citizen, regardless of race, may complain about a race-based gerrymander in federal court.

For the Court, this was only the beginning. The hard part lay ahead. What standards should govern in a case alleging an unlawful racial gerrymander? Would an entire body of law have to be created to provide standards for the district judges actually hearing the challenges in the first instance? And what guidance should be given the courts reviewing the district judges' decisions, the thirteen courts of appeals around the country?

Justice Kennedy shouldered this labor. Building on O'Connor's opinion in the Ruth Shaw case, he worked out the needed standard. He did so in a 1995 case (*Miller v. Johnson*) involving Georgia's congressional redistricting plan. Kennedy wrote that the state could take race into account in the redistricting process; complete race neutrality could not be achieved as a practical matter and did not have to be secured as a constitutional matter. But the state could not make race a "substantial" factor. Allowing race to drive the redistricting decision, he said, would violate equal protection.

Here, the Court assumed a familiar role. By articulating in general terms the basic principle of constitutional law, the Court is able to leave to the lower federal courts the task of filling in the all-critical blanks.

The Court, led by Justices O'Connor and Kennedy, now watched as the lower federal courts applied its new standards to redistricting plans challenged as unlawful racist gerrymanders. These plans did not survive judicial review. States such as Georgia and Texas, in addition to North Carolina, were deemed to have acted unconstitutionally by drawing bizarrely shaped districts so as to create majority-minority districts. State legislatures resumed their redistricting labors, drawing less extreme, bizarre districts but still taking race into account. Mel Watt's district in North Carolina, as finally redrawn in the late 1990s, was more compact, extending from Charlotte to Greensboro, but not extending, as before, all the way to Durham.

The essential message from the Court, now transmitted by federal district and appeals courts, was this: Avoid extremes. That is, avoid bizarre results in the course of trying to achieve a Justice Department–driven goal of maximizing electoral opportunities for previously unsuccessful (or only modestly so) minority groups.

As with affirmative action, the Court has left unanswered questions. New cases will provide occasions for the Court to take up these questions—if it chooses to accept the cases in the first place. This Court tends to move incrementally, making no bold strokes but proceeding cautiously. By doing so, it is able to further elaborate principles—with more time for lawyerly reflection—than it has previously announced.

For now, the Court is only slightly less wary of the use of race in redistricting as it is in affirmative action. It recognizes the demographic reality of race when districts are mapped. There are communities made up mainly of persons of one race or ethnic background. But the Court clearly urges caution in drawing new districts. It is acceptable to craft a plan aimed at improving the chances that a minority might be elected. But a plan deemed extreme when measured against traditional redistricting principles is unlikely to pass muster. Only more moderately drawn plans are going to survive. That became clear, finally, in the spring of 2001 when the Court at long last approved, albeit by a divided vote, a much more moderate plan for North Carolina's Twelfth District. The new Twelfth District, which continues to be represented by Congressman Watt, was more compact than its predecessor plans. Although the new district was more moderate, and thus represented a step in the direction of more traditional line-drawing, the vision of Ruth Shaw and Mel Shimm—restoring a genuine sense of community based on traditional criteria for the sensitive process of drawing political boundaries—was never achieved.

Chapter Ten

★

THE CRIMINAL JUSTICE REVOLUTION: EXCLUDING EVIDENCE FROM CRIMINAL TRIALS

THE WARREN COURT BROUGHT ABOUT a revolution in what is known as "criminal procedure." The term refers in part to the policies that govern police and other law-enforcement officials as they investigate crimes. The Court began this revolution in 1961 in *Mapp v. Ohio,* which extended the Fourth Amendment exclusionary rule to the states. Five years later, the Court handed down *Miranda v. Arizona,* requiring law-enforcement officials to provide warnings to individuals taken into custody.

There were other important criminal procedure cases decided by the Warren Court during the 1960s, but none were as controversial as *Mapp* and *Miranda*. Both decisions provoked vigorous dissenting opinions, academic criticism, and editorial applause. Both required immediate adjustments on the part of police. *Mapp* meant that fully half the states had to change their law-enforcement policies. *Miranda* meant that all the states did.

Miranda, as one supporter of the decision has observed, "galvanized opposition to the Warren Court into a potent political force." In the 1968 presidential campaign, Richard Nixon sought to ride this opposition into the White House. Nixon criticized the Court and promised to use his appointment power to change it. His ideal justice would not be a "super-legislator with a free hand to impose . . . social and political view-points upon the American people," but "a strict constructionist" who saw his "duty as interpreting and not making law." Against a backdrop of rising crime rates, Nixon emphasized that his kind of justice would "strengthen the peace forces against the criminal forces of the land," would appreciate the basic tenets of "law and order," and would be "thoroughly experienced and versed in the criminal laws of the country"—as some others, then sitting on the Supreme Court, by implication were not.

Implicit in Nixon's agenda was the creation of a new Court that would not extend the revolution in criminal procedure and might even roll it back. Among his four appointees were two unstinting critics of *Mapp* and *Miranda:* Chief Justice Warren E. Burger and Associate Justice William H. Rehnquist. Burger wanted to overrule *Mapp* during his seventeen years on the Court but could never summon the necessary votes. Rehnquist, many years later as the chief justice, not only declined an opportunity to overrule *Miranda* but actually wrote the Court's opinion reaffirming its viability.

Mapp and *Miranda* are here to stay. They have survived. In understanding the Court, the question is how, seemingly against the odds, they survived, and why. We examine *Mapp* in this chapter and then, in the following chapter, turn to the remarkable saga of Ernesto Miranda and the case that bears his name.

Mapp was a case about the Fourth Amendment, which secures the freedom from "unreasonable searches and seizures." In particular, *Mapp* was a case about whether this Fourth Amendment right requires the states to adopt the "exclusionary rule," a rule that excludes from admission as evidence items (say guns or drugs) seized illegally by law enforcement.

There is nothing in the Constitution that establishes this rule. It is entirely the product of judges. Early in the last century, the Supreme Court fashioned a rule of evidence—not of constitutional law—that would apply in federal courts only. Under that rule, evidence seized in the course of an unlawful search or seizure (arrest) could not be used in federal court proceedings.

Not surprisingly, resourceful defense lawyers began urging adoption of the rule in state proceedings. The issue languished for years, but in the 1949 case of *Wolf v. Colorado,* the Court rebuffed the effort to extend the rule to the states. Shortly before Earl Warren's arrival, the Court, in its view, was powerless to impose a *federal* rule of evidence on *state* courts. In its *Wolf* decision, the Court recognized a basic principle of federalism and federal judicial power. Federal courts could set their own procedural rules. Those rules would apply in federal courts, but would not be binding on state courts. State court systems thus enjoyed not only their own power but an autonomy not subject to direct control by the federal courts. Thus, the power of the Supreme Court over state courts was limited, reaching *constitutional* but not other matters. So long as they respected basic principles of fairness (due process), state courts were free to order their proceedings as they saw fit. If states wanted an exclusionary rule, they could adopt one legislatively (or through the state supreme courts); indeed, when *Mapp* was decided, half the states had enacted one version or another of the rule. It was not, however, the business of the Supreme Court to impose this or any other procedural rule upon the states.

So matters had stood for decades. Year after year passed with the one rule of evidence governing the federal courts while in many states less stringent rules applied. This was deliberate on the part of the Court. The renowned Benjamin Cardozo made this point emphatically as a judge on New York's highest court. To Judge Cardozo, whom President Hoover appointed to the Supreme Court in 1932, the exclusionary rule made no sense. Why, the judge asked rhetorically, should the criminal go free because the constable blundered? The social cost was too high. Other remedies, such as fines imposed by police-review boards, would be better suited to protecting individual liberties without punishing society.

This was the oddity of the exclusionary rule's operation: It protected only the guilty. It did nothing for an innocent victim of an illegal search. Only if, say, the person subject to a police search was carrying drugs (or some other evidence of criminal activity) would the exclusionary rule be of any help. If, on the other hand, the person subjected to an illegal search (one without probable cause or one, even if probable cause existed, in which there was no justification for dispensing with a search warrant) had nothing pointing to criminal conduct, then no "remedy" was triggered.

But the rule, with its heavy incentive for law enforcement to conduct itself properly, did have the practical effect of enhancing professionalism in federal law enforcement. Thus, FBI agents and other law-enforcement personnel took pains to learn how to conduct themselves in accordance with the rule.

The challenges facing state and local law-enforcement officials, in contrast, were often more formidable. In the gritty world of street crime, snap judgments had to be made by the cop on the beat. Did probable cause exist? The officer needed it to make an arrest or to conduct a search. If probable cause did exist, another question arose: Was there justification for dispensing with a warrant and making a warrantless arrest and then a search (all without the involvement of a detached, neutral judicial officer)? Quite apart from philosophical issues of federal judicial power over the states, the practical effect of imposing the exclusionary rule on all state and local law-enforcement agencies would be enormous. Motions to suppress evidence would become the order of the day in state courts where most criminal cases were tried, for the simple reason that most crimes were state, not federal, offenses.

The Warren Court, however, decided that the states, too, must embrace the exclusionary rule. It did so in a case that started out as a pornography prosecution in state court in Ohio. In Cleveland, police searched the home of Dolly Mapp. They were looking for a fugitive wanted in a bombing. They were acting on a tip that Mapp might be hiding the fugitive. They said they had a warrant but never produced it. The police didn't find their suspect. But they discovered in a trunk allegedly obscene publications. Mapp was convicted under a state law outlawing possession of such materials. She appealed, arguing that the Ohio anti-pornography law was "unconstitutionally vague." She lost in the state supreme court but then took her case to the U.S. Supreme Court. In oral argument in the case, with Dolly Mapp's lawyer in a rather unfocused presentation pushing for exclusion of the evidence admitted at his client's trial, Justice Felix Frankfurter leaned into the microphone and challenged Mapp's lawyer: "Well, Counsel, are you asking us to overrule *Wolf v. Colorado*?" Mapp's lawyer seemed blissfully unaware of the Court's earlier holding (in 1949) rejecting the exclusionary rule's application to the states. Unabashed, the lawyer replied simply: "Well, Your Honor, if it goes against my client, then you should overrule it."

The Warren Court did exactly that in 1961. A five-justice majority, over vehement dissents (including Justice Frankfurter's), reached out to raise and then resolve the

Fourth Amendment exclusionary-rule issue even though it had not been raised by the parties and thus had not been briefed on the merits. Not only did the Court inject into the case an issue that Dolly Mapp and her lawyer had not seen fit to raise, but the Court overruled *Wolf v. Colorado*.

The *Wolf* decision had been on the books since 1949. But that didn't matter. The Warren Court did as it wished. It had the raw power to impose the exclusionary rule upon the states, and the Court was prepared to use this power in order to reform the criminal-justice system.

This somewhat forced birth gave the exclusionary rule, as applied to the states, a shaky parentage. Even so, the rule remained year after year as part of American constitutional law. Editorial pages and civil libertarians hailed it as a good thing because it constrained police. For its part, law enforcement complained that the rule carried an unacceptably high cost. Courts spent much time and attention on motions to suppress the evidence. These motions determined whether the case would die at the outset for lack of evidence or end in a guilty plea when the motion to suppress failed.

Law enforcement bridled at the spectacle of guilty defendants going free due to a legal technicality. And critics of law enforcement said that officers compensated by bending their sworn testimony to conform with the rule's strictures. For example, so-called dropsy cases abounded in narcotics prosecutions. An arresting officer would testify that the suspect threw away the "dropped" contraband and began to run from police, whereupon he was able to catch up to and capture the fleeing suspect. In these cases, the throwaway made the officer's "seizure"—the Fourth Amendment event—perfectly legal, since the suspect could be said to have abandoned any interest in the drugs.

For more than one reason, *Mapp* wasn't good for law

enforcement. *Miranda,* handed down five years later in 1966, only compounded the problems for peace officers. Soon after his election in 1968, having campaigned against the Court's criminal procedure decisions, President Nixon replaced the retiring Earl Warren with Warren Burger, who had given every indication that he would be the kind of judge the new president wanted. A judge on the U.S. Court of Appeals for the District of Columbia Circuit, Burger had been a strong defender of judicial restraint. In dissent after dissent, Judge Burger, who had served as head of the Justice Department's Civil Division under President Eisenhower, railed against opinions flowing from an appellate court dominated by liberal judges such as J. Skelly Wright, a genuine hero from his days as a district judge presiding over New Orleans desegregation issues.

Early on, the new chief justice demonstrated his opposition to *Mapp* and indeed to the entire approach to judging that had produced *Mapp, Miranda,* and the rest. In *Bivens v. Six Unknown Named Agents of Federal Bureau of Narcotics* (1971), a case whose name was destined to strike terror in the hearts of law-enforcement officers, Burger set out the most comprehensive, searching critique of *Mapp* in the entire body of judicial literature. The case before the Court was a hard one. Bivens was an innocent man. But he had been subjected to grossly invasive indignities at the hands of overzealous federal law-enforcement officers. Because he was entirely guiltless, Bivens had no remedy. The exclusionary rule offered no succor, since the misguided federal agents who got the wrong man had, naturally, found no incriminating evidence. And, as we have seen, the exclusionary rule helps only the guilty. Why, then, not sue for damages, for the "tort" (or crime) of violating the individual's privacy interests? Bivens did exactly that, but not under a federal statute. Rather, he invoked the Constitution. Bivens used the Constitution because Congress had not created a remedy for his sort of injury as it had for other kinds of federally caused injuries. For example, if the attorney general's security car injures a visitor otherwise enjoying a trip to the nation's capital, the victim has a remedy for compensatory damages under a duly enacted law, the Federal Tort Claims Act.

With no statutory remedy available, Bivens's lawyers sought damages by alleging a Fourth Amendment violation. The Supreme Court, in a divided judgment, agreed, holding that an individual whose constitutional rights are violated by federal law-enforcement officers—and who is otherwise without a remedy under federal law—may proceed under the Constitution to claim money damages.

The new chief justice wrote a stirring dissent, a classic statement of the need for judicial restraint. The Court, wrote Burger, had engaged in a quintessentially legislative act by creating a new cause of action against officers. The Court, he argued, had no authority to assume "the legislative and policy functions that the Constitution vests in Congress." Burger thus answered the *Bivens* majority—and then he took on *Mapp*, on similar grounds. To Nixon's chief justice, it was fundamentally wrong for courts to get into the legislating business, either by creating a new "*Bivens* action" or by imposing a supervisory rule like the exclusionary rule on the states. Moreover, the chief maintained, the Fourth Amendment exclusionary rule was fundamentally flawed. Echoing Cardozo's earlier critique, Burger bemoaned the high social cost of allowing the guilty to go free because the cop on the beat made a mistake. Fourth Amendment law was becoming more and more technical and complicated, he wrote. Federal trial judges trying to resolve a particular Fourth Amendment issue occasionally found themselves reversed. Appellate judges frequently disagreed with their colleagues on some fine point of Fourth Amendment law. If federal judges sometimes fumbled the Fourth Amendment ball, Burger asked, how could the police officer on the street be expected to maintain an almost superhuman ability always to make the right judgment call on complicated issues involving many facets, such as probable cause? These issues were simply too easy for judges sitting in the quiet of their appellate chambers, with ample time to study and reflect, to second-guess. The world of appellate judging was light-years away from the realities of law enforcement on the streets.

Bivens was one of Chief Justice Burger's proudest judicial moments. He had been in dissent, but bench and bar took notice. His opinion was respectful but vigorous; it was widely seen as a sign of the new chief justice's intention to dismantle the exclusionary rule. After all, it was only 1971. The chief was healthy, vigorous, and spoiling for a fight. Or so it seemed from the tone of his *Bivens* dissent.

But *Mapp* survived Chief Justice Burger, and carries on to this day. Throughout his long tenure, Burger could only gather expressions of discontent about the exclusionary rule. He left office in 1986 with no fewer than five justices having, at various times, expressed concern with both the constitutional foundations and the social costs of the exclusionary rule. But a majority never formed in a single case to reverse *Mapp*.

This failure was a large one. In one of his earliest terms, the chief had sounded the clarion call, only to see year after year pass with opportunities irrevocably lost. Overruling *Mapp* would have been his stamp, an enduring contribution to constitutional law. It would have signaled a return to traditional forms of constitutional interpretation. He well knew that the pundits and commentators would be sharply critical; that loud lamentations would

ensue were this Warren Court "reform" interred—and by
a Nixon appointee to boot. Civil libertarians would be
stirred to anger. The chief was not particularly concerned.
He was an unusual Washington figure, a top government
officer utterly unmoved by negative press. So what if the
New York Times attacked him? When it came to the cultural elite, the midwestern-born-and-bred chief had a
streak of Clint Eastwood in him. The chief called them as
he saw them, period.

Why, then, did he fail to root out this excess of Warren
Court extravagance? The answer is not to be found in
Burger's personality. True, he was less than beloved within
the Court, an unfortunate fact that his intemperate critics
loved to trumpet. But no justice declined to move against
the exclusionary rule because of any animosity toward
Warren Burger.

The reason *Mapp* survived lies in the other selections
that Nixon made. In terms of Nixon's criteria for a justice,
especially those concerning the criminal law, Burger measured up quite well. So did his fourth choice, William
Rehnquist. Nixon's second appointee, Harry Blackmun,
another federal appellate judge, turned out to be a judicial
activist save on criminal justice matters, where at least in
his early years on the Court he often sided with the chief
justice. On this question of *Mapp*'s reversal, it was
Nixon's third choice, Lewis Powell, who let the president
down.

During his tenure on the Court, from 1973 to 1987, the
Burger Court was often the Powell Court. It was moderation, not counterrevolution against the Warren Court, that
characterized the bulk of the Burger Court's work. Powell
labored entirely behind the scenes, without fanfare, and
achieved dramatic success in shaping the Court's jurisprudence. He recruited the smartest law clerks, gave them
marching orders, worked prodigiously hard, and was kind

to everyone in the building. It was a formidable combination. In a courthouse full of towering egos and clashing personalities, Powell was universally respected and admired within the cozy, insular atmosphere that prevailed inside the courthouse walls. He was especially beloved by law clerks, and not just his own.

I had a special fondness for Justice Powell. Back in the clerkship application process, he graciously invited me to Richmond to see him in his summer chambers at the federal courthouse in his hometown. He could not have been kinder. But the eventual answer was no. I didn't quite pass muster with him, but I was finally picked by Chief Justice Burger. The interview had likely been a courtesy and a tribute to the judge for whom I had clerked, David Dyer, who had known Justice Powell for years. They had both been highly successful lawyers in private practice. But even to this reject, Justice Powell remained unfailingly kind. In fact, the justice was genuinely interested in clerks from other chambers. He would gently inquire into your thinking about the future. He even had kindly advice for us twenty-somethings: Find a professional home, and always use that as your base—even if you launch out from time to time in public service or other activities.

In short, Justice Powell made law clerks feel very important. He paid tribute, frequently, to the role of clerks. Not surprisingly, the favor was returned. One of his clerks, a journalist-turned-lawyer destined to serve as chief judge of the U.S. Court of Appeals for the Fourth Circuit (headquartered in Lewis Powell's Richmond), wrote an admiring memoir of his term in Justice Powell's chambers. J. Harvie Wilkinson styled his book, charmingly, *Serving Justice*. Lewis Powell was the most influential member of the Burger Court.

That was especially so on the question as to the future of *Mapp* and the much-criticized exclusionary rule. Indeed, the battle over this issue demonstrated quite early that the Court was being led on the matters that counted most not by the chief justice but by the soft-spoken, genteel Virginian whose instincts and temperament invariably led him to middle ground. He would balance competing interests and come down in or around the middle, eschewing the more rigorous, doctrinally demanding, analytical approach that Justices Antonin Scalia and, later, Clarence Thomas brought to the Court.

Powell ensured the viability of the exclusionary rule by limiting its most unsettling, or at least burdening, implications. Thanks to *Mapp*, state prisoners began filing in the federal courts a steady stream of Fourth Amendment–based challenges to their state court convictions. The justices, upset by the swelling dockets, were concerned. They, and all the federal judges below them, were now experiencing an unanticipated result of the Warren Court revolution in criminal law. Individuals languishing in prison understandably wanted the benefit of a decision like *Mapp*. And, as another part of the Warren Court's legacy, increasingly attractive federal courthouses frowned on quick, summary dismissals of prisoner petitions. Everyone, including convicted prisoners, had a right to his day in federal court.

Jailhouse lawyers found their practices flourishing. State court convictions came under assault in federal district courts around the country. So it was that *habeas corpus*, historically a fairly limited, discrete category of cases in federal court, mushroomed. Under *habeas corpus*, state prisoners whose appeals from state convictions had been exhausted could petition a *federal* court for relief on the basis of a claimed violation of federal constitutional rights. *Habeas* became a growth industry, to the chagrin of increasingly overworked federal judges. Not even the Supreme Court justices were spared. The Court's docket exploded, especially criminal cases. The floodtide of cases, many of them of dubious legal merit, was distracting the Court from larger, more important questions.

In the 1976 case of *Stone v. Powell,* Justice Powell found a solution. Employing the critique of the exclusionary rule set forth by Chief Justice Burger in his *Bivens* dissent, Powell fashioned a compromise: The exclusionary rule would be maintained but could not be employed by state *habeas* petitioners who had already had a fair shot to litigate the Fourth Amendment issue in their state criminal cases. Powell observed that the exclusionary rule was not mandated by the Constitution itself, but designed to deter constitutional violations. Yet what might the rule deter in this context? Powell emphasized that the Fourth Amendment challenge was to a law-enforcement action that had long since been concluded and to state criminal proceedings that had already provided the defendant with his day in court.

For Powell, in this case as in many others, his pragmatic analysis guided constitutional interpretation. He was willing to make policy choices. That is, of course, the business of legislatures, but the Burger Court, influenced primarily by Powell, felt more at home sitting as a legislature than might reasonably have been expected when Nixon launched his project to undo the Warren Court, the most legislative ever. For Powell, and indeed for all justices, the costs of the exclusionary rule were quite high. The fight was over the benefits of the rule. For Justice Powell and the four justices whose allegiance his views commanded, the benefits were quite modest for state prisoners assailing their convictions in federal court.

This middle-of-the-road position was lacking in intellectual consistency. The reasons given for curbing the exclusionary rule could just as easily be used to do away with the rule entirely. But this did not appear to give pause to Powell, the gentlemanly apostle of moderation. His task, as he saw it, was not to fashion the most intellectually coherent and rigorous rule, but to take the existing body of law and proceed in a common-sense, mainstream fashion and come up with a reasonable, presentable result. Justice Powell was acting like Senator Powell.

His approach thus avoided what could be perceived as revolutionary results: the actual overruling of *Mapp v. Ohio*. The chief's position in *Bivens* went too far for the gentleman from Richmond. He was readily willing to sacrifice intellectual rigor for a result that could be persuasively defended to mainstream America. Leading editorial pages, which routinely trumpeted the perceived virtues of confining police excesses, would be muted in what otherwise would be a scathing denunciation of the "right-wing" Court for "turning back the clock" on the progressive reforms fashioned by the Warren Court. Unlike Chief Justice Burger, and like many justices before and after him, Justice Powell was not tone-deaf. The outside world could have a siren song effect on a justice especially sensitive to his place in history, and Justice Powell was very mindful of history.

Powell's approach—find the middle ground and plant the flag firmly there—often prevailed in Fourth Amendment cases as the Court, year after year, carved out exceptions to the exclusionary rule and wove interpretations of the Fourth Amendment so as to find no violation in the first instance.

Justice Sandra Day O'Connor and Justice Anthony Kennedy, the philosophical progeny of Justice Powell, have carried on this tradition. In fact, as a federal appellate judge, Justice Kennedy framed the enormously important exception—the good-faith rule—that many in the criminal defense bar viewed with alarm as swallowing up the Fourth Amendment's basic teaching. Under the good-faith exception, if police acting in good faith secure from a magistrate a search warrant, the evidence resulting from their search is admissible, even if the warrant is ultimately judged defective. In *United States v. Leon* (1982), the Court embraced the good-faith exception.

In the forty years since *Mapp,* law enforcement has simply had to learn to live with the exclusionary rule, as modified. The post-Warren Court was unwilling to try to reverse *Mapp* outright. It would be content to tinker with the exclusionary rule, but not to do away with it. Meanwhile, the surrounding body of Fourth Amendment law has grown to a state of almost Byzantine complexity. Tributaries and branches have emerged, with an entire body of law growing up, for example, about car searches. A moving car, when stopped for a traffic violation, can be searched; but what about containers in the trunk, or how about the highway patrolman opening up the glove compartment? All these questions, and more, have continued to march into the Court for resolution—all thanks to the unwillingness of the post-Warren Court to do away with a jurisprudentially weak and irregularly born exclusionary rule.

Chapter Eleven

★

"You Have the Right to . . .": *Miranda* and the Fifth Amendment

Like the Fourth Amendment's exclusionary rule, the famous *Miranda* rule—fashioned by the Warren Court—has likewise held fast in the Burger and Rehnquist Courts. *Miranda v. Arizona* was a case about the Fifth Amendment, which provides in pertinent part that "no person . . . shall be compelled to be a witness against himself." But the case took the law far beyond the familiar text of the Fifth Amendment. It was lawmaking by judicial interpretation. That it has been upheld by the more conservative Courts tells us how restrained and cautious the Rehnquist Court tends to be.

The now world-famous 1966 case involved a young man named Ernesto Miranda. Twenty-three-year-old Miranda was suspected of kidnapping and raping an eighteen-year-old woman. Arrested at his home, he was taken to a Phoenix police station. He was put in a lineup, but the victim was unable to make a positive identification. Showing less than robust self-confidence, Miranda then asked the police, "How did I do?" An astute policeman was not fully candid. "You flunked," came the ominous reply. After two hours of questioning, Miranda confessed to not only the rape-kidnapping under investigation, but also the robbery and attempted rape of a second victim, as well as the attempted robbery of yet a third. He then wrote out his confession in longhand and signed a prepared statement acknowledging the voluntary character of his incriminating statements. At trial, Miranda's confession was admitted into evidence and he was convicted. After exhausting his state remedies, his case wound its way to the Supreme Court. The Warren Court reversed his conviction on the ground that the confession violated the Fifth Amendment privilege against compelled self-incrimination.

Miranda is the most bitterly debated confession case in American history. Before *Miranda,* the issue of whether a confession should be admitted at trial was governed by a "voluntariness test." Thus, courts inquired whether the confession was involuntary—that is, whether the defendant had been *forced* to incriminate himself. If so, a Fifth Amendment violation had occurred. In pursuing this question, courts looked at the "totality of circumstances." In a word, they looked at everything.

Under the voluntariness test, there was no doubt that Miranda's confession would have been admissible. To be sure, Miranda had not been advised of his right to speak with a lawyer before answering police questions, nor of his right to have a lawyer present during the interrogations. But courts typically had not concluded that a confession obtained under these circumstances was involuntary. More important, the police in *Miranda* had not engaged in the kind of heavy-handed methods that in many cases had led courts to conclude that the confessions received had indeed been "coerced."

In *Miranda,* the Warren Court simply created a new standard and then concluded that the defendant's confession had been obtained under circumstances that failed to satisfy that new standard. Indeed, the opinion began with a statement of the new rule—that police must give a person in custody certain warnings about his or her rights—and in due course proceeded to spell out those warnings. The reader probably knows them: Prior to any questioning, the accused must be warned that he has the right to remain silent; that any statement he does make may be used as evidence against him; that he has the right to the presence of an attorney; that if he cannot afford one, an attorney will be appointed; and that he can waive these rights but only in a knowing manner, yet if he does so and then indicates "in any manner and at any stage" that he wants to consult with an attorney, there can be no further questioning. These are the famous *Miranda* warnings, used by police ever since.

Miranda was the Warren Court at its activist apogee. The decision embodied judicial legislation unapologetically aimed at bringing about reform in the conduct of law-enforcement investigations. It was a bold stroke to protect individual rights against the power of the police.

Miranda, a 5–4 ruling, was then (in 1966) and now (even on rereading) a breathtaking decision. The majority opinion, written by Chief Justice Warren, reads less like a judicial opinion and more like a congressional report. Instead of starting with the facts of the case, including the circumstances of Ernesto Miranda's interrogation by the Phoenix police, Warren started with a panoramic survey of police methods throughout the country. It drew from police manuals, quoted generously from them, and canvassed case law from various states to show appalling examples of police excess. It drew from a report to Congress on the state of law enforcement. The Warren Court proceeded, in short, as if it were Congress, surveying the horizon to determine the state of the country in a particular field or subject matter.

The Court then reached the sweeping conclusion at the heart of *Miranda*'s holding. Interrogation when an individual is in police custody is inherently coercive. The antidote? Procedures and safeguards must be employed to protect the person in custody against these inherent pressures and thus protect his Fifth Amendment privilege against being compelled to be a witness against himself. There would be no exceptions. Legislation tends to build in exceptions to general rules, but *Miranda* did not. No matter who the individual is, no matter how sophisticated, he must, said the Court, be afforded "adequate procedural safeguards." All individuals are presumed vulnerable to skillful police methods designed to elicit confessions.

Chief Justice Warren began the Court's opinion reassuringly. "[O]ur holding is not an innovation in our jurisprudence but is an application of principles long recognized and applied in other settings." This was not so, and surely Warren knew it. He had to justify this revolution in criminal procedure. To do so, the chief drew from the past, the Court's own decisions from yesteryear, in laying out the abiding judicial concern with coerced confessions. But after paying tribute to long-established Fifth Amendment principles (which no one was challenging), the Court took an unusual turn. Painting with a broad brush, the Court devoted page after page to police practices from long ago. It told a tale of violence, of beatings, hangings, whippings, and sustained, protracted questioning incommunicado. It pointed to the *Wickersham Report* to Congress in the early 1930s on "third degree" tactics employed by police. Drawing selectively, the Court described a then recent New York case in which "the police brutally beat, kicked, and placed lighted cigarette butts on the back of a potential witness" under interrogation for the purpose of securing a statement incriminating a third party.

This was a monochromatic, wildly distorted picture.

The Warren Court's recitation of case after dreadful case left the impression that the country was plagued with vicious police violence aimed at wrenching out confessions. A reader could not help but wonder how the new *Miranda* warnings could possibly have any impact in such a law-enforcement jungle. A lawless police department would surely cover up a *Miranda* violation if officers would engage in the kind of egregious misconduct cited by the Court. Take, for example, an Illinois case where the suspect "suffer[ed] from broken bones, multiple bruises and injuries sufficiently serious to require eight months' medical treatment after being manhandled by five policemen." *Miranda* would accomplish nothing in this sort of reign of terror at the police station.

This recitation of horribles was entirely for rhetorical effect. For the Court indicated that police violence wasn't the order of the day, after all. The terrors that the Court had just laid out in the pages of *United States Reports* were "undoubtedly the exception now." A reader might well ask: If this kind of unconscionable cruelty and abuse is the exception, why worry about fashioning a generally applicable, under-all-circumstances rule for every police department in the country?

As it happened, the Court, conceding that bad practices of yesteryear no longer prevailed, was really concerned about *psychological* factors, not physical brutality. "[T]his Court has recognized that coercion can be mental as well as physical, and that the blood of the accused is not the only hallmark of an unconstitutional inquisition."

The problem, the Court opined, was the setting of the interrogation. The suspect was alone. Beatings and similar tactics were largely a thing of the past, but "interrogation still takes place in privacy. Privacy results in secrecy and this in turn results in a gap in our knowledge as to what in fact goes on in interrogation rooms." The Court assumed the role of a congressional oversight committee. In particular, the Warren Court wanted information about the realities of custodial interrogation throughout the country, but it was operating in the dark. The justices had moved entirely into a legislative mode. The *Miranda* Court was not focusing on the facts of the specific case at hand.

To be sure, there are times when courts are called upon to consider a broad set of facts going far beyond a simple dispute between two individuals or a person charged with a crime and the prosecuting authorities. School desegregation cases, by their nature, call upon courts to examine fact patterns in (at times) large, metropolitan districts. What are the city's demographic patterns? What are the conditions of the public schools within the school district? How do facilities and teacher qualifications vary from school to school? And so on.

But a criminal case comes down to specific facts involving identifiable individuals. Fifth Amendment rights are peculiarly personal and individual. At issue in school desegregation is the equality principle, with the state drawing lines based on race or ethnicity. In a criminal case, the individual's personal circumstances are at the core of the case. What happened at the police station? Was that individual's right to be free from having to be a witness against himself violated?

The Court's approach in *Miranda* was the ultimate in class-wide thinking. Earl Warren's opinion imagined the entire class of individuals across the country brought into police custody, and the Court then extrapolated as to the circumstances affecting all of them—including, say, a highly capable criminal defense lawyer who himself was arrested for a crime. They were all lumped together into the same mega-class.

But how to find the facts? In school desegregation cases,

school officials, family members of students, and experts take the stand and testify, or they file detailed affidavits setting forth relevant facts. That process takes place in the context of a trial, where witnesses may be cross-examined. The Warren Court, in contrast, had no mega-trial record before it. Lacking anything other than the specific facts of Ernesto Miranda's interrogation, where he confessed to the rape as well as other crimes, the Court invented the record it wanted.

The "trial record" was a compilation of police manuals and texts. Page after page of the opinion was devoted to the methods of interrogation as set forth in those guides. And the Court was confident in its ability to discern nationwide reality from those manuals: "By considering these texts and other data, it is possible to describe procedures observed and noted *around the country.*" (Emphasis added.) The Warren Court was finding "facts" with no trial, no witnesses, and no opportunity for police departments to respond to the assumption that their methods in daily practice tracked the procedures set forth in the manuals.

The Court then treated the country to a formal primer in police methodology. Location, location, location, the real estate mantra, was also the polestar for successful police interrogation. Quoting from one police manual, the Court emphasized the interrogator's quest for a psychological advantage. And that meant finding the right spot for the questioning to occur: " 'If at all practicable, the interrogation should take place in the investigator's office or at least in a room of his own choice. The subject should be deprived of every psychological advantage. In his own home he may be confident, indignant, or recalcitrant. He is more keenly aware of his rights and more reluctant to tell of his indiscretions of criminal behavior within the walls of his home. . . . In his office, the investigator possesses all the advantages. The atmosphere suggests the invincibility of the forces of the law.'"

The Court marched on to its anti-interrogation conclusion. Even without the use of physical force, "the very fact of custodial interrogation exacts a heavy toll on individual liberty and trades on the weakness of individuals." Tellingly, the Court did not hint, much less conclude, that such confessions (or other statements that tended to inculpate the suspect) were unreliable. A confession extracted from an individual being subjected to beatings and the like was inherently unreliable. But this was not so with respect to confessions obtained under interrogation skillfully designed to get the suspect to commit an act of self-destruction—to confess to what he in fact did, knowing that the penalty for the offense might be quite severe. Reliable, yes, but nonetheless coercive. In-custody interrogation led to an atmosphere of "informal compulsion."

The logic of the Court's conclusion, that in-custody questioning exacted a heavy toll on individual liberty in the form of "informal coercion," seemed to suggest that custodial interrogation should simply be outlawed. If this kind of police tactic was so dangerous to individual liberty, as the Court emphasized, why not just end it? This argument, which echoes more contemporary assaults against the death penalty, was in fact advanced in the companion case to *Miranda* coming out of California. There, Los Angeles lawyer Bill Norris, a future Ninth Circuit Court of Appeals judge, had urged just such a rule.

But the Court would not go that far. Instead, by a 5–4 margin, the Court held that custodial interrogation was so inherently compulsive that specific warnings—the famous *Miranda* litany—had to be given in order to dissipate the otherwise unconstitutional compulsion. Custodial interrogation, although inherently suspect, could continue, but only with safeguards.

Still, the Court was cautious not to carve the specific warnings into constitutional stone. Again and again, the Court throughout its lengthy opinion emphasized the need for adequate "procedural safeguards" to protect the guarantee against compelled self-incrimination. There was no magic in the *Miranda* incantation of rights; to the contrary, the Court invited Congress and state legislatures to come forward with their own protections to ensure the privilege. *Miranda* was not, in short, setting out specific "rights." It was, more narrowly, setting forth particular safeguards to protect a right: the right not to be compelled to incriminate oneself. The Court was essentially saying, "We'll take the first crack at solving this problem of 'informal coercion,' but Congress and state legislatures are welcome to help out."

Justices Harlan and White dissented. Harlan called *Miranda* nothing less than "a dangerous experimentation at a time of a high crime rate that is a matter of growing concern." White scolded the majority for its "deep-seated distrust of confessions." Harlan worried that the Court's doctrine "has no sanction." White worried what *Miranda*'s impact would be upon the criminal justice system. As White feared, *Miranda* immediately led to the release of a number of admitted murderers.

Police across the country were incredulous. They well understood the importance of confessions in solving crimes and the new difficulties in obtaining confessions that would flow from *Miranda*.

In Washington, Senator Sam Ervin of North Carolina proposed to make the pre-*Miranda* voluntariness approach a standard part of the Constitution. Instead, in 1968, a presidential election year that saw Richard Nixon challenging the Warren Court, Congress took up the *Miranda* majority's invitation for legislative bodies to enact laws that would adequately protect the privilege against self-incrimination. In the Crime Control Act of 1968, Congress expressed itself: *Miranda* was not to be the test for determining the admissibility of a confession; instead, a multifactored test would govern. Courts were to consider, for example, the length of time the suspect was subjected to custodial interrogation. This approach was meant to restore the core concept of "voluntariness."

The Justice Department declined, however, to enforce the statute. The department viewed the 1968 measure as a direct slap at the Court, an effort to "overrule" *Miranda* without explicitly saying so. Even so, *Miranda* remained controversial in jurisdictions throughout the country. And on the Supreme Court. Of all the Nixon appointees, William Rehnquist was especially critical of *Miranda*. In one of his early opinions after joining the Court, *Michigan v. Tucker* (1974), Rehnquist observed that the *Miranda* warnings were "not themselves rights protected by the Constitution." In that case and subsequent ones throughout the Burger Court years, Rehnquist helped produce majorities willing to fashion exceptions and limitations to *Miranda*'s reach.

Nonetheless, over time *Miranda* was assimilated into the law-enforcement culture. Even more, its famous warnings became part of American culture, making appearances on television shows and movies involving the criminal justice system. Suspects were to be read their *Miranda* rights—and everyone knew what that meant.

Still, the question of *Miranda*'s constitutional legitimacy remained. *Miranda* raised basic questions about the role of the judiciary in American life. Is it properly within the sphere of courts to fashion specific rules, impose those rules on law-enforcement officials, and enforce them with the sanction that confessions or statements given without the benefit of such warnings will be excluded from evidence? Isn't that, at bottom, a job for Congress and state legislatures or other, more accountable, parts of representative government? How can the least accountable branch of government, justices appointed for life, take on a reform project of such magnitude?

The Warren Court had not worried much about these issues. Chief Justice Warren was a man of action, a former governor, state attorney general, and elected district attorney. He wanted results and was less interested in legal doctrine. But later Courts did worry about doctrine, about the legitimacy of their decisions. Congress shouldn't run foreign policy, the president shouldn't refuse to carry out laws passed by Congress, and the Supreme Court shouldn't try to run the country. These issues loomed large as the post-Warren Courts openly emphasized the search for better doctrine.

I saw the dynamic firsthand as a law clerk to Chief Justice Burger. In the mid-1970s, a decade after *Miranda* was handed down by his predecessor, Chief Justice Burger faced a question flowing out of the then relatively new *Miranda* rule: What happens if an individual goes before the grand jury and, without having received *Miranda* warnings, commits perjury? To Burger, the answer was clear. Perjury was never permitted, period (*United States v. Mandujano*, 1976). If the honest answer to a question from a prosecutor or a grand juror would be incriminating, then the witness had two choices: either invoke the Fifth Amendment privilege and remain silent, or answer truthfully. But lying under oath was not an option, even where there had been a failure to warn an individual of his or her rights. A *Miranda* violation, in short, would not excuse perjury before the grand jury. The Court was unanimous.

As the twenty-first century dawned, the Rehnquist Court had a perfect opportunity to do away with *Miranda*. The issue was this: Had *Miranda* been overruled legislatively by Congress just two years later in the over-whelmingly bipartisan provisions of the 1968 statute? The solicitor general reached the judgment that Congress had unconstitutionally sought to legislate, by statute, a matter that the Court had decided as a question of constitutional law. As a result, the Justice Department, as is its prerogative, refused to defend the statute. The Court therefore appointed a special counsel to argue on behalf of the statute's legality.

The eventual result was foreshadowed during the course of the oral argument in the spring of 2000 as the Rehnquist Court was reconsidering the Warren Court's handiwork. Not one word was said about victims of criminals who gained release by *Miranda*'s application. The social cost of the Warren Court's reform effort was a nontopic during the hour-long, largely academic oral argument. Two months later, the Court, by a staggering 7–2 majority, reembraced *Miranda*. Not only was *Miranda* here to stay, notwithstanding the congressional effort to restore the traditional Fifth Amendment voluntariness approach, but the Court's opinion was written by none other than Chief Justice Rehnquist.

There had been plenty of reason to think Rehnquist was ready to jettison *Miranda*. In the oral argument in the case *Dickerson v. United States,* the chief had appeared skeptical about the pro-*Miranda* position. Dickerson had been convicted of bank robbery and, shortly after his arrest, had made incriminating statements to law-enforcement officers without having been given *Miranda* warnings. On appeal, the Fourth Circuit (based in Richmond) affirmed Dickerson's conviction and concluded that the 1968 statute had supplanted *Miranda*. When Dickerson's lawyer praised *Miranda* as being a clear-cut, predictable rule that was easy for police to apply, the chief was unimpressed: "Well, you say [*Miranda*] provides clear-cut evidence. I looked into the number of cases that we have construing *Miranda,* and there are about 50 of them, so that to say [*Miranda*] is easily applied is just a myth." Not only, then, was *Miranda* still dubious constitutional law, in the chief's mind, it also had not lived up to its supposed promise of certainty and clarity. Someone who had seen the oral argument surely might have thought that if the chief were announcing the opinion of the Court in *Dickerson,* it would come down against *Miranda.* Surely the Court would conclude that Congress has authority to change a nonconstitutional rule. That in fact had been the theme struck hard by Justice Scalia at the April 2000 argument. Congress couldn't overrule the Court in determining the meaning of the Constitution, but it could override a particular judicial convention aimed at serving or vindicating a right protected by the Constitution.

Chief Justice Warren had read his *Miranda* opinion from the bench. Chief Justice Rehnquist did the same in *Dickerson.* He began by stating the *Miranda* warnings themselves. "You have the right to remain silent. . . ."

Courtroom watchers were caught off balance. *Miranda* had not been overruled. Not only had it survived, it now had a new gloss. *Miranda* was, the chief said, a constitutional rule after all. How else, the chief emphasized, could we have applied the rule to the states? The Court would have been powerless to impose a mere procedural rule on the states unless the rule was constitutionally based.

The result was unexpected, as was the 7–2 margin. Justice Scalia, who was joined by Justice Thomas in dissent, wrote powerfully. He began his dissenting opinion ominously: "Those who understand the judicial process will appreciate that today's decision is not a reaffirmation of *Miranda,* but a radical revision of the most significant element of *Miranda* (as of all cases): the rationale that gives it a permanent place in our jurisprudence." Others, who cared only about results, would warmly embrace the decision, Justice Scalia predicted. "Those to whom judicial decisions are an unconnected series of judgments that produce either favored or disfavored results will doubtless greet today's decision as a paragon of moderation, since it declines to overrule *Miranda*." He took the sweeping but short opinion of Chief Justice Rehnquist severely to task. The opinion says nothing, Justice Scalia noted, to the effect that Congress's re-imposition of the voluntariness test is unconstitutional.

Justice Scalia then called the roll of the justices. He noted that "justices whose votes are needed to compose today's majority are on record as believing that a violation of *Miranda* is *not* a violation of the Constitution." He seemed to relish ticking off the names, beginning with Justice Anthony Kennedy, going on to Justice Sandra Day O'Connor, and then closing with Chief Justice Rehnquist himself. Scalia taunted the three justices who he plainly believed should have shared common cause with the two dissenters. The three justices whose shift created the new majority would not forthrightly say that "custodial interrogation that is not preceded by *Miranda* warnings or their equivalent violates the Constitution of the United States." Why not? Because the moderates, now joined by the chief justice, were agnostics on the subject. "[The Court] cannot say that, because a majority of the Court does not believe it." That being so, Justice Scalia concluded, it was the Court that violated the Constitution by failing to give effect to a statute passed by Congress and signed into law by the president. These were strong words, praised for their rhetorical power by Pulitzer Prize–winning columnist Charles Krauthammer: "Some people have John Grisham. Others Tom Clancy. Not me. For sheer power, stiletto prose and verbal savagery, I'll take Antonin Scalia."

What was the Court doing? How could it overrule a statute that embodied an indisputable constitutional principle: that voluntary confessions should be admitted in federal court cases? Certainly, the statute from 1968 was, as Utah law professor Paul Cassell put it, a statute that time forgot. But the statute commanded respect unless it violated the Constitution. To many, the 1968 law represented "an act of defiance by the Congress, ridiculing the Court, an unbelievable hostility to the Court," as Michigan law professor Yale Kamisar wrote. But what if the Court had actually usurped the role of the democratic branches of government? Krauthammer posed the issue this way: "Was the *Dickerson* result of re-embracing *Miranda* . . . arbitrary, willful judge-made law?" It looked like exactly that.

Feelings were running high, almost as high as those in the abortion and religion cases—and as those to come in *Bush v. Gore*. Three justices often in agreement with Scalia and Thomas had broken ranks and embraced a Warren Court icon.

There are two explanations for what happened, and each reveals an important characteristic of the Court and its work. The first is that there is on the Court a deep and abiding respect for maintaining the status of decisions that have caught the public's attention and imagination. The Court had been permitted, year after year, to refine the *Miranda* rule. It had left the decision on the books, and indeed enforced it, but the Court had also crafted numerous exceptions to *Miranda*. The reigning philosophy seemed to be this: *Miranda*'s core should be left, but a majority may nibble at it around the edges. The Court would not expand the decision beyond its basic holding. Throughout these years, too, Congress had sat silently, saying nothing as the Court proceeded in this limiting, moderating fashion. In the meantime, *Miranda* had become part of American culture. The *political* controversy over it had long since abated, replaced by *Roe v. Wade,* and it stood as a constitutional monument erected entirely by the Court. When the assault finally came on the core of *Miranda* itself, the Court proved unwilling to yield to the logic of its own position. Stability when public opinion is genuinely engaged once again proved to be one of the Court's highest values.

The second explanation lies in the Court's view of Congress as an institution largely driven by passing majoritarian sentiments, especially sentiments passionately held by a transient popular majority. The Court doubtless saw the Congress of 1968 as responding to the law-and-order sentiment of an election year. That explained why Congress wrote the anti-*Miranda* rule. But three decades had gone by and nothing else had happened. Federal law enforcement, despite its early objections to *Miranda,* was never anxious to use the 1968 law. Among other reasons, the FBI had long used similar warnings, even prior to *Miranda,* and concerns were raised by agency lawyers as to the constitutionality of the 1968 law. During the Clinton administration, when the issue finally was presented, Attorney General Reno had taken the extraordinary step of directing federal prosecutors around the country not to employ the statute.

Not only that, but a natural self-defense mechanism on the part of the judiciary had set in. The critical fact laid out by Chief Justice Rehnquist was this: By passing the law, Congress had intended to overrule *Miranda.* The court of appeals had said just that. "Based on the statutory language, it is perfectly clear that Congress enacted [the law] with the express purpose of legislatively overruling *Miranda* and restoring voluntariness as the test for admitting confessions in federal court." In the Supreme

Court, Congress's anti-*Miranda* intent proved fatal. *Miranda* would survive.

Krauthammer summed up the anomaly in his postmortem: "Scalia is right that *Miranda* 'is a milestone of judicial overreaching.' And yet *Miranda*, born illegitimate and living on illogic, has turned into one of the glories of American democracy." Why? Because despite its judicial illegitimacy, *Miranda*'s existence says something powerful about the values of the country. "When people around the world go to the movies, they see a bad guy who has just murdered a nun, impaled a policeman and blown up a school, collared by Eastwood or Stallone or Tommy Lee Jones. What are the first words out of the good guy's mouth? 'You have the right to remain silent.' The viewer has to wonder what kind of political paradise America really is. People seeing this in Belgrade and Harare and Kuala Lumpur, places where the *innocent* get whacked and beaten and tortured at the whim of the authorities, can only be awestruck at a country that treats even its monsters with such delicacy."

The Court no doubt knew this: Everyone—the president, Congress, the states, and law-enforcement professionals—would have promptly rallied around the warnings. Few if any elected officials, much less law-enforcement officials, would have said, "We are now directing that all *Miranda* warning cards be appropriately dispensed with for recycling."

Of course, overruling *Miranda* would have been the best result. The appropriate roles of the three branches of government would have been preserved, yet the nation's commitment to safeguarding basic constitutional rights would have been vindicated. Under the most likely scenario, with *Miranda* overruled as a principle of constitutional law, representative institutions of government would have come to a particular view and practice as to what is right and fair in the administration of the criminal justice system. At the same time, if the police erred, then some other remedy would have been triggered rather than allowing dangerous felons like Ernesto Miranda to go free.

But the Court, dominated by the moderates and joined by the chief justice, was unwilling to change course. Stability and structural integrity, rather than fundamental principles, carried the day.

PART THREE

The Powers and Structure of American Government

Chapter Twelve

★

The Power to Make Law: The Statutory Conversation between Court and Congress

In every case, the Supreme Court is asked to interpret federal law, whether a statute passed by Congress or a provision in the Constitution. In most cases, the Court is asked to interpret an act of Congress. In a small number of these cases, there is a constitutional question for the Court. Consider the 1990 flag-burning case, *United States v. Eichman,* in which the defendant argued, successfully, that the new federal law against flag desecration violated his First Amendment speech rights. Others, as we will see in Chapter Thirteen, involve the question of whether Congress has the constitutional authority to pass the particular statute at issue. But the great bulk of the cases in which the Court is asked to interpret an act of Congress do not raise a question of constitutional rights or power. Whether Casey Martin (a handicapped golfer) can play the PGA Tour while using a golf cart, a question decided by the Court in 2001, is an issue involving interpretation of the federal civil rights laws. These are not constitutional but pure statutory cases.

Obviously, the matter of how the Supreme Court and the federal courts generally go about interpreting a federal statute is of no small significance. Do courts simply refer to dictionaries, whether a *Webster's* or a *Black's Law Dictionary* or both, and let lexicographers decide the issue? Does Congress actually define the key words in a statute, say "toxic," or "restraint of trade," or "disability"? Or, in the post-modern age, can it be said with confidence that words, even words set forth in statutes, have meaning that can be discerned?

Much of modern literary scholarship is informed by the deconstructionist philosophy that meaning is elusive at best and illusory at worst. That approach, however popular in universities, is not the way of the law. In particular, the Supreme Court shows no such doubt as it seeks to interpret federal statutes. The philosophy that guides today's Court is emphatically not deconstructionist. The Court's members, across all ideological and philosophical divides, agree that words have meaning and that their meaning can be ascertained by careful, rigorous inquiry. In this respect, the justices are decidedly traditional in going about their work. Whatever inner doubts may plague them, they are not the slightest bit agnostic about meaning, nor do their opinions suggest any serious temptation to enter realms of philosophy. Years ago, as a graduate student at Brown University, I ventured into an epistemology class. The world-renowned professor Roderick Chisholm wrote on the board: "Mary had a little lamb." He then spent the next fifty minutes plumbing the depths of that familiar sentence, noting ambiguities and nuances. That is not the epistemology the justices are interested in. Each is a lawyer of practical bent.

To say the Court agrees that words have discernible meanings does not, of course, mean that the Court is cheerfully unanimous as to what those meanings are. Far from it. Fault lines not only exist, they run deep, as we have already seen. The justices war, for example, over the appropriateness of using "legislative history" to help interpret a statute. Legislative history encompasses congressional committee reports and floor statements by senators and House members during legislative debate.

It is in this arena of the Court's daily work—statutory interpretation—that the appointment of Justice Antonin Scalia has been most dramatically felt, as we noted in Chapter Two. As we saw, Scalia believes that courts are strictly bound by the text and structure of the statute. He is an unabashed textualist. For him, repairing to background legislative materials is inappropriate. "It is simply incompatible with democratic government, or indeed, even with fair government," he wrote in *A Matter of Interpretation,* "to have the meaning of a law determined by what the lawgiver meant, rather than by what the lawgiver promulgated. . . . It is the *law* that governs, not the intent of the lawgiver." In Scalia's approach, virtually all questions about a law's meaning will yield up answers if the judge is sufficiently rigorous and careful in the analysis of its text and structure.

In contrast, Justice Stephen Breyer has argued for a broader approach to interpreting statutes, one that embraces generously all manner of interpretive tools. Disagreeing with Justice Scalia on legislative history, for example, Justice Breyer not only contends that its use is legitimate and important, but insists on taking broadly into account the purposes of Congress in passing the legislation in the first place. This Breyer would do much more freely than the more textually devoted Scalia.

The Court's centrists, Justice O'Connor and Kennedy, largely embrace Scalia's textualist approach in statutory interpretation, though neither is as averse as Scalia is to repairing, when the text and structure of the statute seem ambiguous, to legislative history. Because O'Connor and

Kennedy largely hold the balance of power, Scalia's textualism often prevails.

This development marks a dramatic change in the Court's approach to interpreting statutes. The Burger Court, influenced by Justice Powell, was quite flexible in its reading of federal statutes. Powell, like so many lawyers of his generation, was willing to interpret a statute generously in order to achieve its "remedial purposes." The idea was this: If Congress had passed a law aimed at a particular social evil, then the courts should be willing to interpret the statute liberally in order to achieve its goals.

Few judges take this approach anymore (although the Casey Martin case is an exception that proves the rule). Indeed, all nine justices now focus on text and structure and eschew broad rules of interpretation that do little to constrain judicial discretion.

The antagonism toward "loose" construction is born of basic concerns over judicial power. This concern is part of a broader philosophy that condemns judicial lawmaking as illegitimate. As seen from the textualist perspective, judges usurp power that belongs to the legislative branch when they interpret statutes broadly to reach situations Congress may not have envisioned. The textualist fear is that judges may accomplish by interpretation what one side in Congress was unable to achieve legislatively.

In the textualist view, the way to control judicial power is to remain focused on the words and structure of the statute. Thus, even repairing to legislative history may achieve antidemocratic results. Textualism is rooted in democratic theory. The idea is that, in passing statutes, the members in a representative body have before them only the proposed statute itself, as opposed to transcripts of committee hearings, floor debates, and the like. In addition, once the measure is passed, the people it affects cannot, in reason, be expected to go beyond the literal language and structure of the statute.

At times, the opposition to using legislative history can wreak divisions on the Court even when the justices reach the same bottom-line judgment. In June 2000, for example, the Court unanimously struck down an effort by Massachusetts to regulate in the foreign-policy arena. The Bay State legislature decided that its state agencies should not contract with companies that did business in Burma (now called Myanmar), and passed a law to that effect. The Court unanimously struck down the measure. Among other things, the Court said, the state effort was inconsistent with a later-passed congressional measure that gave discretion to the president in carrying out trade relations with the Southeast Asian pariah country. In his opinion for the Court in *Crosby v. National Foreign Trade Council* (2000), Justice Souter concluded: "Congress clearly intended the federal act to provide the President with flexible and effective authority over economic sanctions against Burma." In support of this interpretation, Souter added commentary from various senators and representatives. From William Cohen (then senator from Maine and later secretary of defense during the Clinton administration) to Arizona Senator John McCain, the footnote made the simple point that "[s]tatements by the sponsors of the federal Act underscore the Act's clarity in providing the President with flexibility in implementing its Burma sanctions policy."

This seemingly innocuous point distressed Justice Scalia. He was fully in agreement with the Court's holding, but he disdained Souter's use of members' commentary. The justices should, Scalia said, look to text and structure, not statements by individual members of the House or Senate. In staccato style, Justice Scalia, joined in his separate opinion by Justice Thomas, rattled off the attack that "it is perfectly obvious on the face of this statute that Congress, with the concurrence of the President, intended to provide Executive Branch flexibility." His opinion dripped with sarcasm. He repeated the "it is obvious on the face of the statute" mantra no fewer than four times in the course of a three-page opinion. There was one additional "it is perfectly obvious from the record," plus five instances of "I therefore see no point in devoting a footnote to the interesting (albeit unsurprising) proposition that . . .". Each of these repetitive phrases underscored Justice Scalia's point that the extensive use of legislative history, especially in footnotes, is wasteful, irrelevant, and ultimately harmful. "[E]ven if all of the Court's invocations of legislative history were not utterly irrelevant, I would still object to them, since . . . the statements of individual members of Congress . . . [are not] a reliable indication of what a majority of both Houses of Congress intended when they voted for the statute before us." He noted that the legislative "debate" largely took place in an empty chamber; specifically, he pointed to a statement during the debate by Senator Mitch McConnell of Kentucky concerning what amendments to take up: "I do not see anyone on the Democratic side in the Chamber." The vacant seats illustrated the textualist point. Half the house (at least) was empty when statements were being made by individual members. What counted, then, was the statute itself, its text and structure. The sea change in judicial interpretation of statutes is especially evident in issues involving federal administrative agencies, such as the Federal Communications Commission or the Environmental Protection Agency. The textualism of the modern Court, albeit modified and softened at times by Justice Breyer's approach, has replaced the culture of deference that previously characterized the Court's analysis of statutes administered by a federal agency.

This culture of deference to federal agencies was an enduring legacy of the New Deal Court. Its high-water mark came in the 1969 case of *Red Lion v. FCC*. The Federal Communications Commission, in regulating the broadcast community, had promulgated a benign-sounding policy known as the "fairness" doctrine. Viewing the airwaves as public property, the policy required television broadcasters, in expressing viewpoints on issues of public policy, to set forth competing opinions. That is, if a broadcaster took a position on an issue of growth in the community, then the broadcaster would be required to allow a competing viewpoint to be aired.

This policy would have been wildly unconstitutional had it been applied to the print media. In fact, five years later the Burger Court by an overwhelming vote struck down a Florida state statute requiring a "right to reply." (*Miami Herald v. Tornillo* [1974]). Thus, if a newspaper were to criticize a public official, then the official had to be given column space to set forth his response. This seemed fair, but it was unconstitutional. The state legislature was purporting to tell the news media what it must print. This struck at the very core of the First Amendment's guarantee of a free press.

Similarly, the fairness doctrine at issue in the *Red Lion* case required broadcasters to publish what they did not want to put on the air. The Court, in an opinion by Justice Byron White, upheld the doctrine. Rejecting the First Amendment challenge on grounds that broadcasters are unlike the printed press (a controversial proposition in its own right, with the ever-increasing concentration of print media), the *Red Lion* Court wrote broadly about the respect and deference owed to an administrative agency charged with interpreting a statute passed by Congress. In the Supreme Court's view, courts should look to the agency's interpretation and accept it unless there were "compelling reasons" to suggest that the agency's view of the statute was wrong.

The *Red Lion* decision, handed down in the final year of the Warren Court, embraced a view of statutory interpretation that suggested a basic institutional limitation on the Court's ability to do its work. Congress, after all, had not simply passed a statute and left it free standing. Rather, it had determined to create an administrative agency, which, at least in theory, would develop its own experience and expertise operating under the statute(s). In fact, the agency itself may have been actively involved in the process of securing the passage of the particular piece of legislation. In that sense as well, in addition to practical operating experience, the agency was seen as knowing best.

The conceptual problem with this deferential approach lay in the way it tugged at our system of separated powers. Why should the agencies have the final say when the issue is one of interpreting statutes? That is ultimately the job of courts. And so it seemed to most judges by the 1980s, especially to adherents of the textualism espoused by Justice Scalia.

The Supreme Court shifted from being a court of deference to one of equal footing with "expert" agencies. Not surprisingly, the shift occurred as the Court's membership changed. In appointment after appointment, experienced judges came to the High Court. No longer were ex-politicians or executive branch officials—those more naturally inclined to heed the wishes of administrative agencies—the nominees of choice. Increasingly, judges, not politicians, were elevated to the nation's highest bench. The Court was becoming the lawyers' court it is today.

Judges felt they could interpret statutes as well as (or better than) executive officers could. There was no need, as a practical matter, to defer to the legal reading embraced by an agency. But more was at stake than issues of agency expertise versus judges asserting their own interpretive powers. Ultimately, the Court was saying, it is up to the judiciary to interpret the law. As a result, administrative agencies had to bow to the courts.

This rule was set forth in the latter years of the Burger Court in the 1984 case of *Chevron v. Natural Resources Defense Council*. As part of the Reagan administration's deregulatory effort, the Environmental Protection Agency had modified its interpretation of one provision of the Clean Air Act. In determining compliance with its administrative pollution regulation, the EPA—in a pro-business shift—changed its interpretation of the underlying federal statute and permitted industrial facilities to be considered as contained within a "bubble" encasing the entire facility. This permitted one smokestack or other pollution source to emit more pollutants than previously as long as the entire facility considered as a whole (or unit) did not increase the level of pollution.

The D.C. Circuit rejected the new EPA regulation. In an opinion by then Judge (and future justice) Ruth Bader Ginsburg, the court of appeals in Washington said that the law, while ambiguous, had to be interpreted in a way that maximized the overriding congressional goal of reducing air pollution.

But the Supreme Court rejected future-justice Ginsburg's approach. The agency could do what it did, said the Court, because the law was not clear and the interpretation embraced by the agency was a "reasonable" understanding of how it might carry out an unclear statute. But in giving the EPA its victory, the Court made clear that it was ultimately the role of the judiciary, not the agency, to be the key interpreter of federal law.

No longer was the culture of deference, highlighted fifteen years earlier in *Red Lion*, in the ascendancy. The

Chevron Court reasoned from first principles. Instead of beginning, as the *Red Lion* Court had done, with the fact that an agency (there, the FCC) existed, that the agency had interpreted the statute in question, and that judges should respect the agency's presumably expert views, the *Chevron* Court began with the statute before it. The law, as passed by Congress, was equally binding on the judiciary and the agency. And the courts, as the final interpreters of federal law (including the Constitution), are not to "delegate" that task to a federal agency—even one filled with experts on the statute in question.

Textualism enabled the Court to embrace first principles. The statute in question had meaning, and that meaning was discernible through careful judicial study. However, if at the end of the interpretive exercise the Court concluded that the statute was ambiguous on the point in question, then and only then would the courts defer to the agency's interpretation—so long as the interpretation was "reasonable."

Today it is the centrist justices who often hold the key to the result in a case of statutory interpretation. Consider the case arising from the Food and Drug Administration's effort during the Clinton administration to regulate tobacco. Tobacco had long been known to have adverse health effects, but no effort had been made by the FDA to regulate cigarettes (and smokeless tobacco).

This was an odd state of affairs. The basic statute had been on the books for decades, the health effects of smoking were known, and the regulatory agency had stayed on the sidelines. Now the agency set aside its prior legal positions and a new, contrary position was fashioned. It was taken through the customary process of giving notice of the proposed action and allowing interested parties to give comments to the agency.

With Justice O'Connor writing for a majority of five

that included Justice Kennedy, the Court concluded that the Clinton administration had exceeded its powers under the key statute. Several elements sealed the legal fate of the anti-tobacco initiative. First, having surveyed with care the structure of the FDA's statute, the Court concluded that, if nicotine truly was what the FDA said it was, then tobacco products would have to be *removed* from the market. Assuming the validity of the FDA's findings concerning the health effects of tobacco, the Court concluded that the agency would not enjoy discretion to allow tobacco products to enter the marketplace without a "reasonable assurance of safety." Yet, that assurance was impossible, given the FDA's conclusion about tobacco's health effects.

So, why not? Why not impose the regulatory death penalty on tobacco? Here, Justice O'Connor wrote, Congress had not been unaware of the issues. In fact, Congress "has foreclosed the removal of tobacco products from the market." In the midst of the debate over tobacco, this long-standing statute loomed large: "The marketing of tobacco constitutes one of the greatest basic industries of the United States with ramifying activities which directly affect interstate and foreign commerce at every point, and stable conditions therein are necessary to the general welfare." Congress, in short, had actually promoted the tobacco industry. Tobacco was seen by Congress as an important industry to the country. How, then, could the agency, with no intervening change of heart by Congress, decide suddenly to regulate the industry? And Justice O'Connor had said that the Court would look to common sense: "[W]e must be guided to a degree by common sense as to the manner in which Congress is likely to delegate a policy decision of such economic and political magnitude to an administrative agency."

In that regard, another fact took on major significance:

Congress had specifically addressed the issue of tobacco and health through legislation on no fewer than six occasions going back to 1965. And what was Congress's reaction to growing scientific knowledge about the tobacco-health relationship? Justice O'Connor put it this way: In the face of information about tobacco's health effects, "[n]onetheless, Congress stopped well short of ordering a ban. Instead, it has generally regulated the labeling and advertisement of tobacco products...". There was in the various statutes passed over the years a "collective premise," namely that "cigarettes and smokeless tobacco will continue to be sold in the United States. A ban of tobacco products by the FDA would therefore plainly contradict congressional policy."

Justice Breyer filed a dissent. Joined by Stevens, Souter, and Ginsburg, Breyer coupled the *literal language* of the statute with its *purposes* to conclude that the FDA was actually within its lawful jurisdiction in asserting power over tobacco. He married literal statutory text—tobacco products are "articles (other than food) intended to affect the structure or any function of the body"—with the congressional purpose of protecting public health. All nine justices thus were comfortable with the same overall approach to interpreting the law. They simply reached different results.

Why? The fundamental reason lay in what the five justices comprising the majority viewed as a huge anomaly. To them, it made little sense, in view of the entirety of the statute and the rich history of congressional legislation affecting tobacco, for the agency after all these years to bring tobacco under its regulatory reach. Looking to the literal language of the statute, in contrast, the dissenters concluded that nicotine fell within that language and that Congress's broad purposes in promoting public health supported the agency's action. Thus, while the majority, led by the centrist justices, thought the agency had over-reached, the dissenters believed the agency was entitled to change its views, particularly in view of the additional information about nicotine that only recently had come to light. In any event, to the dissenters, the Clinton administration was within its rights in changing the government's view. Speaking through Justice Breyer, the dissenters stated: "Early administrations may have hesitated to assert jurisdiction. . . . Commissioners of the [Clinton] administration simply took a different regulatory attitude. Nothing in the law prevents the FDA from changing its policy for such reasons." To the dissenters, that is what elections are all about. Agencies should be able to change their policy views, so long as the governing statute allows such flexibility.

Not surprisingly, the tobacco-regulation case generated far more controversy than most statutory interpretation cases. In the lion's share of such cases, there are few important issues dividing the justices. They also tend to agree on the need for the Court, in effect, to specify details of laws Congress frames in general terms.

The justices, including the textualists, do this quite often. They are "making law" in the same manner as common-law judges who develop the law governing contracts or torts. No more powerful example exists than the federal law governing discrimination. Here, over many years, the Court has quietly developed an elaborate body of law, first on race, national origin, and sex discrimination and, more recently, on age discrimination. None of the justices has seriously objected to this process.

Consider a 2000 case, *Reeves v. Sanderson Plumbing*. In that case, Roger Reeves began working for Sanderson Plumbing, a manufacturer of toilet seats, at the tender age of seventeen. For forty long years, he labored for Sanderson, rising to the level of supervisor in what the company called the Hinge Room. Toilet seats, like doors, need hinges, and Sanderson's Hinge Room produced them. In the summer of 1995, the Hinge Room's top supervisor reported to Sanderson's senior management that production was down in that facility. The fifty-seven-year-old Reeves was blamed—and fired. He had failed, the company said, to discipline misbehaving employees, an especially serious failure for a company whose workforce is unionized. One senior manager testified that maintaining discipline is " 'extremely important when you are dealing with a union' because uneven enforcement across departments would keep the company 'in grievance and arbitration cases, which are costly, all the time.' "

For his part, Reeves complained that this was all a ruse. Charging in a lawsuit that the company had discriminated against him in violation of the Age Discrimination in Employment Act, Reeves introduced evidence showing that he had accurately recorded the attendance and hours of his employees, that disciplining employees was not his responsibility, and that the owner's husband had demonstrated age-biased animus toward him.

The matter went to federal court in 1995. The backdrop of this workaday employment dispute was an elaborate framework devised not by Congress but by the Supreme Court to govern the trial of employment discrimination cases. For its part, Congress had passed a general antidiscrimination law. Like Title VII of the famous 1964 Civil Rights Act prohibiting race, national-origin, and gender-based discrimination, the Age Discrimination in Employment Act was worded in broad, general terms: The statute simply made it "unlawful for an employer . . . to fail or refuse to hire or to discharge any individual or otherwise discriminate against any individual with respect to his compensation, terms, conditions, or privileges of employment because of such individual's age." With Congress having set forth this broad prohibition, it was then up to the courts to fashion specific rules of procedure. Congress was in charge of broad policy strategy, but left it up to the courts to come up with the tactics—the rules to govern these difficult cases. And the judges had done so, led by the Supreme Court in the 1970s in the then burgeoning area of race discrimination in employment. An elaborate procedure had been set up to this effect: The individual complaining of race-based discrimination must meet certain basic requirements, thereby making out a "prima facie" case of discrimination. Then the burden shifts to the employer to come up with a legitimate, nondiscriminatory reason for taking the adverse employment action. At that point, the burden returns to the complaining employee, who, to prevail, must show that the employer's stated reason masks the real one: discrimination. At the end of the day, the complaining party must show, by a preponderance of the evidence, that the employer *intentionally discriminated* against the plaintiff. The Supreme Court imported these procedures from race-discrimination cases to age-discrimination litigation, one of the fastest growing branches of civil rights litigation.

To the chagrin of the business community, the Court in the spring of 2000 used Roger Reeves's case to enhance the chances of plaintiffs like him. Given the state of the evidence, a unanimous Court held, Reeves could properly win before a jury. In fact, he had done just that. The jury in Mississippi had listened to the evidence and ruled in his favor. But appellate courts across the country had been troubled by allowing cases like his too readily to "go to the jury." So a number of courts had said, in effect, that more is required of the employee than establishing a prima facie case, coupled with sufficient evidence to disbelieve the employer's stated legitimate reason for its decision. Rather, the employee also has to come up with evidence of intentional discrimination.

In the *Reeves* case, the Supreme Court said this was unjustified. Speaking through Justice O'Connor, the Court
unanimously concluded that once the employee had established his case under the burden-shifting rules, then the
case could go to the jury, which could then find in favor
of the employee. The lower courts had been requiring the
employee to prove too much. After all, if the employee
showed that the company's stated reason was untrue, then
the jury should be able to *infer* that the company's real
reason was a discriminatory one. As O'Connor put it: "In
appropriate circumstances, *the [jury] can reasonably infer
from the falsity of the explanation that the employer is
dissembling to cover up a discriminatory purpose.*"

Here, the Court simply made up the law of discrimination. It didn't apologize for it, nor criticize Congress for
having left this exercise in "interstitial lawmaking" to the
judiciary. This is an anomaly, asking courts, in effect, to
fill in the blanks of what Congress had done. But as a
practical matter, it is impossible for Congress to anticipate
each and every aspect of a law. The best Congress can do
at times is provide a basic set of policy choices, and a general framework within which specific cases can be resolved. It thus must fall to the judiciary to do the rest of
the lawmaking. Our system of government has grown entirely comfortable with Congress passing a law and then
anticipating, without saying so in the law itself, that the
judiciary will take over and finish the legislation.

That unanimity can ever be achieved under these circumstances is remarkable. This is, after all, the judiciary
doing what we understandably assume Congress will do.
One would think that it's Congress that sets up the framework, and then the judiciary steps in to resolve the
specifics of the individual cases within the framework that
Congress has seen fit to establish. Little would we suspect
that the judiciary would be in an informal joint venture—

a joint construction contract—with Congress, with few rules to guide the courts in carrying out their part of the building project.

Not surprisingly, unanimity on the Court frequently breaks down here, as elsewhere. Not only is there a good deal of running room for judges, but no unifying principles, such as the equality principle, bind the justices together. They are, in this context, sailing in less charted waters. They are more like common-law judges, with the ebbs and flows that characterize the development of English and American law over the centuries.

The enduring point is that these now commonplace exercises in lawmaking reveal a Court engaged in "making the law"—indeed making it up. Congress does not mind, even if the law the Court makes is not what most members like. Only if Congress strongly disagrees does it write new law.

Statutory interpretation, then, is best understood as a matter of dialogue. It is a conversation between Congress and the courts. And the creativity required—and contemplated—in this exercise renders what many observers dismiss or ignore: one of the most lively areas of the Court's work, affecting the lives and liberties of the American people.

Chapter Thirteen

★

THE REHNQUIST COURT AND THE FEDERAL REPUBLIC

CHRISTY BRZONKALA'S DAYS as an undergraduate at Virginia Tech ended in 1994 when she said she had been raped in her dormitory by two varsity football players. Brzonkala sued her assailants under a federal law, the Violence Against Women Act (VAWA). Congress had passed the measure after no fewer than four years of hearings during which it assembled evidence pointing to, in the words of a Senate report, "a national tragedy played out every day in the lives of millions of American women at home, in the workplace, and on the street." Not only was the human toll grave but the economic effects were hugely negative, among them foreclosed job and educational opportunities. VAWA created a new civil remedy for women like Christy Brzonkala—specifically, the right to sue perpetrators of violence for money damages.

Anyone knowing as little about Christy Brzonkala's lawsuit as I have just related might fairly wonder whether hers was really a "federal" case. After all, some matters, regardless of how pressing they might be, have long been considered "local" in nature. States and subordinate units of government—counties and cities—handle local matters.

To cite an obvious example: The states, not the federal government, address the myriad questions involving marriage, divorce, and child custody. Is violence against women a matter for the states, or may Congress also deal with it?

These are questions of federalism, one of structure under the Constitution. What is the constitutional distribution of power between the federal government and the states? The Constitution does not confer on Congress a general power to address every issue it wants to. Instead, the Constitution specifies the powers it gives to Congress.

This isn't an accidental feature. When the framers met in Philadelphia in 1787, they intended to create a national government of limited powers. The framers began Article I—on Congress—this way: "All legislative Powers herein granted shall be vested in a Congress of the United States." The framers then spelled out those legislative powers. Their understanding was that Congress had only those powers (and any others the people might grant it through constitutional amendments). For the framers, the "enumerated powers," as they called them, and what may reasonably be implied to be within those powers and those "necessary and proper" to carry out the enumerated powers, were the sum of it. Powers that were not enumerated, they also agreed, belonged to the states and ultimately the people.

James Madison, rightly regarded as the Father of the Constitution, summarized what it meant to enumerate powers. During the Constitutional Convention he wrote: "The powers delegated by the proposed Constitution to the federal government are few and defined. Those which are to remain in the State governments are numerous and indefinite." In 1791, the Tenth Amendment was added to the Constitution. It stated what everyone in Philadelphia had assumed to be the case: "The powers not delegated to the United States by the Constitution, nor prohibited by it to the States, are reserved to the States respectively, or to the people."

"Enumerated powers" and the Tenth Amendment are key elements of federalism. Federalism, as Madison's statement shows, concerns the division or distribution of power between the federal government and the states. Madison thought that dividing power between two sovereigns would be better than having just one, because the one would help limit the other. This way, liberty, the ultimate end of the Constitution, would have what Madison called a "double security." This is at the core of the Constitution's genius: The existence of two governments would better promote liberty than would a single unit.

Many provisions of the original Constitution were written with federalism concerns in mind. So were many of the twenty-seven amendments added over the following two centuries. Indeed, federalism runs through the entire document, in words but also in theory. Like separation of powers, it is a basic structural principle.

Christy Brzonkala's lawsuit provoked a debate over this principle. The debate wasn't about the merits of her claim but about the constitutionality of the new federal law she used to state her claim. Congress had never seen fit to pass a general assault statute applicable anywhere and everywhere in the country. Assault had been a matter for the states to deal with, in such laws as they might frame and direct prosecutors to enforce. Thus the question: What authority did Congress have to enact the Violence Against Women Act?

Congress answered that question when it passed the law in 1994. In its view, Congress was acting on the basis of its Article I power to regulate interstate commerce (the Commerce Clause) and its power under section 5 of the Fourteenth Amendment to enforce civil rights.

But the Supreme Court, by a vote of 5–4, held in 2000 that Congress lacked authority to create a federal cause of action for victims of gender-animated bias. The Court, in an opinion authored by Chief Justice Rehnquist, said that violence against women, however serious a social problem it might be, was not interstate commerce, and thus was not a matter Congress could regulate in this manner.

Christy Brzonkala's case is one in a series of federalism decisions in which the Rehnquist Court has sided against Congress. The nature of the issue in these cases has varied, as have the constitutional bases for the Court's decisions. The Court has discerned and enforced limits on federal power under the Commerce Clause and under section 5 of the Fourteenth Amendment. It has also enforced the prerogatives of the states provided by the Tenth and Eleventh Amendments.

To repeat: All of these cases are federalism cases, and in them the Court has found laws of Congress unconstitutional. But these are not the only cases the Court has decided that affect federalism. Civil liberties and civil rights cases involving a state law or action also have consequences for federalism. Consider that whenever the Court holds, for example, that the law of a state violates the First Amendment, it denies that state the power to have that law—that is, to govern itself in a particular way. Recall the 1989 flag-burning case from Texas. At issue was whether a Texas statute outlawing flag desecration violated the First Amendment. The Court by a vote of 5–4 said the law was unconstitutional. The law thus could have no more effect. Today, however much the Texas legislature might want to regulate what someone might do to the American flag, it can't pass a law that denies the right to burn it.

During the same term the Court decided Christy Brzonkala's case, it also ruled—as it usually does every term—in a series of cases involving disputes over civil liberties and civil rights arising from the states. And, as typically happens each term, many of these cases went against the states. State laws were found invalid under the First, Sixth, Fourteenth, and Fifteenth Amendments.

Cases like these are not the ones people have in mind, however, when they talk about the Rehnquist Court's federalism cases. Cases like these are not the controversial ones, at least from a federalism perspective. The cases concerning federalism that have deeply divided the Court and that have provoked debate in law review articles and on the nation's op-ed pages are those, like Brzonkala's, in which the Court has found that Congress lacked constitutional authority to pass a law or that a law of Congress unconstitutionally invaded state prerogatives.

These cases deserve a closer look. Their importance derives from the fact that in these cases the Court is making what might be called structural repairs to our constitutional system. Here, though, it is worth pausing to clarify the meaning of federalism. Say the word and many people immediately will think of "states' rights" and conjure up the image of Alabama Governor George Wallace invoking those rights in his effort to block the admission of black students to the University of Alabama. The states, of course, are not free anymore to discriminate on grounds of race. That is good for federalism, for now it is possible to consider the role of the states in our constitutional system without having to see the matter through a racial lens. Significantly, not one of the Court's recent federalism cases has involved race.

During my service as solicitor general, I saw another version of "states' rights" that can also be distinguished from true federalism. This version of states' rights was at the heart of a case I argued in 1989. In the 1980s the nation debated what our foreign policy should be toward Central America. Several governors, including Michael

Dukakis of Massachusetts and Rudy Perpich of Minnesota, ordered the National Guard units within their states not to participate in military training exercises in Honduras. The governors had taken this action as a way of expressing their disapproval of U.S. aid to rebel forces in Nicaragua. Congress passed a law to prevent these states from conducting their own foreign policies. The governors challenged the law and lost. The Rehnquist Court's decision in *Perpich v. Department of Defense* (1990) recognized that under the Constitution the federal government, not the states, has the authority to conduct foreign affairs. This was an entirely sensible resolution, vindicating national power over that of the states.

Just as federalism need not be a mask for racism (or any other kind of oppression), it should not be identified with state efforts to assume obviously federal tasks, such as running U.S. foreign policy. Federalism, properly understood, is an essential part of our constitutional system. And the proper way to understand federalism is in Madisonian terms—as the division of power between the national government and the states so that there is a "double security" for liberty.

A major federalism challenge facing Madison and his colleagues at the founding lay in the fact that the states were islands of stubborn economic protectionism. No small part of the original constitutional design was to obliterate parochialism in matters of trade and commerce and create a vast common market of the states. Indeed, the Commerce Clause, which was at issue in the *Brzonkala* case, was framed with precisely this goal in mind, for economic liberty would be in jeopardy if the states were able, without limitation, to regulate commercial activities involving several states.

Federalism challenges differ from era to era, and today a narrow majority of five justices regards as the challenge for our time the tendency of Congress to legislate on a great many subjects—too many, according to the majority's view of the Constitution. It surely appears to the Rehnquist majority that Congress acts as though its powers were not limited by the Constitution, as though it could legislate on any subject it chose.

The explanation for Congress's view lies, at least in part, in the history of the Court's treatment of the New Deal. During FDR's first term, the Court found several pivotal New Deal measures unconstitutional because Congress had exceeded its authority under the Commerce Clause or because it had violated the Tenth Amendment. But the Court famously changed its mind, starting in 1937, and declined to condemn New Deal legislation. In the process, it also read out of the Commerce Clause virtually any limits that provision might impose upon Congress, and it found the Tenth Amendment an empty one. In the ensuing decades, Congress legislated on more and more matters. The Court did not disturb this centralizing trend. Nor did many parties try to challenge it, their chances seeming completely nil.

Nonetheless, the trend was bound eventually to produce a response, and the source of that response was bound to be the increasingly conservative Republican Party. In his critical comments about the Court in 1968, Richard Nixon didn't mention federalism as such. His focus, as we saw in earlier chapters, was on law and order—the Warren Court's controversial criminal justice decisions. But it was not surprising that the justices he appointed proved receptive to challenges to the centralizing tendencies since the New Deal. In 1976—for the first time in four decades—the Court, with all four Nixon appointees in the five-justice majority, struck down an act of Congress on federalism grounds.

The case was *National League of Cities v. Usery.* At

issue was a 1974 law that extended the maximum-hours and minimum-wage provisions of the Fair Labor Standards Act to most state and municipal employees. Congress had enacted the statute on the basis of its power to regulate interstate commerce. The Court did not find that Congress had exceeded its Commerce Clause authority, but instead held that the law violated the Tenth Amendment. Congress, said the Court, had unconstitutionally intruded into an "attribute of state sovereignty."

Writing the Court's opinion was Nixon appointee William Rehnquist, who had long been known for his interest in a federalism that would reinvigorate the role of the states. But if the case demonstrated the difference it makes who sits on the Court, it did not start a trend. The case left unclear where the line should be drawn between permissible and impermissible federal intrusions upon the states. After a decade of efforts to clarify the distinction, the Court overruled *National League of Cities* in the 1985 case of *Garcia v. San Antonio Metropolitan Authority.*

Here, too, the vote was 5–4. Nixon appointee Blackmun, who had voted with the majority in *National League of Cities,* wrote the Court's opinion. Blackmun set forth an understanding of what has been called "process federalism," one in which the balance of power between the states and the federal government can be left, without need of judicial review, to the political process. "The Framers," Blackmun wrote, "chose to rely on a federal system in which special restraints on federal power over the States inhered principally in the workings of the National Government itself, rather than in discrete limitations on the objects of federal authority. State sovereign interests, then, are more properly protected by procedural safeguards inherent in the structure of the federal government [such as that senators represent states] than by judicially created limitations on federal power." The Tenth

Amendment thus could not be construed by judges to limit what Congress might do. Nor could any of the enumerated powers, including the power to regulate interstate commerce in particular, be read to constrain Congress. "The political process," wrote Blackmun, "ensures that [federal] laws that unduly burden the States will never be promulgated."

The dissenters disagreed with Blackmun's view that state interests were adequately represented in the federal structure, pointing out that senators, thanks to the Seventeenth Amendment, are elected by the people of the states, not by their state representatives. They also invoked *Marbury v. Madison* to say that the Court must have a role in federalism disputes. Justice Rehnquist expressed hope that the Court would someday revive the principle of federalism it had upheld in *National League of Cities* but was now casting aside. "The Court today surveys the battlefield of federalism and sounds a retreat," wrote Justice O'Connor, then in her fourth year on the Court. "I share Justice Rehnquist's belief that this court will in time again assume its constitutional responsibility." She was right.

Garcia returned the law of federalism to where it had been before *National League of Cities.* But as I write, the law has shifted again, thanks to changes in the Court's membership. Since *Garcia,* six new justices have been appointed: Scalia and Kennedy (by Reagan), Souter and Thomas (by Bush), and Ginsburg and Breyer (by Clinton). Of these new justices just one, Clarence Thomas, has taken views of federalism at odds with those of his predecessor (Marshall). Thomas thus has facilitated the emergence of the five-justice majority in favor of federalism.

The Five Friends of Federalism are Chief Justice Rehnquist and Justices O'Connor, Scalia, Kennedy, and Thomas; the Four Foes are Justices Stevens, Souter, Ginsburg, and Breyer. For years, the two sides have fought pitched battles over constitutional doctrine, and the majority has struggled mightily in search of coherent principles to justify its decisions. Justices in both camps have candidly observed the difficulty that the Court has had throughout its history in coming up with sensible, useful principles with solid roots in the Constitution itself. They have also fought the battle—defined by Blackmun in his *Garcia* opinion—over whether the Court has any role at all in enforcing federalism. The Four Foes have adamantly and consistently rejected the decisions of their five colleagues. Moreover, they have eagerly anticipated a reversal of those decisions. In the *Christy Brzonkala* case, Justice Souter, writing bitterly in dissent, taunted the majority by suggesting that their citadel of federalism would soon fall. And of course it could collapse when the next justice joins the Court—if that justice is willing to join the Four Foes and replaces one of the Five Friends.

The majority's critics are also found outside the Court. The majority stands accused of judicial activism. This charge is the most searing (other than an accusation of outright corruption or utter incompetence) there is, for the Court is said to be doing what it says, in its holdings, Congress is doing: acting at odds with the Constitution. Has the Court placed itself over the Constitution? Is it making itself the supreme law? Is it acting to suit its own desires and predilections? Such questions deserve an answer.

A 1995 case marks the beginning of the Court's much-debated effort to revive federalism. The social context of the case was and unfortunately remains a familiar one: gun-related incidents in and around schools. Such incidents were on the rise in the late 1980s, and Congress decided to investigate. It found that 4 percent of high-school students (and 6 percent of inner-city high-school students) carried a gun to school at least occasionally; that 12 percent of urban high-school students had had the unsettling experience of having had guns fired at them; and that 20 percent of city high-schoolers had been threatened with guns. Invoking its authority to regulate interstate commerce, Congress decided to address the issue by passing the Gun-Free School Zones Act, which made it a crime to possess a firearm in and around a school. Though no one much saw this as a problem at the time, Congress had, by passing the law, regulated an admittedly dangerous but decidedly local activity.

The challenge to the new law came from Alfonzo Lopez, a senior at Edison High School in San Antonio. An anonymous tipster told school authorities that Lopez had arrived at the school with a concealed .38-caliber handgun. The authorities confronted him, found the weapon, and turned him over to state law-enforcement officers, who in turn decided he should be prosecuted under the new federal law. But his lawyers thought his case belonged in state court, there being a state law covering the same matter, and the federal district judge agreed. (Note the irony: It is not the state but Lopez who challenged the law.) Eventually Lopez's case rose to the Supreme Court, and with the Friends and Foes of Federalism dividing 5–4, the Court held that Congress had exceeded its power under the Commerce Clause.

Lopez marked the first time in over fifty years that the Court had found a federal law in violation of the Commerce Clause. As we mentioned in Chapter One, the clause has played a major role in our constitutional history. According to one scholar, the clause spawned more litigation between 1789 and 1950 than any other constitutional provision. The Court's first effort to interpret the clause came in 1824 with *Gibbons v. Ogden* (the case holding that New York's grant of a monopoly on steamship service across the Hudson River to New Jersey conflicted with federal law). During much of the nineteenth century, the Court was asked to review state regulatory initiatives challenged as unconstitutional burdens on interstate commerce. In the late nineteenth and early twentieth centuries, with Congress more frequently regulating the economy, the Court was asked the opposite question: whether new federal laws unconstitutionally burdened the states.

The key issue for the Court concerned the scope of the congressional power to regulate commerce "among the states." The line the Court attempted to draw was between "interstate commerce," on the one hand, and, on the other hand, state and local matters beyond the reach of Congress. The Court decided that Congress could regulate railroads that crossed state lines and criminalize the driving of a stolen car from one state to another. But the Court also decided that because some activities weren't "commerce," Congress couldn't regulate them. These activities included manufacturing, agriculture, and mining. "Commerce succeeds to manufacture, and is not part of it," the Court said in one case. And, in another: "Mining brings the subject matter of commerce into existence. Commerce disposes of it."

The Commerce Clause wasn't the only part of the Constitution that stood in the way of national regulatory schemes. There was also the Tenth Amendment. Both parts of the Constitution were in play in the "sick chicken" case, *Schechter Poultry Corp. v. United States* (1935). At issue was the constitutionality of the National Industrial Recovery Act. Passed in 1933, the law was Roosevelt's first and most important response to the Great Depression. The far-reaching measure declared a national emergency and directed industry groups to draw up codes designed to lift wages and spur business recovery. Schechter Poultry in Brooklyn, New York, was found guilty of violating the wage-and-hour provisions of its industry's code and also of selling unfit chicken. Schechter's produce came from out of state, but the company sold it only in Brooklyn. It sued, and the Court unanimously agreed that NIRA was unconstitutional, a violation of the Commerce Clause (and also the Tenth Amendment). The Court drew a distinction between activities with direct effects on interstate commerce and those with only indirect effects: Congress may regulate the former but not the latter. Schechter Poultry, the Court concluded, was engaged in intrastate commerce.

Schechter Poultry was among a series of anti–New Deal decisions that ultimately drove President Roosevelt to make an audacious proposal whereby the Court's membership would quickly increase to fifteen, the new members being ones he would get to appoint. FDR's court-packing plan was vehemently and widely criticized. It proved unnecessary, because within a month after he had proposed it the Court shifted course and began upholding New Deal initiatives. Retirements then gave FDR opportunities to appoint justices. Roosevelt filled the vacancies with appointees who shared his philosophy, and by 1941 the Court had revised much of its doctrine, on federalism especially. The Court abandoned its Commerce Clause distinctions between manufacturing and commerce and between direct and indirect effects. It embraced a much broader understanding of the clause: Congress may regulate any activity affecting commerce, whether directly or indirectly. Does the activity in question, the Court now asked, have a close, substantial relationship to interstate commerce? If so, Congress may regulate it.

But now, decades later in *Lopez*, the Court had finally said that Congress may not regulate. The case was not an easy one for the two justices so often in the middle on the Rehnquist Court, O'Connor and Kennedy. In a separate opinion, they made clear their anguish, even as they also made clear that they wanted a principled way to decide federalism cases. A New Deal case called *Wickard v. Filburn* (1942) summoned their attention. Roscoe Filburn lived in Ohio, where he had a small farm of twenty-three acres. Filburn had a herd of dairy cattle and some poultry, and sold milk, eggs, and poultry in nearby markets. He planted winter wheat on his farm, none of which he sold. Instead, he fed the wheat to his livestock and ground it into flour for his family. Filburn, however, ran afoul of a new federal regulation by planting twelve acres of wheat more than it permitted. The government charged him 49 cents each for the 239 bushels he had harvested from the twelve acres. Filburn sued, and it is not hard to understand his objection: He had more or less gardened in his own (large) backyard. Surely Congress had no power to regulate how much he needed to grow for his own family and his livestock. Surely what he did was "local" and not part of interstate commerce. Surely Congress lacked the power to regulate a situation like his.

The New Deal Court, however, was unmoved and rendered a unanimous decision against the small farmer in Ohio. For the justices, it was enough that the regulated activity be one that "substantially affects" commerce. The qualifier was important: An orange tree beside your driveway might not be "interstate commerce," as long as you harvest the oranges and squeeze them at home. But Filburn's winter-wheat farming was different. It could substantially affect commerce—and therefore could be an object of congressional regulation—if many other farmers did as he did. And in fact many did: Roughly 20 percent of all wheat grown in the nation did not leave the farm but was used and consumed at home. The actions of these farmers, taken together, affected overall demand for wheat and in turn its price.

Thus was born the "cumulative effects" approach to determining whether an activity qualified as interstate commerce and could be regulated by Congress. In *Lopez,* this definition of interstate commerce was advanced in behalf of the Gun-Free School Zones Act. Antonio Lopez had in his possession, while on school grounds, a .38-caliber handgun. Could he be regarded in the same manner as the New Deal Court had viewed Roscoe Filburn? That is, might a cumulative-effects analysis of Lopez's gun possession lead to the conclusion that his activity could be regulated?

For Chief Justice Rehnquist, the two cases were not close. Rehnquist juxtaposed Filburn's activity to Lopez's. The former, he said, involved commerce while the latter obviously did not. Moreover, on its own terms, the Gun-Free School Zones Act did not have anything to do with commerce.

The chief justice discussed the fact that in passing the law Congress had failed to show that gun possession near schools had a "substantial effect" on interstate commerce. Rehnquist said that findings to this effect weren't necessary and emphasized that Congress may legislate however it pleases. But the lack of findings made it harder, he continued, for the Court to review the constitutionality of the statute. Congress had provided nothing to explain why it believed it was acting on the basis of its enumerated power to regulate interstate commerce.

Rehnquist then responded to what defenders of the law argued: that possession of firearms does in fact substantially affect commerce since an educational process handicapped by violence will result in a less productive citizenry. This proved too much, the chief concluded, for Congress could on this argument regulate virtually anything in education or in law enforcement. It could even decide to run the nation's schools. But that could not be what the Constitution permits. The Commerce Clause was not meant to be a license for Congress to exercise a national police power.

Rehnquist's opinion may well have reflected a concern he had expressed in his annual state-of-the-judiciary statements, namely that the modern Congress often rushes to pass a law in order to appear responsive to whatever problem seems to have caught the public's attention. As a result, Congress has federalized problems that historically were addressed by cities and counties. The problem of school violence fell into this category. Congress had deemed it a problem requiring a national response. And by passing the Gun-Free School Zones Act, Congress basically placed the burden on the federal courts, thus expanding their jurisdiction. The irony attending the passage of the Gun-Free School Zones Act was that state legislatures had not exactly ignored the problem of school violence. The states, too, had responded with their own laws.

These political facts likely informed the Court's deliberations. One justice, however, remained entirely on a theoretical level. Justice Clarence Thomas, who emerged during the 1990s as the most ardent defender of a pristine approach to constitutional interpretation, crafted a remarkable opinion in which he hammered away at what he saw as modern-day revisionism. The honest justice, in his view, had to be willing to admit that since the New Deal the Court had misinterpreted what the Commerce Clause originally meant. Justice Thomas wanted the Court to return to basics. The text of the Constitution, he said, confers on Congress the power to regulate commerce "among the states." Commerce, he continued, had a well-understood and limited meaning when the Constitution was framed and ratified. In addition, the structure of the Constitution likewise signaled a limited power by Congress. The Court had interpreted the power correctly for 130 years, until the New Deal, when a Court stocked with Roosevelt appointees removed the limits on the power by embracing the notion that anything that "substantially affects" commerce may be regulated by Congress. That doctrine, he said, was at odds with the original meaning of the Commerce Clause and would permit Congress to become the national policeman as well as the national educator.

Justice Thomas knew, however, that the pristine past was lost. No one was willing to reopen settled law, and stability, he also knew, was important in the law. His approach would be radical, and this was a Court inclined to moderation.

The two justices who generally ensured the Court's moderation were O'Connor and Kennedy. Precisely because of their moderation they were unwilling to accept Justice Thomas's invitation to reopen long-settled issues. For them, *doctrinal stability overrode the argument that the New Deal approach to enumerated powers needed to be revisited.*

At the same time, O'Connor and Kennedy were unwilling to ignore federalism concerns and simply allow Congress to do as it wished. Doing that would have been, for them, an immoderate position. The states were an important feature of the constitutional design, they said, and Congress historically had made a genuine effort to determine the impact of a proposed law upon the states. They cited, for example, the civil rights legislation of the 1960s. Congress studied the pertinent issues carefully and came to a considered conclusion of how to legislate on behalf of civil rights without upsetting the delicate balance of power between the states and Washington. In more recent years, the two justices continued, Congress in a number of instances had not shown similar care. The federal courts could not fail to respond if it could be shown that Congress had crossed constitutional lines. That would be a dereliction of judicial duty.

Kennedy and O'Connor joined the majority because they found constitutional lines that Congress had crossed. The Gun-Free Schools Zone Act, they decided, invaded what had traditionally been a state function and local prerogative. Nor was it a law, in their view, that the Commerce Clause authorized. Gun possession in or near a school, the justices said, was dangerous and criminal (under state law), but it was not a commercial activity or tied closely, like Roscoe Filburn's wheat-farming years earlier in Ohio, to commercial arrangements.

Kennedy and O'Connor noted that the dissenters in *Lopez,* like the majority ten years earlier in *National League of Cities,* believed that because the economy was seamless and not a respecter of state lines, Congress could regulate almost anything. To Kennedy and O'Connor, the dissenters' view proved too much. It would not protect federalism but promote centralization and thus erode traditional state functions.

The four dissenters were Justices Stevens, Souter, Ginsburg, and Breyer. Recall that Stevens and Souter were appointed by Republican presidents (Nixon and Bush respectively), Ginsburg and Breyer by President Clinton. Souter and Breyer both filed opinions. Souter concluded that Congress had simply exercised a power confided to it by the Constitution. But this begged the question. The power Congress has to regulate interstate commerce is not a power that permits Congress to decide what is to count as interstate commerce. If Congress declares napping or snoring to be "commerce," that surely does not make it so. Souter's opinion held no allure for O'Connor and Kennedy, because it contained no principle limiting Congress. Souter invoked judicial restraint, but his version would allow Congress under the rubric of regulating commerce to do anything it wanted.

Justice Breyer, likewise, said nothing to allay the moderates' concern about centralization of power. Because the problem of school violence was so acute, said Breyer, Congress could not be faulted for trying to do something about it. Congress, he continued, was on solid ground in asserting that education affected the nation's economic prosperity. Congress could nationalize education, he said.

Two days after issuing its decision in *Lopez*, the Court handed down its judgment in another federalism case, *Printz v. United States*. In 1983 Congress had drawn on its power to regulate interstate commerce to pass the Brady Bill, named for White House press secretary James Brady. Brady had been gravely wounded by John Hinckley during the latter's attempt in March 1981 to assassinate President Reagan. The law directed local law-enforcement officials to conduct background checks on individuals attempting to buy weapons. Two sheriffs, one from Arizona and the other from Montana, sued, claiming that Congress had exceeded its powers. They did not say that Congress could not, under its power to regulate commerce, require gun registration. Their argument, rather, was that Congress had stepped over the federalism line by ordering state and local officials to become firearms registrars for the federal government. In violation of federalism, Congress had commandeered the officials of a sovereign state.

Once again, the Court was deeply fractured, dividing as in other federalism cases along the same 5–4 lines. This time the most quotable member of the majority, Justice Scalia, shouldered the responsibility of writing the Court's opinion. Scalia, as was his wont, became a teacher of American history. Never had Congress, he said, ordered state and local law-enforcement officials to carry out federal functions. To the contrary, history showed that Congress had always *asked* state officials to be of assistance. Moreover, Scalia continued, federalism was, for the framers, a principal means of securing liberty. For Congress to compel state officials to execute federal law was as abhorrent to liberty as would be an effort by the state governments to require federal officials to carry out their laws.

O'Connor's struggle to achieve balance and moderation was again on display. She wrote a short, concurring opinion in which she said that the Court's decision should not prevent Congress from achieving its goals. The problem as she saw it was that Congress had gone too far. It had been, in short, immoderate.

The signature issue of the Rehnquist Court—the protection of the federal structure ordained at the founding— was secure. The moderates would not be swayed, but they would continue their search for theory—legal principles and doctrines that would help explain more fully and persuasively the lines they were ardently determined to draw between what is national and what is local in a federal republic.

Chapter Fourteen

★

PRESIDENTS: THE COURT AND THE EXECUTIVE BRANCH

CONGRESS LEGISLATES IN ITS PROPER DOMAIN. Unless the president vetoes the law (subject to Congress's override) or the Constitution (as interpreted by the Supreme Court) stands in the way, Congress can do as it sees fit.

But the president is different. At every turn, the president is constrained by a body of law, as passed by Congress, and the Constitution, as interpreted by the Supreme Court. Uniquely in our system of government, the president is subordinate to the two other branches. The irony is that the American people tend, naturally, to view the president as uniquely powerful—as supreme—in our structure of government. This is especially so in a time of national tragedy, such as that ushered in by the terrorist attacks of September 11, 2001, and the ensuing war against terrorism. But this perception is imperfect at best. At critical junctures in our history, the Supreme Court has served as the final arbiter of what the president can lawfully do.

This principle was stated forcefully—and definitively—by the Supreme Court the year before Earl Warren was appointed chief justice. The setting was the Korean Conflict.

Labor strife in the steel industry had led to walkouts, slowdowns, and threats of strikes, which threatened the production of steel vital to the war effort. In a bold stroke, President Truman directed the secretary of commerce to take control of the steel mills to keep them in production. In a case challenging Truman's action, the Supreme Court held that the president had exceeded his constitutional and statutory powers. The Court considered in detail the role of Congress, which had passed various laws permitting the president to take certain actions to restore labor peace. Canvassing a wide array of such laws, the Court found no support for the president taking, even in a time of war, the extraordinary step of temporarily seizing control of private industry. President Truman dutifully obeyed the Supreme Court's command. The Steel Seizure case, as it was called, confirmed that the president was ultimately subordinate to Congress and the Supreme Court in the conduct of domestic affairs.

During his tenure as chief justice, Earl Warren had little occasion to confront delicate issues concerning the role and scope of presidential power. But his successor, Warren Burger, was confronted with pivotal cases concerning executive power. The setting was Watergate, and the issue involved the Nixon tapes. The attention of the country was riveted on the drama, with impeachment looming. Senator Howard Baker, the Tennessee Republican and future majority leader, during the hearings conducted by the Senate Select Committee on Watergate, asked the famous question, "What did the president know, and when did he know it?" Was the president aware of the break-in by political operatives into the Watergate offices of the Democratic National Committee? Even if he had no advance knowledge, did the president participate in a cover-up scheme that might constitute an obstruction of justice?

Two investigations were underway on parallel tracks.

Senator Sam Ervin of North Carolina presided over the Special Committee. Television brought the colorful chairman, his committee members, and a string of witnesses before the nation. John Dean, counsel to the president, broke ranks with the White House and testified, in effect, that President Nixon had been directly involved in a conspiracy to obstruct justice. Meanwhile, just five blocks away, a federal grand jury was investigating. Due to laws requiring grand jury secrecy, the specifics of what was occurring in the grand jury were unknown to the outside world. But in the quiet of the courthouse halls was brewing a legal dispute that at once demonstrated the supremacy of the High Court's authority and spelled doom for the Nixon presidency.

In its investigation, the Senate Committee had uncovered a telltale fact: President Nixon had installed an elaborate voice-taping system in the Oval Office. The president's voice was on untold hours of tape. The tapes were, of course, potentially critically important evidence in the criminal investigation. The tapes could tell the story of whether the president himself had committed crimes.

It had seemed unthinkable. The "third-rate burglary," as the White House dismissively referred to the episode, had spun out of control. Instead of getting the facts out and coming to grips with them, the White House, including the president and his closest, most powerful aides, had embarked on a systematic effort to obstruct justice. A conspiracy had been born, with the president in the middle.

In response to mounting pressure from Congress, Archibald Cox had taken over the federal criminal investigation into Watergate as special prosecutor appointed by the attorney general. For its part, the Justice Department had been compromised in the course of its investigation into the matter. Sensitive investigative information had inappropriately found its way from the department's Criminal Division to White House officials. The wall of confidentiality between professionals at the Justice Department and politicians at the White House had been breached, and the bruised agency had to step aside and allow an outsider to take over the investigation.

The outsider was a partisan Democrat. A respected Harvard law professor and former solicitor general, Cox had attacked the Nixon administration's civil rights policy in a speech only weeks before his appointment. He was independent and determined. Cox wanted the tapes. As a special prosecutor, he had no choice but to gather the information as thoroughly as possible.

On behalf of the federal grand jury investigating Watergate, Cox issued a subpoena for the tapes. This, in the White House's perspective, constituted a massive invasion into the privacy of a sitting president. The grand jury's powers were broad, to be sure, but the president was unique in our governmental structure. His responsibilities were so important that surely no court would permit such a wholesale assault on the core of executive authority. This was, after all, only one of thousands of federal criminal investigations across the country. In the White House's view, Cox had lost perspective. He was a one-case prosecutor, assisted by a rabidly anti-Nixon, liberal staff of prosecutors anxious to bring down a conservative president.

President Nixon directed his lawyers to fight the subpoena. The White House contended that the Constitution provided a legal privilege—"Executive privilege"—that protected the president's conversations and communications. But it was to no avail. The District Court in Washington, D.C., with Chief Judge John J. Sirica presiding, was determined to get the facts. The criminal justice system had needs as well, and the president would simply have to bend. Dismayed, the president appealed to the

United States Court of Appeals in Washington. But President Nixon again lost. In an elaborate, scholarly opinion, the Court of Appeals rejected outright the president's claim to absolute immunity from the grand jury's process. The president's duties—and his need for confidential advice—could not prevent the grand jury's work. The president, in short, was not above the law. The grand jury had a duty to gather the facts, it had determined it needed the information on the tapes, and its wide-ranging right to that evidence could not be abridged.

Steeped in the art of political compromise, Nixon advanced a middle ground. Instead of turning over the raw tapes, written transcripts would be prepared and presented to the grand jury, with excisions to protect sensitive national security information and matters implicating personal and family privacy. Cox refused the offer. There would be no substitutes or compromises: The grand jury (and the special prosecutor's staff) wanted the tapes, not substitutes.

This, Nixon concluded, was beyond the pale. The special prosecutor had rejected a perfectly reasonable compromise. The special prosecutor was an "inferior officer," in the words of the Constitution. He was in the executive branch, and there was only one head of that branch: the president. The president cannot order judges around, nor can he order Congress to take action. He can only litigate in the courts, like anyone else, and try to persuade and cajole the Congress, just like others. But a special prosecutor appointed by the attorney general was different. The president could order the attorney general to take action, say, to dismiss an antitrust or civil rights case that the president disliked. It could not be denied, then, that a single-mission special prosecutor could be fired when he engaged, as Cox did, in an act of disobedience to a direct order of the president.

Like any head of a corporation or a college, the president had to be in control of his own department. The point had been made clear soon after the Civil War. President Andrew Johnson had been impeached for defying the radical Tenure of Office Act, passed by the Reconstruction Congress in the wake of the Civil War. The purpose of the act, passed over the president's veto, was to regulate the executive powers of the president, in particular to limit his power to remove subordinate officials. Johnson openly challenged the new law when he fired his disloyal secretary of war, Edwin Stanton, a darling of the radical Reconstructionists who then dominated Congress. That firing was illegal under the Tenure of Office Act, since it expressly required that a cabinet officer, duly confirmed by the Senate, could not be removed without Senate approval. Johnson regarded the statute as an unconstitutional affront to the powers of the presidency.

The House of Representatives responded by impeaching Johnson. The Senate, following a full-blown trial (complete with actual witnesses giving live testimony), fell a vote short of convicting him. Just barely, Johnson survived. Whatever his qualities as a person or as president, he had fought hard for the rightful powers of office. The judiciary had not had occasion to step in.

But the Court's role in our structure of government was more central when, a century later, the presidency again came under assault. Cox's extremism, as the White House saw it, was yet another chapter in the unfolding history of struggle for power in a nonparliamentary system of government where divisions of power counted greatly. The founding generation had viewed separation of powers— and the related system of checks and balances—as fundamental to maintaining the liberties of the people. The power of the British Crown, coupled with the excesses of Parliament, had left the founding fathers with a keen eye for structure. Indeed, creating the right structure of government was the basic task at the Constitutional Convention in Philadelphia in 1787.

The upshot was what James Madison, the primary architect of the constitutional structure, called "balanced government." The secret to maintaining liberty was not in a bill of rights, which Madison regarded as mere "parchment barriers." Bills of rights were necessary and appropriate with respect to state governments that could directly affect the liberties of the people. But the new central government would not pose such a threat to liberty, Madison believed, because of the separation of powers and the enumeration, within those three separate powers, of their respective authorities and responsibilities. In the very structure of the Constitution framed in Philadelphia lay adequate protection for liberty.

Nixon was steeped in all of this. He was not only a lawyer but also a veteran of both Congress and the executive branch. He had served in both the House and the Senate, then as vice president under President Eisenhower for eight years. He knew a congressional power grab when he saw one, and he likewise knew when historic presidential prerogatives were under attack. To Nixon, Cox's snubbing of the proposed compromise about the tapes was unjustified.

The controversial result of Nixon's resistance was the Saturday Night Massacre. The new attorney general, Elliot Richardson, had promised the Senate Judiciary Committee during his own confirmation hearings that he not only would appoint Archibald Cox as the special prosecutor but that he also would protect Cox's independence. Cox had made his judgment, right or wrong, about the need for the tapes. Compromise was out. Nixon wanted Cox fired. In a hastily called meeting with the number-two officer at the department, Deputy Attorney General

William Ruckelshaus, and the number-three officer, Solicitor General Robert Bork, Richardson made it clear: He could not, in good conscience, fire Cox. The president had the power to do so and to direct his attorney general to carry out the directive. But Richardson had made a moral commitment to the Senate. As a matter of honor, Richardson would have to resign.

Ruckelshaus felt the same way. As deputy attorney general, he had made his own promises about the special prosecutor's independence. Like the attorney general, the deputy felt he had no choice but to resign. That left the issue with Solicitor General Bork, who had not had occasion to make such moral commitments. The three officers discussed the options. The AG and the DAG would resign, the solicitor general would become the acting attorney general (by operation of law) and then carry out the president's order. There was no other realistic choice. Otherwise, the hemorrhaging at the department would continue. Both the former attorney general, John Mitchell, and the former deputy attorney general, Richard Kleindienst, were under investigation and soon would be under federal criminal indictment. For the Justice Department, Watergate had led to one disaster after another.

Bork dutifully carried out Nixon's order by firing Cox, but Nixon could not win politically. Weakened by public revulsion to the firing of Cox, Nixon promised that the Watergate investigation would not, as he had intended, be returned to the Justice Department. He would accede to the growing demand, voiced by members of Congress, that the investigation be handled by an outside prosecutor. No insider, even though the person was a career prosecutor protected by the civil-service laws, could be trusted. The replacement was quickly named: a prominent Texas Democrat, Leon Jaworski, who had been a lawyer and confidant of President Johnson. Like Cox, Jaworski could be counted on to press the investigation aggressively.

Jaworski picked up where Cox had left off. As trials of the seven Watergate defendants loomed in federal district court in Washington, Jaworski made a strategic judgment. He wanted the tapes for trial. Again, Nixon refused. The resulting dispute over the tapes quickly arrived at the Supreme Court. The case was argued in early July 1974 and decided just two weeks later. The result was surprising: A unanimous Court, speaking through a chief justice appointed by President Nixon, held that the tapes had to be turned over.

The Court well understood the stakes. Its decision could doom the Nixon presidency. But it would also affect Nixon's successors, since the Court would have to sort out the relative powers of the presidency when the operation of the Oval Office touched on the needs of a separate branch, the judiciary.

The Nixon Court engaged in a classic method of deciding cases: balancing. Balance had to be maintained, in the Court's view, lest a terrible injury ensue to our system of government. The Court, speaking through Chief Justice Burger, first accepted the main submission by President Nixon. The principle of executive privilege did indeed exist, the Court concluded, and the principle protected the confidentiality of conversations and discussions involving the president. The idea of "privilege" was simple: As with attorney-client privilege, conversations falling within the ambit of "executive privilege" could be protected from investigators, grand juries, or prosecutors. The reason had to do with the president's powers. For the president to carry out his responsibilities, he had to have the candid advice of his staff. Advisers would be afraid to speak forthrightly if they knew their conversations could be forcibly disclosed. For the sake of the effective functioning of government, a privilege, grounded in the constitutional separation of powers, must be recognized by the judiciary.

But that was only the first part of the analysis. The Court went on to note the needs of the criminal justice system. That system depended upon access to information. The justice system was, at its best, a search for truth, and care had to be taken not to interfere with the truth-seeking process.

Both branches of government had powerful claims. The Court split the difference. In the absence, the Court wrote, of a claim by the president that he was seeking to protect highly sensitive information (such as military or diplomatic secrets), the president's generalized claim of privilege had to bend to a specific, justified request for information from the judicial branch. And here the prosecutor had made a showing to Judge Sirica that the information in the tapes was highly relevant to a nationally watched criminal trial of high government officials. That point carried the day. A "generalized, undifferentiated" interest by the president in confidentiality had to yield to a demonstrated, specific need by the judicial branch to do justice in a criminal case.

This was an odd sort of "privilege." Unlike privileges rooted in the common law (such as the attorney-client privilege), this privilege was grounded in the Constitution itself, specifically in the structural design of separated powers. Each branch, separate from the others, had to do its job. Executive privilege was an important tool in permitting the presidency to operate as the founders intended. Yet that privilege could be trumped by the interest of another branch: the judiciary.

Privileges grounded in the common law were absolute (with a handful of exceptions), so much so that the Supreme Court was destined to hold, in the late 1990s, that the common-law attorney-client privilege survived

the death of the client. The Court held this in a case growing out of the Whitewater investigation: the death of Vincent Foster, Jr., the deputy White House counsel in the
Clinton administration. The attorney-client privilege, in
short, was strong. The common-law privilege, even after
the client's death, would trump the interest of a federal
grand jury in gathering all potentially pertinent information to its inquiry.

Executive privilege, in contrast, was weak (unless,
again, military or diplomatic secrets were at issue). It
would have to bend to the needs of a single trial, or, as the
court of appeals had held in an earlier phase of the Watergate controversy, to the interests of the federal grand
jury. The irony was stark: The president enjoyed virtually
absolute confidentiality were he consulting with his private lawyer (to secure legal advice, as opposed to general
policy or political advice), but he possessed only a qualified privilege if he were talking with his chief of staff.

The president nonetheless dutifully obeyed the Court's
order, turned over the tapes, and within two weeks resigned. *United States v. Nixon* had brought the Nixon
presidency to a shattering conclusion.

Nixon stands for the following: All persons are under
the law. The law (as interpreted by the courts) is supreme.
Since the president is under the law, he can be ordered to
give over tapes, just as Thomas Jefferson, while president,
was ordered by Chief Justice John Marshall to turn over
documents for evidence in the treason trial of Aaron Burr.

The Court's supremacy was also manifest in the most
important executive-powers case decided by the Rehnquist Court, *Morrison v. Olson*. At issue was the constitutionality of the special prosecutor act, which came to be
known as the independent counsel statute. The statute was
a direct response to the firing of Archibald Cox. Passed by
Congress in 1978, the law required the attorney general to

apply to a Special Division of the United States Court of Appeals in Washington for appointment of a "special prosecutor," later called "independent counsel," when allegations of wrongdoing were made against a high-level executive branch official, including the president.

The Reagan administration fought the law, first in Congress and then in the courts. In round one, the Justice Department urged Congress not to reauthorize the statute when it first came up for renewal in 1983. At senior levels, department officials—beginning with my mentor and former law partner, Attorney General Bill Smith—focused on the statute's costs and benefits. Inside the Reagan Justice Department, where I was serving at the time, we well understood that the law was aimed at ensuring a fair, vigorous investigation into wrongdoing when allegations were made about a senior executive branch official. But this apparent "benefit" came at a high cost. At the core, we felt, the statute was unconstitutional; it intruded improperly into the functions of the executive branch. Among the fundamental responsibilities of the executive branch was the faithful enforcement of the law, including investigating and prosecuting federal crimes. The statute was aimed directly at that very function: the president's ability to control criminal investigations and prosecutions at the federal level.

Speaking through the then associate attorney general, future New York City Mayor Rudy Giuliani, the Department of Justice, under Attorney General Smith's leadership, urged Congress to allow this feature of the post-Watergate "reforms" to expire in accord with its built-in sunset provisions. But Congress disagreed, the law was re-enacted in 1983, then again in the late 1980s, and then, finally—and fatefully—in 1994.

Along the way, the issue of the statute's constitutionality found its way into federal court. *Morrison v. Olson* was the watershed. This was round two in the battle over the statute, and the Reagan administration again weighed in, this time through written briefs and oral arguments. By this point I was serving on the court of appeals in Washington, and I stepped aside as the case wended its way into our court. Embracing the Reagan administration's attack on the statute, the court of appeals struck down the law as unconstitutional on a variety of grounds. I was gratified since this was precisely the position that the Reagan Justice Department under Bill Smith had championed in Congress five years before.

But this was not to be the last word. In 1988, in a sweeping decision, the Rehnquist Court reversed my court's judgment, upheld the law, and said that Congress had the power to control the president's exercise of authority over the executive branch. In particular, the Court, speaking through Chief Justice Rehnquist, upheld Congress's power to limit the president's authority over appointments of executive branch officials. Even though the independent counsel was an executive branch official exercising only executive authority, the president's power to appoint—and remove—such an official could be narrowed by Congress.

This was an extraordinary result, crafted by an overwhelming 7–1 majority (Justice Kennedy, newly arrived at the Court, did not participate). The Court upheld the law through a balancing and weighing process. This intrusion by Congress into the powers of the presidency was limited, the Court assured the country, to a particular set of circumstances that would not substantially interfere with the orderly functioning of the executive branch. Looming in the background was Judge Lawrence Walsh's far-reaching Iran-Contra investigation and then, in the 1990s, the Whitewater investigation culminating in President Clinton's acknowledgment, on his last day in office, of responsibility to the criminal justice system. In a prescient dissent, Justice Scalia attacked the law as entirely inimical to a system of separated powers; the country would rue the day the Court upheld this system of congressionally ordained investigations of executive branch officials.

The die was thus cast for the 1997 case *Clinton v. Jones,* the controversial lawsuit brought by Paula Corbin Jones against the president that eventually found its way to the Rehnquist Court. The enduring result in that most famous of sexual harassment cases, ultimately dismissed by Chief Judge Susan Webber Wright, was foreshadowed by the *Nixon* case and to a certain extent by *Morrison v. Olson.* From *Nixon* came the principle that the president had to stand before the bar of justice just like anyone else. Applied to the Paula Jones contest, the president could not claim an exemption from civil process. He would have to deal with lawsuits brought against him in his private capacity (as opposed to his official capacity as the president), just like other citizens. From *Morrison* came the point that executive power was not so broad as to be without significant limitations that Congress saw fit to impose.

Like President Nixon's resistance to subpoenas, the effort by President Clinton's lawyers to create a new form of "immunity" from private civil litigation was doomed from the outset. Paula Jones's suit, grounded in the federal statutory law of sexual harassment and civil rights, was assailed by his private lawyers as a distraction to a busy president. The Supreme Court was respectful, but ultimately unpersuaded. As in the *Nixon* case, the Court rejected President Clinton's claim by a unanimous vote.

As in *Nixon,* the Court was unanimous on this proposition: The federal judicial system has its own pressing needs. Just as the president is not given an exemption from the federal tax laws, he likewise does not enjoy any sort of constitutional immunity from lawsuits brought against him as an *individual*.

This did not mean that the president was powerless, left to the whim of any judge in the country who might be presiding over private litigation involving the president. To the contrary, the Rehnquist Court, speaking through Justice Stevens, emphasized that the unique responsibilities of the president required judges to be highly respectful of the extraordinary demands on his time and attention. Judges would have to accommodate the president's schedule.

This was not just politeness by one branch toward another. This was institutional respect born of the nature of the presidency. Chief Justice Marshall in the Aaron Burr case had made this corollary clear: The president was fully subject to the law (as interpreted by the courts), like all others in our representative democracy, but he would be accorded every courtesy due the nation's chief executive. He was not to be treated like just any other litigant.

There was another potential source of relief, however. Congress could, if it so chose, step in and legislate. This was a lesson from *Morrison,* and the parallel principle of congressional supremacy operating within its sphere. If, as pundits predicted, the president found himself subject to time-consuming, distracting litigation, then Congress could, by statute, provide for relief (consistent with basic due process demands). Years before, Congress had done just that in connection with the military. Especially for service personnel stationed far away from home, the burdens of litigation would at times become unmanageable. Basic fairness required some sort of dispensation. And Congress did what legislative bodies customarily do; the Article I Branch made a study of the issue and crafted a statute that struck a balance between the interests of service personnel, on the one hand, and fairness to litigants bringing lawsuits against those personnel on the other. Congress, in short, could weigh competing interests and craft a statute that reflected its considered sense of fair play. This was, in a different setting, the approach of the Rehnquist Court in *Morrison v. Olson.*

Constitutional decision-making, however, seemed different from a run-of-the-mill equity case. This was the judiciary interpreting rights and responsibilities—or powers—under the Constitution. This seemed far afield from a judge "sitting in equity" determining the best remedy in resolving a dispute, to take a commonplace example, between two property owners when the underlying issue was the legality of an intrusion (or trespass) by one person onto the property of the other. To import the methods and mind-sets of equitable decision-making seemed likely to enhance judicial power at the expense of Congress and the presidency. The judiciary, not the two political branches, would weigh matters in the balance and then come to judgment.

But this was the methodology the Court saw fit to use when it came to interpreting the powers and prerogatives of the presidency. The result was indeed to enhance judicial power, and in the process, to maximize judicial flexibility in the exercise of that power. The Court's moderation served ironically to expand judicial authority—to ensure the Supreme Court's role as the authoritative, final voice in the framework of representative government. The stage was set for *Bush v. Gore.*

Chapter Fifteen

★

Bush v. Gore

THE ENDURING QUALITY of the Supreme Court's supremacy under the leadership of Chief Justice Rehnquist has nowhere been more manifest than in the case that resolved the 2000 presidential election, *Bush v. Gore*. Given the high stakes and the political context, it was unsurprising that the cries of foul were both loud and heartfelt. There was a genuine sense in many quarters that the Court had assumed an overtly political role, with Republican appointees cobbling together a majority of votes to give the election to George W. Bush.

The decision and reaction seemed, ironically, like a page drawn from the stormy history of the Warren Court or the Burger Court in its most controversial decision, *Roe v. Wade*. Typical of the reaction, although expressed in terms of sorrow, not anger, was that of New York Congressman Jose Serrano, who stated in a March 2001 hearing on the Supreme Court's budget that the Court "broke my heart by getting involved with a political decision."

Indeed, the most significant fact in the Rehnquist Court's role in the presidential election litigation was that it chose, twice, to become involved at all. It could have simply declined to hear the case. There would have been criticism of the Court, to be sure, for forsaking its duty to decide important issues, but the criticism would not have been particularly serious and certainly not enduring. Rarely if ever does the Court find itself engulfed in controversy by virtue of deciding not to decide. It is widely viewed as commendable when the Court approaches its work with prudence and caution, including staying away from issues that bitterly divide the country. And prudence and caution have characterized much of the work of this Court of lawyers, not politicians.

As a result, many Court watchers, myself included, did not expect the Court to step into the swirl of litigation that came out of the closeness of the presidential vote in Florida. At first glance, the lawsuit seemed to revolve around very specific aspects of Florida election laws, such as how and when to conduct an election "protest" procedure and then a "contest" of the election results. The body of Florida statutes governing elections seemed quite complicated. More than that, the duty of interpreting Florida election law fell, naturally, to the Florida state courts, not the federal courts.

To be involved at all, the federal courts needed a federal "hook," a claim under federal statutes or the Constitution. Otherwise, the federal courts, including the Supreme Court, would have no power over the matter. Just as Congress cannot regulate those matters entrusted to the states in our federal system, so too the federal courts cannot, as a general matter, stray beyond the boundaries of federal law and insert themselves into state-law controversies.

Then again, a presidential election was at stake. Although the Florida courts were interpreting that state's law, the context was overwhelmingly federal. Control of the White House would be determined by Florida's twenty-five electoral votes, so a strong "federal interest" overlay the state courts' interpretation of state law.

One federal interest lay in the Constitution itself. Article II, section I of the Constitution entrusts the method of determining a state's presidential electors to the legislatures of the various states. This delineation of power proved important in the *Bush v. Gore* litigation. Nothing in the Constitution prohibits, for example, a state legislature from deciding how to cast the state's electoral votes for president. Tradition, common sense, and obvious political considerations ensure that the popular vote will be the method for determining a state's position on who the next president should be. Nonetheless, as the Florida litigation continued week after week in the wake of the November 7 election, the Florida legislature—not without controversy—went into session to carry out its responsibility. If litigation gridlock resulted, with the dispute continuing between the state's highest court and the Florida secretary of state (who had certified Governor Bush as the winner based on the original count and the machine recount), then the Florida legislature seemed poised to step in and designate the state's electors. The heavy assumption was that the Republican-controlled legislature would designate George W. Bush as the victor and send a slate of electors to Washington to vote for Bush. It would then have been up to Congress to decide whether to recognize that slate. That untidy, politically divisive result was made possible by the Constitution. Governor Bush's advocate at the time, Ted Olson, who then became President Bush's solicitor general, made much of this point in his oral argument before the Court in the initial case, *Bush v. Palm Beach County Canvassing Board*. In his view, the framers of the Constitution did not want the state judiciary to be a pivotal institution in the presidential election process. He argued the point this way:

The framers of the Constitution debated long and hard. It was one of the longest debates that took place during the formation of the Constitution. Where should [the power to select the president] be lodged, in the Federal legislature, in the state legislature, at the ballot booth or what. The one thing that was discussed and rejected by virtually everyone is that the power to select the manner in which electors would be appointed would be in the state judiciary.

In addition to the Constitution, there was another "hook" for federal courts—a little-known statute passed by Congress well over a century earlier in the aftermath of the controversial presidential election of 1876. That election took place against the backdrop of the Civil War, Lincoln's assassination, and the Reconstruction of the South. The eventual winner, Republican Rutherford B. Hayes, was locked in a close contest with New Jersey Democrat Samuel Tilden. Cries of election fraud, theft, and the like erupted as several southern states, including Florida, designated competing slates of electors. The contest was eventually decided in a hastily arranged compromise that threw the election to Hayes in exchange for his commitment to pull the remaining Northern troops out of the defeated South, thereby bringing Reconstruction to an end. The confusion and chaos surrounding the Tilden-Hayes contest moved Congress to fashion the soon obscure law that suddenly loomed, 124 years later, in the seesaw battle between Vice President Gore and Governor Bush. The 1876-era statute was worded in a convoluted way, but it in effect guaranteed finality to the choice of a state's electors if that choice was made under a system of state law in place prior to election day. Issues abounded as to the precise meaning of the old law, but the important point for the Supreme Court's purposes was that this was a federal law that looked to the relevant body of state law for determining the means of choosing electors for the electoral college.

The federal constitutional and statutory provisions established a federal interest sufficient to justify the Court's involvement. The provisions together concerned the presidency, and of course one of the two candidates had invited the Court to step in. Somehow, perhaps, it may have been viewed within the Court as not quite right for the justices to remain aloof when the request for review was coming from a major-party candidate and the issues were of the highest national moment. In any event, the Court simply agreed, as is its practice, to review the case with no expression or statement of views by any member of the Court.

But also what appeared to be at work was a sense, among at least some of the justices, that the Florida courts had gone too far. The state laws governing election protests had seemed relatively clear, yet the Florida Supreme Court had stitched together—by creative interpretation—a statutory scheme that looked quite different from the one enacted by the Florida legislature. In the process, the highest state court had inadvertently waved a red flag. In its opening opinion, that court had, oddly, denigrated the importance of the specific text of the various state statutes, which were admittedly complicated. The court emphasized instead the value and importance, under the Florida Constitution, of the voter's intent. The state constitution thus was seen as perhaps more important to the resolution of the challenge mounted by Vice President Gore than the specifics of the relevant laws passed by the state legislature. At the very least, the state constitution would provide a lens through which the entire state election code would be examined.

This judicial perspective was understandable, since a

constitutional provision is obviously superior to a statute. This proved, however, to be a land mine destined to blow up in the U.S. Supreme Court just a few days later. Ted Olson made effective use of the point in his argument: "[T]he Florida Supreme Court said we are not going to be bound by technical statutory requirements or what the [state] supreme court called hyper-technical statutory requirements. Instead, we are going to resort to the will of the people . . . and we are going to partially rewrite the statute." The critical point for Olson was that the state constitution could not be used to override a state statutory scheme. The explanation lay in the primacy given by Article II of the federal Constitution to the state legislatures, not to the ultimate sovereign, the people, speaking through the language of their own state constitution.

Compared to that somewhat theoretical dispute, the "pregnant and hanging chad" controversy (that is, mere indentations and partial perforations on punch-card ballots in the places where small paper squares were to be detached entirely to indicate a vote) riveting the nation's attention seemed trumped up and artificial. No one was alleging fraud, ballot stuffing, or the like in Palm Beach County, the epicenter of the original dispute. Perhaps some senior citizens were confused by the butterfly ballot. But no one seriously disputed that the instructions on how to use the ballot were clearly set forth. Not only that, but Florida case law, scant though it was, held that such chads did not count as votes.

The oral argument proved to be dramatic. Assembled in the courtroom on December 1, 2000, was not only Ted Olson (one of the nation's premier lawyers) for Governor Bush, but Laurence Tribe, one of the nation's leading constitutional scholars, representing Vice President Gore. Alongside these titans were two lesser-known but able advocates: Joe Klock, a private practitioner from Miami representing Florida's secretary of state, Katherine Harris; and a lawyer from the Florida Attorney General's Office, Paul Hancock. The Florida executive branch was divided, with the Attorney General's Office vigorously defending the state supreme court's decision over the secretary of state's opposition.

All this was transmitted immediately after the argument by audio, a remarkable lifting of the curtain surrounding the Court's work. Millions heard the voices of the justices, in oral argument, for the first time. Here was the Court working with remarkable speed and great ability—and now in a way accessible to the interested public.

Ted Olson began for Governor Bush. His message was simple and powerful: The Florida Supreme Court had changed the rules in midstream. Specifically, through judicial interpretation, the Florida Supreme Court had changed the date for the state's certification of a winner in order to permit a manual recount of ballots in several contested counties. That change in state law, he maintained, worked a violation of both federal law and the Constitution. Olson began this way: "Two weeks after the November 7 presidential election, the Florida Supreme Court overturned and materially rewrote portions of the carefully formulated set of laws enacted by Florida's legislature to govern the conduct of that election." This set of laws had federal constitutional significance, Olson maintained. "[Florida's] laws have been formulated by the Florida legislature pursuant to an express delegation of authority ... by the United States Constitution." The Florida Supreme Court however, had failed to understand this basic limitation of the state judicial power. Again and again, Olson emphasized the federal Constitution: "Article II of the Constitution ... vests authority to establish the rules exclusively in the legislatures of the States."

In addition, Olson maintained, the federal statute dating back to the 1876 Hayes-Tilden election required state courts to show caution in interpreting state law. Emphasizing the historical context of the presidential election in 1876, Olson emphasized that Congress had wanted stability and predictability. Put laws in place prior to the election, Congress was telling the states, and then choose electors based on settled laws. To be consistent with federal law, states should not change the election rules in midstream.

Olson was strongly challenged throughout his opening presentation by the Court, including the two pivotal justices, O'Connor and Kennedy. It looked grim for the Bush team. Around the country, Court watchers listening in via the Internet were predicting that the Bush assault on the Florida Supreme Court's judgment would fall short. But the breakthrough for Olson actually came during Professor Tribe's presentation. Elegantly presented, Tribe's theme was likewise straightforward: Florida's courts were simply doing what courts do all the time—interpreting statutes, and making a complex statutory scheme work harmoniously. This soothing assurance drew immediate fire from several justices, including the pivotal ones in the center, Justices O'Connor and Kennedy. What the state supreme court had done, both justices suggested (echoing Olson's argument), was to change critical provisions of the state election law. In particular, the specific date for certifying an election had been shifted, from seven days after the election (November 14) to nineteen days after (November 26). In probing how and why the Florida high court changed the certification date, two other members—Chief Justice Rehnquist and Justice Scalia—introduced into the proceedings an obscure Supreme Court case from the late nineteenth century, *McPherson v. Blacker*. The case was almost entirely unknown, even to constitutional scholars, and had not figured prominently in the briefs. Of practical significance, however, under that old, long-forgotten case, a state supreme court could not properly rely on a state constitutional provision so as to intrude into the primacy of state legislatures (as ordained by Article II) in fashioning specific laws governing the conduct of presidential elections.

The fast-moving argument turned, again and again, to a close analysis of the language in the state supreme court's opinion. Exactly what had the Florida Supreme Court determined and how? By this stage in the argument, the justices were practically arguing with one another, using their questions to Professor Tribe to send messages to their colleagues. The Supreme Court's house seemed hopelessly divided, an unfortunate development at best in view of deep institutional concerns that the Court would be perceived as playing politics. To make matters worse, the state supreme court had been unanimous in its judgment establishing new deadlines and procedures to govern the increasingly controversial and chaotic recount.

In the middle of Professor Tribe's argument, almost as an aside, Justice Ruth Bader Ginsburg pointed to a possible compromise. The justices' arguments back and forth about the specific meaning of the state supreme court's ruling—in particular whether that court had in fact relied on the Florida constitution in interpreting state statutes (thus triggering the *McPherson v. Blacker* decision)—led this former professor of procedure to suggest sending the case back to the state supreme court for clarification. It was as if Justice Ginsburg were thinking aloud. Her questions, laced with telling comments and telegraphs of her views, had been strongly supportive of Professor Tribe's defense of the Florida Supreme Court's work and its methodology. But there was, at the least, ambiguity in that court's opinion. After stoutly defending the state supreme court's reasoning, Justice Ginsburg suddenly observed: "I suppose there would be a possibility for this Court to re-mand [to the state supreme court] for clarification."

Phase one of the presidential-election litigation was ef-fectively decided by that one passing comment. The Court had found, through the insight of one of its members, a controversy-free way to achieve unanimity in the midst of what appeared to be unbridgeable inconsistencies in the justices' underlying views.

This interim resolution was sealed when Olson took the podium for a four-minute rebuttal. He seized upon the ref-erence to *McPherson v. Blacker* made by Rehnquist and Scalia and then turned back to specific passages of the state supreme court's opinion to show that the court had not just referred to the Florida constitution, but had actu-ally relied upon it in fashioning its decision. The last pocket of potential resistance came in a question from Jus-tice Souter, who with seconds remaining in the argument said this: "As I look in the conclusion [of the state supreme court's opinion] . . . there is nothing there about the Florida Constitution. It's only about the Florida elec-tion code. . . . There is not one word in that paragraph that says anything about the Florida Constitution." That, of course, meant that the state supreme court might not have used the state constitution to interpret what the leg-islature had done. If so, the Article II problem had been solved.

Olson had the perfect retort: "The very second para-graph [of the conclusion] refers to the Florida Constitu-tion and the right to vote."

The argument was over. Like clockwork, it ended ex-actly on schedule, at 11:30 A.M.

Three days later, on December 4, 2000, the Court unan-imously sent the case back to the Florida Supreme Court for further consideration. The basis for the send-back was the Court's "considerable uncertainty" as to exactly what the grounds were for the state supreme court's decision. In particular, what was the role of the Florida Constitution in the Florida court's interpretation of the state legislature's authority under Article II of the Constitution? What consideration was given, as well, to the Hayes-Tilden statutory reform passed by Congress over a century earlier? Justice Ginsburg had shown the way.

Of particular note: Not a single justice suggested that the Court should simply stand aside and allow the process in Florida to run its course. All nine justices agreed, at least implicitly, that the Court was to have a principal role in resolving who the next president would be. There was not a hint that, since this dispute was all part and parcel of high-stakes politics, the Court should stay away from the political arena. That expression would eventually come—after the second round of litigation—only from Justice Breyer.

The remaining process unfolded quickly. The Florida Supreme Court took a second look at the issues and, only four days after the U.S. Supreme Court's remand, issued a deeply divided opinion staying the course. By a 4–3 vote, Florida's justices ordered manual counting to continue in Miami-Dade County, the inclusion of additional votes for Vice President Gore in two counties, and then manual recounts in all other Florida counties where "undervotes" (ballots not showing a choice for president) had not been subject to manual tabulation. This time, there were vehement dissents. The state supreme court's prior unanimity had badly broken down.

Once again, Governor Bush sought expedited review in Washington, the Supreme Court agreed, and argument was set for Monday, December 11. Only eight days had passed since the Court had resolved the initial round of the Florida litigation.

In the rush of events, it seemed as if everyone was

scrambling, with confusion suddenly reigning. At oral argument, Joe Klock, the experienced lawyer for Katherine Harris, bungled the justices' names in a rather odd way. He had been at the podium only days before, yet he referred, strangely, to Justice Souter as Justice Brennan, a name from yesteryear. It was as if the Court had undergone a time warp and the Warren or Burger Court was once again sitting. Klock then confused yet another pair of justices' names, prompting Justice Scalia to point out before asking a question: "I'm Scalia." The courtroom erupted with laughter.

Even if fatigued, Ted Olson, once more at the podium for Governor Bush, again hammered hard at the Florida Supreme Court. Now, with a fractured state supreme court judgment, Olson charged that court with having brought about "wholesale revisions" and a "major restructuring" of Florida law. Professor Tribe, in contrast, had not been asked to make the return visit on behalf of the Gore team; instead, Vice President Gore decided to look to his lead lawyer throughout the Florida courts, the nationally renowned David Boies. Although a master of the facts in the litigation, Boies was unaccustomed to the speedy give-and-take in the Supreme Court. His amiable tendency casually to agree with the questioner came through repeatedly in his presentation. One of his answers, deep in the argument, was especially unhelpful to the Gore cause. Telegraphing the ultimate outcome, Justice Kennedy asked Boies: "Do you think in the contest phase, there must be a uniform standard for counting the ballots?" Boies readily responded: "I do, Your Honor. I think there must be a uniform standard." He proceeded to argue that a uniform standard was in fact in place—"[t]he standard is whether or not the intent of the voter is reflected by the ballot."

This was far too general and amorphous to satisfy the

Court, and the case was resolved on that very point. Vice President Gore lost the case on grounds of inequality. The next evening, the Court issued its opinions. In the lead opinion, joined by five of the nine justices, the Court grounded its result on the equality principle. In that unsigned opinion, which to Court watchers had the look and feel of an Anthony Kennedy opinion, the five justices concluded that the recount procedures ordered by the Florida Supreme Court were not specific enough to ensure equal treatment of all affected voters. The pivotal conclusion, reflecting a concession by David Boies at the podium that morning, was this: "As seems to have been acknowledged at oral argument, the standards for accepting or rejecting contested ballots might vary not only from county to county but indeed within a single county from one recount team to another."

The majority pointed to various examples. "A monitor in Miami-Dade County testified at trial that he observed that three members of the county canvassing board applied different standards in defining a legal vote. And testimony at trial also revealed that at least one county changed its evaluative standard during the counting process. . . . This is not a process with sufficient guarantees of equal treatment."

Equality, not Article II of the Constitution, or the Hayes-Tilden-era statute, or even whether the Florida courts had run roughshod over the state legislative election scheme (as condemned by *McPherson v. Blacker*)— the various points so strongly pushed by Governor Bush's lawyers—was the Court's chosen principle for deciding the case. Seven justices, cutting across the Court's ideological spectrum, agreed with the substance of the equality-based critique of the vote-counting morass in Florida. Justice Souter and Justice Breyer, although disagreeing with the Court's highly aggressive bottom line, calling a complete halt to the recount process, nonetheless agreed that the vote-counting procedure contemplated by the Florida Supreme Court was simply too open to inconsistencies in actual practice and administration. Ironically, and uncharacteristically, Justices Stevens and Ginsburg were entirely dismissive of the equal-protection claim. As they saw it, the Florida courts were well within their appropriate sphere in interpreting the state election code so as to vindicate the fundamental interest of each voter in having his or her vote count. Equality principles, however powerful they might be to these two justices in other contexts, were simply not worrisome to them in this setting.

Equality, in short, carried the day even in the face of vehement criticisms from within the Court itself. Powerful enough to unite (to a limited extent) seven justices of differing judicial persuasions, it resolved the presidential-election dispute. And the actual decision was remarkably aggressive: an order to the Florida Supreme Court to cease and desist from any further action. There was not a trace of deference to the prerogatives of a state court system. Everyone well knew the inevitable result: Vice President Gore would have to concede, as he did, gracefully, less than forty-eight hours later.

There can be little doubt that, at least at the pivotal center of the Court, where Justices O'Connor and Kennedy sit, equality was seen as the anchor that would ultimately justify, at a moral and political level, what the Court had boldly done. Equality would justify the Court's intrusion into presidential politics and, at the least, minimize the institutional damage inexorably flowing from the Court's involvement with a high-stakes political controversy.

Something else appeared to influence the Court's decision: the freewheeling exercise by the Florida Supreme Court of its judicial power. Article II of the Constitution mandated supremacy of state legislatures in the electoral-selection process. But the Florida Court did not seem particularly sensitive to the Article II requirement and the deference it might have owed to state legislative choices in determining procedures for selecting presidential electors. The justices pressed David Boies to acknowledge a duty by the state supreme court to be respectful of the legislature's choices. Justice Kennedy put it this way to Boies:

> You are responding as though there were no special burden [on the Florida courts] to show some deference to legislative choices. In this one context, not when courts review laws generally for general elections, but in the context of selection of presidential electors, isn't there a red flag up here, watch out?

Boies cheerfully conceded the point. His response was considerably less than a full-throated defense of the state supreme court's majority: "I think there is [a special burden] in a sense, Your Honor, and I think the Florida Supreme Court was grappling with that." Suffice it to say that the majority was unmoved by Boies's tepid defense. It is not unreasonable to think that more than a few justices regarded the Florida Supreme Court as an activist one, determined to assert itself over the Constitution and federal law in order to determine the outcome of the presidential election, weeks after it had taken place. Indeed, it was not lost on the Court that in its second decision the Florida justices narrowly divided, and that Florida's chief justice had been sharply critical of what he regarded as the majority's abusive exercise of power.

In *Bush v. Gore,* the Supreme Court thus was rebuking the Florida Supreme Court. The federal Supreme Court was using its judicial power to reject an exercise of judicial power by the state Supreme Court. The federal Supreme Court provided constitutional reasons for its action, but it is apparent that the federal justices were also concerned that the state justices had simply glided past what the U.S. Court had unanimously said during the first round of litigation on December 3. As Justice O'Connor stated, "I did not find really a response by the Florida Supreme Court to this Court's remand in the case a week ago. It just seemed to kind of bypass it and assume that all those changes and deadlines were just fine and they would go ahead and adhere to them, and I found that troublesome."

Again and again, throughout the course of the oral argument, the justices expressed concern that the state supreme court had glided past what the U.S. Supreme Court had directed at the conclusion of round one. The Florida court had, as one justice put it, "contraven[ed] our vacating of their prior order." The authority of the nation's highest court had been, at least implicitly, challenged by Florida judges who doubtless felt keenly that they, and only they, should be the final interpreters of their own state's election law. Like the Gore team, the Florida judges underestimated the Supreme Court's determination to protect its authority—first stated in *Marbury v. Madison*—to be the ultimate expositor of the law of the land.

Brushed aside in the process, ironically, was Justice Stephen Breyer's eloquent dissent urging restraint and prudence on the part of the High Court. Courts needed to be cautious in going about their work, he emphasized. Even though, in Justice Breyer's view, equal-protection concerns were triggered by the Florida court's work, the federal courts would be well advised to sit on the sidelines when the core questions at issue were so inextricably wrapped up in politics. Drawing from criticisms of the Warren Court's raw activism, Justice Breyer gently suggested, in his characteristically elegant way, that his colleagues had allowed themselves to be drawn into the "political thicket," precisely the warning issued to the Warren Court by one of its most outspoken dissenting members, Justice Felix Frankfurter. Remarkably, the *Bush v. Gore* majority touched on this criticism of their judgment only briefly, and at the very end of its opinion:

> None are more conscious of the vital limits on judicial authority than are the Members of this Court, and none stand more in admiration of the Constitution's design to leave the selection of the President to the people, through their legislatures, and to the political sphere. When contending parties invoke the process of the courts, however, it becomes our unsought responsibility to resolve the federal and constitutional issues the judicial system has been forced to confront.

Notwithstanding this gesture toward restraint, one is left with the impression that the Court, by virtue of its independence, remains aloof from the strong sense that it had usurped power and intruded into the province of both the states (or at least Florida) and the Congress in resolving the ultimate political question in American politics: who the president shall be.

In this decisive sense, the Supreme Court proved beyond doubt its enduring position in the governmental pantheon. It is first among equals.

★ ★ ★

Acknowledgments

My indebtedness is broad and deep. To my beloved family, especially Alice, who unfailingly helped and guided me on an unaccustomed (for me) solitary path, I am ever thankful. To those kind enough to read the manuscript at various stages, and provide invaluable insights throughout, my sense of moral obligation to you is very high. Terry Eastland in particular was enlightened by the thoughful criticisms and comments of Stephen Bates and Brett Kavanaugh as to earlier drafts and, more recently, by the insights of Kannon Shanmugam of Kirkland & Ellis in later iterations of the manuscript. Grant Dixton, my most recently arrived colleague at Kirkland & Ellis, has been particularly helpful in the final stages of preparation. Along the way, portions of the book were examined closely by two of my beloved former teachers at the Duke Law School, Robinson Everett and Melvin Shimm. Throughout the process, Kim Martines, my assistant at Kirkland & Ellis, was patient and consummately skilled in laboring over the incessant changes that flooded her desk.

A particular note of thanks for kindness and hospitality of a very high order is due to Mark Grady, dean of the George Mason University School of Law, who made me warmly welcome on campus in Arlington during the months of intense reflection and writing. In addition, my many colleagues and friends at George Mason, including several student research assistants, were steady companions during my exploration of the institution that is largely enshrouded in mystery to the American people. To the George Mason community, I am deeply in your debt.

★ ★ ★

The Constitution of the United States

We the people of the United States, in order to form a more perfect union, establish justice, insure domestic tranquility, provide for the common defense, promote the general welfare, and secure the blessings of liberty to ourselves and our posterity, do ordain and establish this Constitution for the United States of America.

Article I

Section 1. All legislative powers herein granted shall be vested in a Congress of the United States, which shall consist of a Senate and House of Representatives.

Section 2. The House of Representatives shall be composed of members chosen every second year by the people of the several states, and the electors in each state shall have the qualifications requisite for electors of the most numerous branch of the state legislature.

No person shall be a Representative who shall not have attained to the age of twenty five years, and been seven years a citizen of the United States, and who shall not, when elected, be an inhabitant of that state in which he shall be chosen.

Representatives and direct taxes shall be apportioned among the several states which may be included within this union, according to their respective numbers, which shall be determined by adding to the whole number of free persons, including those bound to service for a term of years, and excluding Indians not taxed, three fifths of all other Persons. The actual Enumeration shall be made within three years after the first meeting of the Congress of the United States, and within every subsequent term of ten years, in such manner as they shall by law direct. The number of Representatives shall not exceed one for every thirty thousand, but each state shall have at least one Representative; and until such enumeration shall be made, the state of New Hampshire shall be entitled to chuse three, Massachusetts eight, Rhode Island and Providence Plantations one, Connecticut five, New York six, New Jersey four, Pennsylvania eight, Delaware one, Maryland six, Virginia ten, North Carolina five, South Carolina five, and Georgia three.

When vacancies happen in the Representation from any state, the executive authority thereof shall issue writs of election to fill such vacancies.

The House of Representatives shall choose their speaker and other officers; and shall have the sole power of impeachment.

Section 3. The Senate of the United States shall be composed of two Senators from each state, chosen by the legislature thereof, for six years; and each Senator shall have one vote.

Immediately after they shall be assembled in consequence of the first election, they shall be divided as equally as may be into three classes. The seats of the Senators of the first class shall be vacated at the expiration of the second year, of the second class at the expiration of the fourth year, and the third class at the expiration of the sixth year, so that one third may be chosen every second year; and if vacancies happen by resignation, or otherwise, during the recess of the legislature of any state, the executive thereof may make temporary appointments until the next meeting of the legislature, which shall then fill such vacancies.

No person shall be a Senator who shall not have attained to the age of thirty years, and been nine years a citizen of the United States and who shall not, when elected, be an inhabitant of that state for which he shall be chosen.

The Vice President of the United States shall be President of the Senate, but shall have no vote, unless they be equally divided.

The Senate shall choose their other officers, and also a President pro tempore, in the absence of the Vice President, or when he shall exercise the office of President of the United States.

The Senate shall have the sole power to try all impeachments. When sitting for that purpose, they shall be on oath or affirmation. When the President of the United States is tried, the Chief Justice shall preside: And no person shall be convicted without the concurrence of two thirds of the members present.

Judgment in cases of impeachment shall not extend further than to removal from office, and disqualification to hold and enjoy any office of honor, trust or profit under the United States: but the party convicted shall nevertheless be liable and subject to indictment, trial, judgment and punishment, according to law.

Section 4. The times, places and manner of holding elections for Senators and Representatives, shall be prescribed in each state by the legislature thereof; but the Congress may at any time by law make or alter such regulations, except as to the places of choosing Senators.

The Congress shall assemble at least once in every year, and such meeting shall be on the first Monday in December, unless they shall by law appoint a different day.

Section 5. Each House shall be the judge of the elections, returns and qualifications of its own members, and a majority of each shall constitute a quorum to do business; but a smaller number may adjourn from day to day, and may be authorized to compel the attendance of absent members, in such manner, and under such penalties as each House may provide.

Each House may determine the rules of its proceedings, punish its members for disorderly behavior, and, with the concurrence of two thirds, expel a member.

Each House shall keep a journal of its proceedings, and from time to time publish the same, excepting such parts as may in their judgment require secrecy; and the yeas and nays of the members of either House on any question shall, at the desire of one fifth of those present, be entered on the journal.

Neither House, during the session of Congress, shall, without the consent of the other, adjourn for more than three days, nor to any other place than that in which the two Houses shall be sitting.

Section 6. The Senators and Representatives shall receive a compensation for their services, to be ascertained by law, and paid out of the treasury of the United States. They shall in all cases, except treason, felony and breach of the peace, be privileged from arrest during their attendance at the session of their respective Houses, and in going to and returning from the same; and for any speech or debate in either House, they shall not be questioned in any other place.

No Senator or Representative shall, during the time for which he was elected, be appointed to any civil office under the authority of the United States, which shall have been created, or the emoluments whereof shall have been increased during such time: and no person holding any office under the United States, shall be a member of either House during his continuance in office.

Section 7. All bills for raising revenue shall originate in the House of Representatives; but the Senate may propose or concur with amendments as on other Bills.

Every bill which shall have passed the House of Representatives and the Senate, shall, before it become a law, be presented to the President of the United States; if he approve he shall sign it, but if not he shall return it, with his objections to that House in which it shall have originated, who shall enter the objections at large on their journal, and proceed to reconsider it. If after such reconsideration two thirds of that House shall agree to pass the bill, it shall be sent, together with the objections, to the other House, by which it shall likewise be reconsidered, and if approved by two thirds of that House, it shall become a law. But in all such cases the votes of both Houses shall be determined by yeas and nays, and the names of the persons voting for and against the bill shall be entered on the journal of each House respectively. If any bill shall not be returned by the President within ten days (Sundays excepted) after it shall have been presented to him, the same shall be a law, in like manner as if he had signed it, unless the Congress by their adjournment prevent its return, in which case it shall not be a law.

Every order, resolution, or vote to which the concurrence of the Senate and House of Representatives may be necessary (except on a question of adjournment) shall be presented to the President of the United States; and before the same shall take effect, shall be approved by him, or being disapproved by him, shall be repassed by two thirds of the Senate and House of Representatives, according to the rules and limitations prescribed in the case of a bill.

Section 8. The Congress shall have power to lay and collect taxes, duties, imposts and excises, to pay the debts and provide for the common defense and general welfare of the United States; but all duties, imposts and excises shall be uniform throughout the United States;

To borrow money on the credit of the United States;

To regulate commerce with foreign nations, and among the several states, and with the Indian tribes;

To establish a uniform rule of naturalization, and uniform laws on the subject of bankruptcies throughout the United States;

To coin money, regulate the value thereof, and of foreign coin, and fix the standard of weights and measures;

To provide for the punishment of counterfeiting the securities and current coin of the United States;

To establish post offices and post roads;

To promote the progress of science and useful arts, by securing for limited times to authors and inventors the exclusive right to their respective writings and discoveries;

To constitute tribunals inferior to the Supreme Court;

To define and punish piracies and felonies committed on the high seas, and offenses against the law of nations;

To declare war, grant letters of marque and reprisal, and make rules concerning captures on land and water;

To raise and support armies, but no appropriation of money to that use shall be for a longer term than two years;

To provide and maintain a navy;

To make rules for the government and regulation of the land and naval forces;

To provide for calling forth the militia to execute the laws of the union, suppress insurrections and repel invasions;

To provide for organizing, arming, and disciplining, the militia, and for governing such part of them as may be employed in the service of the United States, reserving to the states respectively, the appointment of the officers, and the authority of training the militia according to the discipline prescribed by Congress;

To exercise exclusive legislation in all cases whatsoever, over such District (not exceeding ten miles square) as may, by cession of particular states, and the acceptance of Congress, become the seat of the government of the United States, and to exercise like authority over all places purchased by the consent of the legislature of the state in which the same shall be, for the erection of forts, magazines, arsenals, dockyards, and other needful buildings;— And

To make all laws which shall be necessary and proper for carrying into execution the foregoing powers, and all other powers vested by this Constitution in the government of the United States, or in any department or officer thereof.

Section 9. The migration or importation of such persons as any of the states now existing shall think proper to admit, shall not be prohibited by the Congress prior to the year one thousand eight hundred and eight, but a tax or duty may be imposed on such importation, not exceeding ten dollars for each person.

The privilege of the writ of habeas corpus shall not be suspended, unless when in cases of rebellion or invasion the public safety may require it.

No bill of attainder or ex post facto Law shall be passed.

No capitation, or other direct, tax shall be laid, unless in proportion to the census or enumeration herein before directed to be taken.

No tax or duty shall be laid on articles exported from any state.

No preference shall be given by any regulation of commerce or revenue to the ports of one state over those of another: nor shall vessels bound to, or from, one state, be obliged to enter, clear or pay duties in another.

No money shall be drawn from the treasury, but in consequence of appropriations made by law; and a regular statement and account of receipts and expenditures of all public money shall be published from time to time.

No title of nobility shall be granted by the United States: and no person holding any office of profit or trust under them, shall, without the consent of the Congress, accept of any present, emolument, office, or title, of any kind whatever, from any king, prince, or foreign state.

Section 10. No state shall enter into any treaty, alliance, or confederation; grant letters of marque and reprisal; coin money; emit bills of credit; make anything but gold and silver coin a tender in payment of debts; pass any bill of attainder, ex post facto law, or law impairing the obligation of contracts, or grant any title of nobility.

No state shall, without the consent of the Congress, lay any imposts or duties on imports or exports, except what may be absolutely necessary for executing its inspection laws: and the net produce of all duties and imposts, laid by any state on imports or exports, shall be for the use of the treasury of the United States; and all such laws shall be subject to the revision and control of the Congress.

No state shall, without the consent of Congress, lay any duty of tonnage, keep troops, or ships of war in time of peace, enter into any agreement or compact with another state, or with a foreign power, or engage in war, unless actually invaded, or in such imminent danger as will not admit of delay.

ARTICLE II

Section 1. The executive power shall be vested in a President of the United States of America. He shall hold his office during the term of four years, and, together with the Vice President, chosen for the same term, be elected, as follows:

Each state shall appoint, in such manner as the Legislature thereof may direct, a number of electors, equal to the whole number of Senators and Representatives to which the State may be entitled in the Congress: but no Senator or Representative, or person holding an office of trust or profit under the United States, shall be appointed an elector.

The electors shall meet in their respective states, and vote by ballot for two persons, of whom one at least shall not be an inhabitant of the same state with themselves. And they shall make a list of all the persons voted for, and of the number of votes for each; which list they shall sign and certify, and transmit sealed to the seat of the government of the United States, directed to the President of the Senate. The President of the Senate shall, in the presence of the Senate and House of Representatives, open all the certificates, and the votes shall then be counted. The person having the greatest number of votes shall be the President, if such number be a majority of the whole number of electors appointed; and if there be more than one who have such majority, and have an equal number of votes, then the House of Representatives shall immediately choose by ballot one of them for President; and if no person have a majority, then from the five highest on the list the said House shall in like manner choose the President. But in choosing the President, the votes shall be taken by States, the representation from each state having one vote; a quorum for this purpose shall consist of a member or members from two thirds of the states, and a majority of all the states shall be necessary to a choice. In every case, after the choice of the president, the person having the greatest number of votes of the electors shall be the Vice President. But if there should remain two or more who have equal votes, the Senate shall choose from them by ballot the Vice President.

The Congress may determine the time of choosing the electors, and the day on which they shall give their votes; which day shall be the same throughout the United States.

No person except a natural born citizen, or a citizen of the United States, at the time of the adoption of this Constitution, shall be eligible to the office of President; neither shall any person be eligible to that office who shall not have attained to the age of thirty five years, and been fourteen Years a resident within the United States.

In case of the removal of the President from office, or of his death, resignation, or inability to discharge the powers and duties of the said office, the same shall devolve on the Vice President, and the Congress may by law provide for the case of removal, death, resignation or inability, both of the President and Vice President, declaring what officer shall then act as President, and such officer shall act accordingly, until the disability be removed, or a President shall be elected.

The President shall, at stated times, receive for his services, a compensation, which shall neither be increased nor diminished during the period for which he shall have been elected, and he shall not receive within that period any other emolument from the United States, or any of them.

Before he enter on the execution of his office, he shall take the following oath or affirmation:—"I do solemnly swear (or affirm) that I will faithfully execute the office of President of the United States, and will to the best of my ability, preserve, protect and defend the Constitution of the United States."

Section 2. The President shall be commander in chief of the Army and Navy of the United States, and of the militia of the several states, when called into the actual service of the United States; he may require the opinion, in writing, of the principal officer in each of the executive departments, upon any subject relating to the duties of their respective offices, and he shall have power to grant reprieves and pardons for offenses against the United States, except in cases of impeachment.

He shall have power, by and with the advice and consent of the Senate, to make treaties, provided two thirds of the Senators present concur; and he shall nominate, and by and with the advice and consent of the Senate, shall appoint ambassadors, other public ministers and consuls, judges of the Supreme Court, and all other officers of the United States, whose appointments are not herein otherwise provided for, and which shall be established by law: but the Congress may by law vest the appointment of such inferior officers, as they think proper, in the President alone, in the courts of law, or in the heads of departments.

The President shall have power to fill up all vacancies that may happen during the recess of the Senate, by granting commissions which shall expire at the end of their next session.

Section 3. He shall from time to time give to the Congress information of the state of the union, and recommend to their consideration such measures as he shall judge necessary and expedient; he may, on extraordinary occasions, convene both Houses, or either of them, and in case of disagreement between them, with respect to the time of adjournment, he may adjourn them to such time as he shall think proper; he shall receive ambassadors and other public ministers; he shall take care that the laws be faithfully executed, and shall commission all the officers of the United States.

Section 4. The President, Vice President and all civil officers of the United States, shall be removed from office on impeachment for, and conviction of, treason, bribery, or other high crimes and misdemeanors.

ARTICLE III

Section 1. The judicial power of the United States, shall be vested in one Supreme Court, and in such inferior courts as the Congress may from time to time ordain and establish. The judges, both of the supreme and inferior courts, shall hold their offices during good behaviour, and shall, at stated times, receive for their services, a compensation, which shall not be diminished during their continuance in office.

Section 2. The judicial power shall extend to all cases, in law and equity, arising under this Constitution, the laws of the United States, and treaties made, or which shall be made, under their authority;—to all cases affecting ambassadors, other public ministers and consuls;—to all cases of admiralty and maritime jurisdiction;—to controversies to which the United States shall be a party;—to controversies between two or more states;—between a state and citizens of another state;—between citizens of different states;—between citizens of the same state claiming lands under grants of different states, and between a state, or the citizens thereof, and foreign states, citizens or subjects.

In all cases affecting ambassadors, other public ministers and consuls, and those in which a state shall be party, the Supreme Court shall have original jurisdiction. In all the other cases before mentioned, the Supreme Court shall have appellate jurisdiction, both as to law and fact, with such exceptions, and under such regulations as the Congress shall make.

The trial of all crimes, except in cases of impeachment, shall be by jury; and such trial shall be held in the state where the said crimes shall have been committed; but when not committed within any state, the trial shall be at such place or places as the Congress may by law have directed.

Section 3. Treason against the United States, shall consist only in levying war against them, or in adhering to their enemies, giving them aid and comfort. No person shall be convicted of treason unless on the testimony of two witnesses to the same overt act, or on confession in open court.

The Congress shall have power to declare the punishment of treason, but no attainder of treason shall work corruption of blood, or forfeiture except during the life of the person attainted.

ARTICLE IV

Section 1. Full faith and credit shall be given in each state to the public acts, records, and judicial proceedings of every other state. And the Congress may by general laws prescribe the manner in which such acts, records, and proceedings shall be proved, and the effect thereof.

Section 2. The citizens of each state shall be entitled to all privileges and immunities of citizens in the several states.

A person charged in any state with treason, felony, or other crime, who shall flee from justice, and be found in another state, shall on demand of the executive authority of the state from which he fled, be delivered up, to be removed to the state having jurisdiction of the crime.

No person held to service or labor in one state, under the laws thereof, escaping into another, shall, in consequence of any law or regulation therein, be discharged from such service or labor, but shall be delivered up on claim of the party to whom such service or labor may be due.

Section 3. New states may be admitted by the Congress into this union; but no new states shall be formed or erected within the jurisdiction of any other state; nor any state be formed by the junction of two or more states, or parts of states, without the consent of the legislatures of the states concerned as well as of the Congress.

The Congress shall have power to dispose of and make all needful rules and regulations respecting the territory or other property belonging to the Untied States; and nothing in this Constitution shall be so construed as to prejudice any claims of the United States, or of any particular state.

Section 4. The United States shall guarantee to every state in this union a republican form of government, and shall protect each of them against invasion; and on application of the legislature, or of the executive (when the legislature cannot be convened) against domestic violence.

ARTICLE V

The Congress, whenever two thirds of both houses shall deem it necessary, shall propose amendments to this Constitution, or, on the application of the legislatures of two thirds of the several states, shall call a convention for proposing amendments, which, in either case, shall be valid to all intents and purposes, as part of this Constitution, when ratified by the legislatures of three fourths of the several states, or by conventions in three fourths thereof, as the one or the other mode of ratification may be proposed by the Congress; provided that no amendment which may be made prior to the year one thousand eight hundred and eight shall in any manner affect the first and fourth clauses in the ninth section of the first article; and that no state, without its consent, shall be deprived of its equal suffrage in the Senate.

Article VI

All debts contracted and engagements entered into, before the adoption of this Constitution, shall be as valid against the United States under this Constitution, as under the Confederation.

This Constitution, and the laws of the United States which shall be made in pursuance thereof; and all treaties made, or which shall be made, under the authority of the United States, shall be the supreme law of the land; and the judges in every state shall be bound thereby, anything in the Constitution or laws of any State to the contrary notwithstanding.

The Senators and Representatives before mentioned, and the members of the several state legislatures, and all executive and judicial officers, both of the United States and of the several states, shall be bound by oath or affirmation, to support this constitution; but no religious test shall ever be required as a qualification to any office or public trust under the United States.

Article VII

The ratification of the conventions of nine states, shall be sufficient for the establishment of this Constitution between the states so ratifying the same.

Done in convention by the unanimous consent of the states present the seventeenth day of September in the year of our Lord one thousand seven hundred and eighty seven and of the independence of the United States of America the twelfth. In witness whereof We have hereunto subscribed our Names,

G. Washington-Presidt. and deputy from Virginia
New Hampshire: John Langdon, Nicholas Gilman
Massachusetts: Nathaniel Gorham, Rufus King
Connecticut: Wm: Saml. Johnson, Roger Sherman
New York: Alexander Hamilton
New Jersey: Wil: Livingston, David Brearly,
    Wm. Paterson, Jona: Dayton
Pennsylvania: B. Franklin, Thomas Mifflin,
    Robt. Morris, Geo. Clymer, Thos. FitzSimons,
    Jared Ingersoll, James Wilson, Gouv Morris
Delaware: Geo: Read, Gunning Bedford jun,
    John Dickinson, Richard Bassett, Jaco: Broom
Maryland: James McHenry, Dan of St Thos. Jenifer,
    Danl Carroll
Virginia: John Blair—, James Madison Jr.
North Carolina: Wm. Blount, Richd. Dobbs Spaight,
    Hu Williamson
South Carolina: J. Rutledge, Charles Cotesworth
    Pinckney, Charles Pinckney, Pierce Butler
Georgia: William Few, Abr Baldwin

The Conventions of a number of the States having, at the time of adopting the Constitution, expressed a desire, in order to prevent misconstruction or abuse of its powers, that further declaratory and restrictive clauses should be added, and as extending the ground of public confidence in the Government will best insure the beneficent ends of its institution;

Resolved, by the Senate and House of Representatives of the United States of America, in Congress assembled, two-thirds of both Houses concurring, that the following articles be proposed to the Legislatures of the several States, as amendments to the Constitution of the United States; all or any of which articles, when ratified by three-fourths of the said Legislatures, to be valid to all intents and purposes as part of the said Constitution, namely:

AMENDMENT I*

Congress shall make no law respecting an establishment of religion, or prohibiting the free exercise thereof; or abridging the freedom of speech, or of the press; or the right of the people peaceably to assemble, and to petition the government for a redress of grievances.

AMENDMENT II

A well regulated militia, being necessary to the security of a free state, the right of the people to keep and bear arms, shall not be infringed.

AMENDMENT III

No soldier shall, in time of peace be quartered in any house, without the consent of the owner, nor in time of war, but in a manner to be prescribed by law.

*The first ten amendments, in effect since 1791, constitute the Bill of Rights.

AMENDMENT IV

The right of the people to be secure in their persons, houses, papers, and effects, against unreasonable searches and seizures, shall not be violated, and no warrants shall issue, but upon probable cause, supported by oath or affirmation, and particularly describing the place to be searched, and the persons or things to be seized.

AMENDMENT V

No person shall be held to answer for a capital, or otherwise infamous crime, unless on a presentment or indictment of a grand jury, except in cases arising in the land or naval forces, or in the militia, when in actual service in time of war or public danger; nor shall any person be subject for the same offense to be twice put in jeopardy of life or limb; nor shall be compelled in any criminal case to be a witness against himself, nor be deprived of life, liberty, or property, without due process of law; nor shall private property be taken for public use, without just compensation.

AMENDMENT VI

In all criminal prosecutions, the accused shall enjoy the right to a speedy and public trial, by an impartial jury of the state and district wherein the crime shall have been committed, which district shall have been previously ascertained by law, and to be informed of the nature and cause of the accusation; to be confronted with the witnesses against him; to have compulsory process for obtaining witnesses in his favor, and to have the assistance of counsel for his defense.

Amendment VII

In suits at common law, where the value in controversy shall exceed twenty dollars, the right of trial by jury shall be preserved, and no fact tried by a jury, shall be otherwise reexamined in any court of the United States, than according to the rules of the common law.

Amendment VIII

Excessive bail shall not be required, nor excessive fines imposed, nor cruel and unusual punishments inflicted.

Amendment IX

The enumeration in the Constitution, of certain rights, shall not be construed to deny or disparage others retained by the people.

Amendment X

The powers not delegated to the United States by the Constitution, nor prohibited by it to the states, are reserved to the states respectively, or to the people.

Amendment XI (1798)

The judicial power of the United States shall not be construed to extend to any suit in law or equity, commenced or prosecuted against one of the United States by citizens of another state, or by citizens or subjects of any foreign state.

Amendment XII (1804)

The electors shall meet in their respective states and vote by ballot for President and Vice-President, one of whom, at least, shall not be an inhabitant of the same state with themselves; they shall name in their ballots the person voted for as President, and in distinct ballots the person voted for as Vice-President, and they shall make distinct lists of all persons voted for as President, and of all persons voted for as Vice-President, and of the number of votes for each, which lists they shall sign and certify, and transmit sealed to the seat of the government of the United States, directed to the President of the Senate;—The President of the Senate shall, in the presence of the Senate and House of Representatives, open all the certificates and the votes shall then be counted;—the person having the greatest number of votes for President, shall be the President, if such number be a majority of the whole number of electors appointed; and if no person have such majority, then from the persons having the highest numbers not exceeding three on the list of those voted for as President, the House of Representatives shall choose immediately, by ballot, the President. But in choosing the President, the votes shall be taken by states, the representation from each state having one vote; a quorum for this purpose shall consist of a member or members from two-thirds of the states, and a majority of all the states shall be necessary to a choice. And if the House of Representatives shall not choose a President whenever the right of choice shall devolve upon them, before the fourth day of March next following, then the Vice-President shall act as President, as in the case of the death or other constitutional disability of the President. The person having the greatest number of votes as Vice-President, shall be the Vice-President, if such number be a majority of the whole number of electors appointed, and if no person have a majority, then from the two highest numbers on the list, the Senate shall choose the Vice-President; a quorum for the purpose shall consist of two-thirds of the whole number of Senators, and a majority of the whole number shall be necessary to a choice. But no person constitutionally ineligible to the office of President shall be eligible to that of Vice-President of the United States.

AMENDMENT XIII (1865)

Section 1. Neither slavery nor involuntary servitude, except as a punishment for crime whereof the party shall have been duly convicted, shall exist within the United States, or any place subject to their jurisdiction.

Section 2. Congress shall have power to enforce this article by appropriate legislation.

AMENDMENT XIV (1868)

Section 1. All persons born or naturalized in the United States, and subject to the jurisdiction thereof, are citizens of the United States and of the state wherein they reside. No state shall make or enforce any law which shall abridge the privileges or immunities of citizens of the United States; nor shall any state deprive any person of life, liberty, or property, without due process of law; nor deny to any person within its jurisdiction the equal protection of the laws.

Section 2. Representatives shall be apportioned among the several states according to their respective numbers, counting the whole number of persons in each state, excluding Indians not taxed. But when the right to vote at any election for the choice of electors for President and Vice President of the United States, Representatives in Congress, the executive and judicial officers of a state, or the members of the legislature thereof, is denied to any of the male inhabitants of such state, being twenty-one years of age, and citizens of the United States, or in any way abridged, except for participation in rebellion, or other crime, the basis of representation therein shall be reduced in the proportion which the number of such male citizens shall bear to the whole number of male citizens twenty-one years of age in such state.

Section 3. No person shall be a Senator or Representative in Congress, or elector of President and Vice President, or hold any office, civil or military, under the United States, or under any state, who, having previously taken an oath, as a member of Congress, or as an officer of the United States, or as a member of any state legislature, or as an executive or judicial officer of any state, to support the Constitution of the United States, shall have engaged in insurrection or rebellion against the same, or given aid or comfort to the enemies thereof. But Congress may by a vote of two-thirds of each House, remove such disability.

Section 4. The validity of the public debt of the United States, authorized by law, including debts incurred for payment of pensions and bounties for services in suppressing insurrection or rebellion, shall not be questioned. But neither the United States nor any state shall assume or pay any debt or obligation incurred in aid of insurrection or rebellion against the United States, or any claim for the loss or emancipation of any slave; but all such debts, obligations and claims shall be held illegal and void.

Section 5. The Congress shall have power to enforce, by appropriate legislation, the provisions of this article.

Amendment XV (1870)

Section 1. The right of citizens of the United States to vote shall not be denied or abridged by the United States or by any state on account of race, color, or previous condition of servitude.

Section 2. The Congress shall have power to enforce this article by appropriate legislation.

Amendment XVI (1913)

The Congress shall have power to lay and collect taxes on incomes, from whatever source derived, without apportionment among the several states, and without regard to any census of enumeration.

Amendment XVII (1913)

The Senate of the United States shall be composed of two Senators from each state, elected by the people thereof, for six years; and each Senator shall have one vote. The electors in each state shall have the qualifications requisite for electors of the most numerous branch of the state legislatures.

When vacancies happen in the representation of any state in the Senate, the executive authority of such state shall issue writs of election to fill such vacancies: Provided, that the legislature of any state may empower the executive thereof to make temporary appointments until the people fill the vacancies by election as the legislature may direct.

This amendment shall not be so construed as to affect the election or term of any Senator chosen before it becomes valid as part of the Constitution.

AMENDMENT XVIII (1919)

Section 1. After one year from the ratification of this article the manufacture, sale, or transportation of intoxicating liquors within, the importation thereof into, or the exportation thereof from the United States and all territory subject to the jurisdiction thereof for beverage purposes is hereby prohibited.

Section 2. The Congress and the several states shall have concurrent power to enforce this article by appropriate legislation.

Section 3. This article shall be inoperative unless it shall have been ratified as an amendment to the Constitution by the legislatures of the several states, as provided in the Constitution, within seven years from the date of the submission hereof to the states by the Congress.

AMENDMENT XIX (1920)

The right of citizens of the United States to vote shall not be denied or abridged by the United States or by any state on account of sex.

Congress shall have power to enforce this article by appropriate legislation.

AMENDMENT XX (1933)

Section 1. The terms of the President and Vice President shall end at noon on the 20th day of January, and the terms of Senators and Representatives at noon on the 3d day of January, of the years in which such terms would have ended if this article had not been ratified; and the terms of their successors shall then begin.

Section 2. The Congress shall assemble at least once in every year, and such meeting shall begin at noon on the 3d day of January, unless they shall by law appoint a different day.

Section 3. If, at the time fixed for the beginning of the term of the President, the President elect shall have died, the Vice President elect shall become President. If a President shall not have been chosen before the time fixed for the beginning of his term, or if the President elect shall have failed to qualify, then the Vice President elect shall act as President until a President shall have qualified; and the Congress may by law provide for the case wherein neither a President elect nor a Vice President elect shall have qualified, declaring who shall then act as President, or the manner in which one who is to act shall be selected, and such person shall act accordingly until a President or Vice President shall have qualified.

Section 4. The Congress may by law provide for the case of the death of any of the persons from whom the House of Representatives may choose a President whenever the right of choice shall have devolved upon them, and for the case of the death of any of the persons from whom the Senate may choose a Vice President whenever the right of choice shall have devolved upon them.

Section 5. Sections 1 and 2 shall take effect on the 15th day of October following the ratification of this article.

Section 6. This article shall be inoperative unless it shall have been ratified as an amendment to the Constitution by the legislatures of three-fourths of the several states within seven years from the date of its submission.

AMENDMENT XXI (1933)

Section 1. The eighteenth article of amendment to the Constitution of the United States is hereby repealed.

Section 2. The transportation or importation into any state, territory, or possession of the United States for delivery or use therein of intoxicating liquors, in violation of the laws thereof, is hereby prohibited.

Section 3. This article shall be inoperative unless it shall have been ratified as an amendment to the Constitution by conventions in the several states, as provided in the Constitution, within seven years from the date of the submission hereof to the states by the Congress.

AMENDMENT XXII (1951)

Section 1. No person shall be elected to the office of the President more than twice, and no person who has held the office of President, or acted as President, for more than two years of a term to which some other person was elected President shall be elected to the office of the President more than once. But this article shall not apply to any person holding the office of President when this article was proposed by the Congress, and shall not prevent any person who may be holding the office of President, or acting as President, during the term within which this article becomes operative from holding the office of President or acting as President during the remainder of such term.

Section 2. This article shall be inoperative unless it shall have been ratified as an amendment to the Constitution by the legislatures of three-fourths of the several states within seven years from the date of its submission to the states by the Congress.

Amendment XXIII (1961)

Section 1. The District constituting the seat of government of the United States shall appoint in such manner as the Congress may direct:

A number of electors of President and Vice President equal to the whole number of Senators and Representatives in Congress to which the District would be entitled if it were a state, but in no event more than the least populous state; they shall be in addition to those appointed by the states, but they shall be considered, for the purposes of the election of President and Vice President, to be electors appointed by a state; and they shall meet in the District and perform such duties as provided by the twelfth article of amendment.

Section 2. The Congress shall have power to enforce this article by appropriate legislation.

Amendment XXIV (1964)

Section 1. The right of citizens of the United States to vote in any primary or other election for President or Vice President, for electors for President or Vice President, or for Senator or Representative in Congress, shall not be denied or abridged by the United States or any state by reason of failure to pay any poll tax or other tax.

Section 2. The Congress shall have power to enforce this article by appropriate legislation.

AMENDMENT XXV (1967)

Section 1. In case of the removal of the President from office or of his death or resignation, the Vice President shall become President.

Section 2. Whenever there is a vacancy in the office of the Vice President, the President shall nominate a Vice President who shall take office upon confirmation by a majority vote of both Houses of Congress.

Section 3. Whenever the President transmits to the President pro tempore of the Senate and the Speaker of the House of Representatives his written declaration that he is unable to discharge the powers and duties of his office, and until he transmits to them a written declaration to the contrary, such powers and duties shall be discharged by the Vice President as Acting President.

Section 4. Whenever the Vice President and a majority of either the principal officers of the executive departments or of such other body as Congress may by law provide, transmit to the President pro tempore of the Senate and the Speaker of the House of Representatives their written declaration that the President is unable to discharge the powers and duties of his office, the Vice President shall immediately assume the powers and duties of the office as Acting President.

Thereafter, when the President transmits to the President pro tempore of the Senate and the Speaker of the House of Representatives his written declaration that no inability exists, he shall resume the powers and duties of his office unless the Vice President and a majority of either the principal officers of the executive department or of such other body as Congress may by law provide, transmit within four days to the president pro tempore of the Senate and the Speaker of the House of Representatives their written declaration that the President is unable to discharge the powers and duties of his office. Thereupon Congress shall decide the issue, assembling within forty-eight hours for that purpose if not in session. If the Congress, within twenty-one days after receipt of the latter written declaration, or, if Congress is not in session, within twenty-one days after Congress is required to assemble, determines by two-thirds vote of both Houses that the President is unable to discharge the powers and duties of his office, the Vice President shall continue to discharge the same as Acting President; otherwise, the President shall resume the powers and duties of his office.

AMENDMENT XXVI (1971)

Section 1. The right of citizens of the United States, who are 18 years of age or older, to vote, shall not be denied or abridged by the United States or any state on account of age.

Section 2. The Congress shall have the power to enforce this article by appropriate legislation.

AMENDMENT XXVII (1992)

No law varying the compensation for the services of the Senators and Representatives shall take effect until an election of Representatives shall have intervened.

INDEX